"*The Synergy Solution* is an instant M&A classic. In their no-nonsense approach, Sirower and Weirens describe in great detail the discipline and hard work required throughout the M&A process to realize the promised value from deals and avoid the pitfalls. I highly recommend this book for any leader who wants to play the acquisition game."

—**BOB SWAN**, Operating Partner, Andreessen Horowitz;
former CEO, Intel Corporation

"*The Synergy Solution* provides a complete how-to on M&A. If you only read one book, make it this one—from case studies to practical examples, readers can connect with the fundamentals and, at the same time, learn what to expect from a real-life merger or acquisition."

—**MARK LITTLE**, President and CEO, Suncor Energy

"Finally, a definitive guide on M&A and the creation of shareholder value that makes sense. From M&A strategy and communicating with investors to the details of integration and change, *The Synergy Solution* delivers what it promises. A must-read for CFOs and senior executives involved in M&A."

—**FRANK D'AMELIO**, CFO and Executive Vice President,
Global Supply, Pfizer

"*The Synergy Solution* is an important achievement and a revealing and comprehensive book on mergers and acquisitions. Packed with data and details, it will be of great interest to directors who are evaluating M&A proposals as they fulfill their governance duties, as well as to senior executives who will be called upon to formulate these deals and successfully execute them."

—**SCOTT BARSHAY**, Chair of Corporate Department, Paul, Weiss,
Rifkind, Wharton & Garrison

"*The Synergy Solution* is a powerful resource revealing the end-to-end development and successful execution of M&A strategies—including the art and the science of getting deals done and done right. This is the practical guidebook to read if you're considering M&A or building a career in this field."

—**JOHN LO**, CFO, Tencent

"One of the enduring mysteries of finance over the last quarter century has been the persistent belief among CEOs and boards that despite the significant amount of M&A activity that results in value destruction, 'our deal will be different.' In this comprehensive book, two leading M&A experts lay out with clarity and persuasiveness a detailed approach for how your deal can, in fact, be different. A must-read for every practitioner—and every student."

—**RAGHU SUNDARAM**, Richard R. West Dean and
Edward I. Altman Professor of Credit & Debt Markets,
NYU Stern School of Business

"Growth and M&A ideas abound, so leaders must exercise great discipline as they negotiate deals and commit precious financial and human capital. This excellent book elegantly weaves insights across the elements of successful M&A and will serve as an essential primer for boards as they face the challenges of not only assessing proposed deals—with forward-looking growth synergies—but also holding management accountable for delivering tangible results."

—**TERESA BRIGGS**, board member, DocuSign, ServiceNow,
Snowflake, and Warby Parker

"With *The Synergy Solution*, Sirower and Weirens provide an insightful, accessible, and extremely useful road map for senior management and boards that are considering or executing M&A activity. All potential acquirers should be able to answer the straightforward questions that structure *The Synergy Solution*. Sirower and Weirens guide readers through the many considerations necessary to avoid bad deals and realize the potential of good ones. Their book is a must-read. Acquirers ignore it at their peril."

—**MARK W. NELSON**, Anne and Elmer Lindseth Dean and Professor of Accounting, Johnson Graduate School of Management, Cornell University

"Trust is foundational to any well thought-out M&A transaction. *The Synergy Solution* explores step by step not only the practical aspects of conducting a successful M&A transaction but also the rigors of the communication and announcement processes relevant to building, from day one, that trust between business leaders and stakeholders."

—**SANDRA SUCHER**, professor, Harvard Business School; coauthor, *The Power of Trust*

THE SYNERGY SOLUTION

MARK L. SIROWER
JEFFERY M. WEIRENS

THE SYNERGY SOLUTION

HOW COMPANIES WIN THE MERGERS AND ACQUISITIONS GAME

HARVARD BUSINESS REVIEW PRESS
BOSTON, MASSACHUSETTS

The web addresses referenced in this book were live and correct at the time of the book's publication but may be subject to change.

Library of Congress Cataloging-in-Publication Data

Names: Sirower, Mark L., 1962– author. | Weirens, Jeffrey M., author.
Title: The synergy solution : how companies win the mergers and
    acquisitions game / Mark L. Sirower, Jeffrey M. Weirens.
Description: Boston, Massachusetts : Harvard Business Review Press, [2022] |
    Includes index.
Identifiers: LCCN 2021034676 (print) | LCCN 2021034677 (ebook) |
    ISBN 9781647820428 (hardcover) | ISBN 9781647820435 (ebook)
Subjects: LCSH: Consolidation and merger of corporations. |
    Corporations—Valuation. | Business planning. | Corporate reorganizations.
Classification: LCC HD2746.5 .S57 2022 (print) | LCC HD2746.5 (ebook) |
    DDC 658.1/6—dc23
LC record available at https://lccn.loc.gov/2021034676
LC ebook record available at https://lccn.loc.gov/2021034677

ISBN: 978-1-64782-042-8
eISBN: 978-1-64782-043-5

The paper used in this publication meets the requirements of the American National Standard for Permanence of Paper for Publications and Documents in Libraries and Archives Z39.48-1992.

MARK SIROWER
To my daughter Ellen, you will always be the heart of my heart

JEFFERY WEIRENS
To my favorite merger ever, Julie, and our three synergies—Sierra, Aurora, and Skylar
$1+1=5$

Imagine being on a treadmill. Suppose you are running at 3 mph now, but you are required to run at 4 mph next year and 5 mph the year after. Synergy would mean running even harder than this expectation while competitors supply a head wind. Paying a premium for synergy—that is, for the right to run harder—is like putting on a heavy pack. Meanwhile, the more you delay running harder, the higher the incline is set. This is the acquisition game.

—Mark L. Sirower, *The Synergy Trap* (1997)

In some mergers there are truly major synergies—though often times the acquirer pays too much to obtain them—but at other times the cost and revenue benefits that are projected prove illusory. Of one thing, however, be certain: if a CEO is enthused about a particularly foolish acquisition, both his internal staff and his outside advisors will come up with whatever projections are needed to justify his stance. Only in fairy tales are emperors told that they are naked.

—Warren Buffett, *Berkshire Hathaway 1997 Annual Report*

CONTENTS

FOREWORD

Mergers and acquisitions continue to be a mainstay of global business strategies. Corporations and their stakeholders, and the economy overall, can reap significant benefits—as long as attention is paid to all the vital elements that make these transactions successful. It can be challenging, but it can be done.

With more than two decades of experience practicing and leading M&A at Deloitte Consulting LLP, advising on both public and private global transactions, I know the breadth of work required to envision, execute, and implement a successful merger or acquisition. While many transactions might look good on paper, it's the combination of strategy and delivering results that lead to success. M&A involves substantial risk, so understanding all the moving parts from the beginning and getting them right requires capable leadership and strong executional ability.

There are many lessons for successful M&A, but virtually all of them revolve around trust. That's easy to say but hard to earn. Combining two entities to create something better is hard. It takes accountability, responsibility, commitment, and clarity. Embarking on a major transaction means inspiring and building trust with your board, your investors, your employees on both sides, your customers, and other crucial stakeholders that will be vital for your success.

I've known Mark Sirower and Jeff Weirens for more than 20 years and worked closely with both of them while I oversaw Deloitte LLP's Consulting practice. They are truly two of the leading minds on M&A and have advised on and assisted Deloitte clients through many hundreds of transactions across the M&A life cycle.

That's what makes *The Synergy Solution* such an important book. As Sirower and Weirens describe, M&A is a process—a "cascade," as they call it—and one that starts long before a deal as leaders refresh the vision of the future for their company. CEOs and their executive teams need to keep abreast of the changes and opportunities that exist in their markets and think of M&A not just as doing a deal but as a connected chain of actions that have to be led and managed in order to realize that vision for success. The ambitious scope of this book, and the detailed advice throughout, make it an illuminating read for all acquirers, regardless of their experience.

The authors ask a lot from leaders who are considering M&A. Do you understand the risks of what can go wrong, and the potential rewards if you get it right? What is your long-term M&A strategy, and have you done all the homework required to test your ideas before you value a target? What is your Day 1 plan for communicating to stakeholders why a transaction makes strategic and financial sense when you announce the deal to the public? Is your organization prepared for all the challenges ahead before and after the deal closes? How do you best anticipate the needs of your employees and customers and the uncertainty that lies ahead for them? *The Synergy Solution* answers all of these questions and many more.

This book is *the* definitive M&A text that every C-suite leader—and everyone who aspires to the C-suite—needs right now. Whether it's a traditional merger or acquisition to expand your markets and achieve efficiencies or you're filling capability gaps in what you need to compete and delight your customers, this book will help you get the right deals done—and vastly increase your chances for success. From strategy to valuation to integration to achieving an issue-free Day 1 and beyond, *The Synergy Solution* covers everything business leaders need to understand about what a strategic move might mean for their organization and how to prepare and execute on it successfully—as well as build trust in the process.

The Synergy Solution offers timeless insights about the mechanics of success throughout the M&A process. It is the most comprehensive, practical, and hands-on guide ever written for M&A deals. The best organizations care about culture, purpose, the future of their workforce, and the common good, but, ultimately, they have to take care of their customers and deliver results. All these factors are critical to a successful M&A deal—making this kind of work that much more complex, but also that much more meaningful.

Whether it's your first deal or your hundredth, the principles outlined in *The Synergy Solution* will help you to achieve greater clarity and focus around intent. As a result, you will be better positioned to emerge from the integration process with a high-performing, sustainable culture and employees who are committed to its growth and success for years to come.

Punit Renjen
CEO, Deloitte Global

THE
SYNERGY
SOLUTION

CHAPTER 1

The Acquisition Game

Once upon a time, mergers were sexy. They were perfectly glamorous. Filled with flamboyant corporate raiders, junk bonds, and coercive hostile takeovers of the 1980s and the all-stock mega-deals of the 1990s internet boom, mergers and acquisitions (M&A) grabbed front-page headlines seemingly every day.

But something went wrong. And "synergy" was getting a bad name.

By the early 1990s, evidence began to emerge from prominent academics and consulting firms that a majority of deals actually hurt the shareholders of corporate acquirers, several even resulting in bankruptcies.[1] In October 1995, *BusinessWeek* published the groundbreaking story "The Case Against Mergers," based on research showing that fully 65 percent of major deals destroyed value for the buyers' shareholders. Acquirers were regularly overpaying for alleged synergies, and investors knew it.[2]

Unfortunately, acquirers continue to disappoint today.

Yet few other tools of corporate development and growth can change the value of a company—and its competitive future—as quickly and dramatically as a major acquisition. Material M&A deals are major "life events" in the story of a company's history. Although the welfare of employees and customers are paramount, any deal's success will ultimately be judged like any other major capital investment decision: Did the allocation of capital and resources create superior shareholder returns relative to competitors?

Most material acquisitions even today do not deliver on their promises and hurt the shareholders of the acquirer. Although the shareholders of selling companies routinely benefit from the significant premiums that acquirers pay, returns to the shareholders of acquirers, on average, fall far short of expectations. Instead of giving investors the reason to buy more of their shares, acquirers are often giving them clear reasons to sell. And initial market reactions of investors, positive or negative, are on balance a reliable forecast and indicative of future results. Acquisitions usually fail, and investors can smell a rat.[3]

The questions are *Why?* and *What do we do about it?*

Our hypothesis is that these systemic failures are the result of a lack of preparation, methodology, and strategy. Most companies don't have a real M&A strategy in place. They haven't thought through the deals they believe are the most important versus a universe of others they have no business even looking at—they have few priorities. They jump into an auction or hire a banker who comes up with a few available acquisition targets and promises of synergies. Teams are quickly assembled to perform whatever operational or commercial diligence they can complete in a compressed time frame while the CEOs and bankers negotiate the price. They present the deal to the board, often with little consideration of how the synergies will actually be delivered, but with an urgency to approve. The implicit threat is that if the board can't see their way to approving the deal, there may be nothing else this good on the horizon. One prominent CEO called it the "Wow! Grab it! acquisition locomotive."[4]

Announcement Day arrives in the form of a carefully staged conference call packed with journalists and analysts—and plenty of excitement.

Then investors react. For the majority of companies, it's a harsh surprise, with the acquirer's stock dropping—investors (who include employees, who are also owners) feel the pain immediately.

Despite all the hard work that both the acquirer and target do, investor reactions tend to be right on the mark. The promised synergies never develop, or at least not at a level to have justified the price; employees don't understand how the deal will impact their futures; and the new company is a mess, destroying significant value for the firm and its shareholders. They rarely recover their losses.

We want to improve your odds for successful M&A. *The Synergy Solution* aims to change how companies—managers, executives, and boards—think about and approach their acquisition strategies. Beginning with the well-accepted foundation of the economics of the M&A performance problem, we'll guide acquirers through how to develop and execute an acquisition strategy that both avoids the pitfalls that so many companies fall into and creates real, long-term shareholder value. We're not looking to make mergers sexy again. But we are aiming to make mergers work—for acquirers and for their shareholders.

Then and Now: The Evidence

While some claim that things have gotten better—that companies and their managers are better at evaluating acquisitions and realizing the predicted synergies—we've discovered that, empirically speaking, things aren't much better at all. Moreover, investors continue to listen carefully to the details of what acquirers tell them about their major deals.

We updated Mark's landmark study of the 1990s merger wave (the basis of a *BusinessWeek* cover story), and our findings support the case that even after all the deal activity of the past several decades—and all of that opportunity to learn—there is still plenty of room for improvement.[5]

Let's take a closer look.

For our study, we drew from well-known data sources Thompson ONE and S&P's Capital IQ and examined more than 2,500 deals valued at $100M or more that were announced between

January 1, 1995, and December 31, 2018. We used publicly available data so that anyone can replicate our results. We excluded those deals where the acquirer's share price could not be tracked on a major US stock exchange. Using the rationale that a deal had to be material, we excluded those deals in which the market capitalization of the seller was less than 10 percent of the acquirer's. Finally, we culled deals in which the acquirer subsequently announced another significant acquisition within a year.

That yielded a sample of 1,267 deals representing $5.37 trillion of equity value and $1.14 trillion of acquisition premiums paid over the 24 years of our study. The average equity market capitalization, five days before announcement, was $9.3B for acquirers and $3.8B for sellers. The average market capitalization of sellers relative to their acquirer was 46 percent. These were by any measure very significant deals for acquirers. The average premium paid was 30.1 percent, or $902M.

We measured how acquirers performed around deal announcement using the 11-day total shareholder return (five trading days before to five days after) and how they performed over the course of a year post-announcement (including the announcement period). While one year may seem a short period in which to judge success or failure, the first year is critical to deliver performance promises because it signals the credibility of those promises.[6]

We examined both raw total shareholder return (stock price appreciation plus dividends) and total shareholder return relative to each acquirer's industry peers within the S&P 500, as classified by Capital IQ.[7] We report the industry-adjusted total shareholder returns (often called RTSR, or relative total shareholder return).

What did we find? The key results for our sample of 1,267 deals are outlined below.

Acquirers, on average, underperform their industry peers

Average returns to acquirers for these major acquisitions around deal announcement were –1.6 percent, with 60 percent of deals viewed negatively and 40 percent viewed positively by the market. One year later, the average returns for these acquirers were slightly worse at –2.1 percent, and 56 percent of acquirers lagged their industry peers. As with any study on M&A, there is a wide range of results, so these are just the averages.[8] Our overall results certainly suggest we should stop using the still widely cited statistic on M&A performance that 70 to 90 percent of deals fail.[9]

That said, acquirer performance was pretty bad in the 1980s and 1990s merger waves where nearly two-thirds of deals destroyed value for the acquirer.[10] *There is some encouraging news here.* When we split our sample into three eight-year periods covering three merger waves—1995–2002, 2003–2010, and 2011–2018—we found that acquirers have improved from 64 percent negative deal reactions to 56 percent in the most recent merger wave, and initial market reactions have improved from –3.7 percent to nearly zero; but one-year returns remain challenged, with a –4.2 percent one-year return in the latest eight-year period. (See appendix A for detailed data and results of the study.)

Despite what might be an encouraging sign, we're still not out of the woods. To put it bluntly, while M&A, on average, may be getting slightly better, it's just "less negative" overall.

Let's de-average these results and look deeper.

Initial investor reactions are persistent and indicative of future returns

Many observers believe that stock market reactions to deal announcements are mere short-term price movements and don't offer predictions of future success or failure. One CEO famously said, after a near 20 percent drop in the company's share price on the day of a major acquisition announcement, "You don't make this kind of move, and judge its success, by the short-term stock price."

To explore the assertion that initial investor reactions don't matter, we divided initial reactions into a positive reaction portfolio and a negative reaction portfolio. If market reactions don't matter, then both portfolios should trend to zero. They don't.

One year later, the portfolio of 759 deals that began with a negative reaction of –7.8 percent earned an even stronger negative return of –9.1 percent. The portfolio of 508 deals that began positively with a return of +7.7 percent maintained a strong positive return of +8.4 percent. A closer look shows that 65 percent of the initially negative deals were still negative, and 57 percent of initially positive deals were still positive a year after announcement. So, while a positive start is no guarantee of future success, especially if companies do not subsequently deliver on promises, a negative start is very tough to reverse, with nearly two-thirds of deals still negative a year later. And it's even tougher for negative reaction deals that use stock as currency: Nearly three out of four all-stock deals (or 71%) that were initially negative were still negative a year later.[11]

Bottom line: *Initial market reactions matter.*

Delivering results after a good start pays off big—and the opposite is true

Deals that began in a positive direction—and actually delivered—dramatically outperformed deals that began poorly and were persistently negative—what we call the "persistence spread." In the year following announcement, acquirers whose deals were met initially with a negative investor reaction, and continued to be perceived negatively, posted an average return of –26.7 percent; whereas acquirers whose deals initially received, and continued to receive, a favorable response, returned an average of +32.7 percent—a persistence spread, or difference in returns, of nearly 60 percentage points.

Not only do initial investor reactions matter a lot, they matter a lot in a way that should be very important to acquirers.

Figure 1-1 illustrates the general pattern of returns to acquirers. These findings are not accidental. Investor reactions are

FIGURE 1-1

Shareholder returns to acquirers

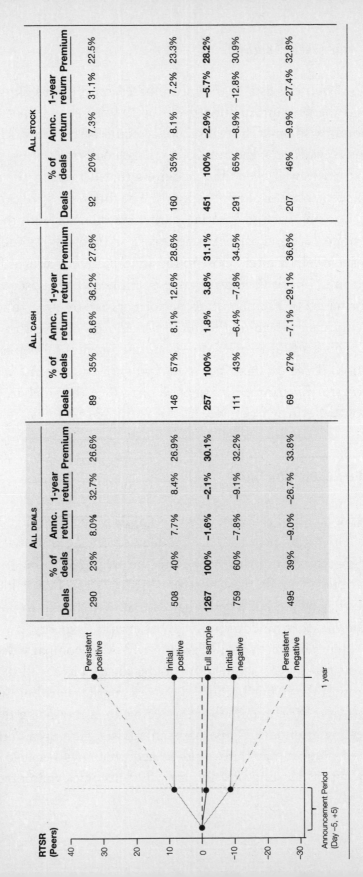

powerful forecasts of the future based on previous expectations and the new information given by the company about the economic wisdom of the transaction. Acquirers that truly deliver and show evidence of their ability to make good on their promises do extremely well over time; acquirers that deliver on the negative expectations do extremely poorly. The differences are enormous.

Looking back, the initial market reactions of both the persistent positive and persistent negative portfolios (8.0% and −9.0%, respectively) are very close to the announcement returns for overall initial positive and negative portfolios. The subsequent performance of the persistent performers is largely a function of acquirers confirming the initial perceptions of investors.

This leads us to ask a question fundamental to the rest of this book: *Based on this data, would you rather start with a positive investor reaction or a negative one?* (See the sidebar, "Shareholder Returns from M&A" for additional findings.)

The Acquisition Game

How can this be? Everyone knows by now you shouldn't pay "too much" for an acquisition, that acquisitions need to make "strategic sense," and that corporate cultures need to be "managed carefully." But do these nostrums have any practical value? What do they mean, anyway? What does it really mean to pay a premium? More fundamentally, what even is "synergy"?

Here's how it typically goes in M&A: A company decides to grow through an acquisition, not because it has a well-developed growth thesis but because the stock market is riding high and lots of other companies in the sector are announcing deals and getting attention. Or perhaps an adviser puts on a convincing presentation that the would-be acquirer buys because organic growth is leveling off, and the CEO becomes enamored of the deal.

Shareholder Returns from M&A

- **Acquisition premiums matter.** The average premium paid
  for targets across the whole sample was 30.1 percent,
  with an average premium of 32.2 percent paid by the
  initially negative portfolio and 26.9 percent paid by the
  initially positive portfolio. Not surprisingly, the average
  premium paid by the persistently negative performers was
  33.8 percent whereas the persistently positive performers
  paid an average premium of only 26.6 percent. The difference in premiums is even more striking for all-cash and
  all-stock deals for the persistently negative versus the
  persistently positive portfolios (36.6% vs. 27.6% for
  all-cash deals and 32.8% vs. 22.5% for all-stock deals,
  respectively).

- **Cash deals outperform stock deals by a lot.** All-cash deals
  (20% of deals) markedly outperformed all-stock deals
  (36% of deals). At announcement, the returns for all-cash
  deals beat all-stock deals by +4.7 percent (+1.8% vs. −2.9%,
  respectively). Moreover, 57 percent of cash deals received
  positive market reactions versus only 35 percent for stock
  deals, and the performance gap only widened over the
  course of a year to 9.5 percent as cash deals beat their
  peers by +3.8 percent while stock deals lagged their peers
  by −5.7 percent. This finding reaffirms the widely reported
  result on the underperformance of stock deals. The
  contrast is also illustrated with 46 percent of stock deals
  in our sample receiving initial and persistent negative
  returns versus 27 percent of cash deals. Combo deals—a
  mix of cash and stock—yielded announcement returns of
  −2.1 percent (with only 36% receiving a positive reaction)

(continued)

and one-year returns of −1.9 percent with a similar persistence spread as the overall sample of 1,267 deals (see appendix A for additional details).

· **Sellers are the biggest beneficiaries of M&A transactions.** While buyers on average lost, shareholders of selling companies earned an average 20 percent peer-adjusted return from the week before deal announcement to the week after. That contrasts with the average announced premium of 30 percent because of negative market reactions for acquirers on stock and combo deals, which reduced the amount actually received by sellers.

· **M&A transactions create value at the macroeconomic level.** Mergers create value for the economy. We calculated a measure for both buyers and sellers based on the 11-day peer-adjusted dollar return, for both, around deal announcement. The average total shareholder value added (TSVA) is simply the sum of those dollar returns for buyers and sellers. While buyers lost on average $285M, sellers gained an average $469M for a TSVA of $184M for all deals. (The TSVA is $333M for all-cash deals and $11M for all-stock deals.) The TSVA has improved over our three periods from nearly zero in the first period to $424M in the last, again with the majority of those gains going to sellers.

We also calculated a TSVA percentage based on total market capitalization of buyers and sellers. In the aggregate, we find value creation (TSVA) of roughly +1.45 percent at announcement based on the combined changes in market capitalization. Cash deals yielded a combined return of +3.73 percent, while stock deals had a combined change of +0.07 percent—a large difference—and a return of +2.05 percent for combo deals.

When acquirers play the acquisition game, they enter a unique business gamble where they pay an up-front premium for some distribution of potential outcomes—the synergies. If acquirers do not fully understand the performance promises they are making up front, or do not have the capabilities to deliver on those promises, or if the synergies are illusory, they will have engineered failure right from the beginning—something investors can and do recognize right at announcement.

Let's start with some simple examples that will illustrate the point.

Imagine there is an apartment you truly want to own on a lovely block of Greenwich Village in New York City. Sure, it's expensive, but you really want it. You and all your friends agree that it is better to live there than where you live now. You'll feel better. What's more, the apartment is a fixer-upper, and you figure you can increase the $1M appraised value by at least 25 percent. Unfortunately, you are dealing with an unmotivated seller who is asking $1.5M for the apartment. But you have spent so much time searching for the right place, and this one is a perfect fit. (Besides, all of your friends have apartments so much nicer than the one in which you currently reside.)

Do you go ahead with the transaction price of $1.5M? It depends on whether feeling better about your apartment is worth $250,000 to you. Because even if you make the improvements you think are possible and even if they add 25 percent to the appraised value, you will have permanently sacrificed $250,000 right at the point of purchase.

Or suppose you just arrived in Las Vegas, a trip you have been planning for a long time. You have read all the books about the various casino games, and you are sure you will make a killing. On the way to the casino, an attractive hotel employee beckons you to a room to play a very special game. You are offered the following payoff distribution: A fair coin will be flipped where heads (H) = $20,000 and tails (T) = $0. It will cost you $9,000 to play the game. Thus,

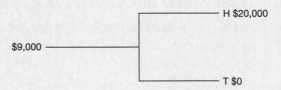

You think for a moment and realize that according to the law of averages, if you could play this particular game 100 times, you could make a lot of money—$100,000. That is, you pay to play whether you win or lose, and you expect to win 50 times for a net gain of $100,000 [(50 × $20,000) − (100 × $9,000)]. On the other hand, you also realize you could be wiped out after just a couple of plays before the law of averages sets in.

The essential lesson here is that we have to be very clear about the distribution of payoffs before we pay the price to play the game.

These examples illustrate the acquisition game. The acquisition premium is paid up front and we know it with certainty. The actual post-merger integration (PMI) will yield some uncertain stream or *distribution* of realized payoffs or synergies *sometime in the future*. Executives need to consider the likelihood of different scenarios of these payoffs (the synergies), or they may actually know more about the payoffs in blackjack than for a given acquisition. Stripped to its essentials, then, an acquisition is a traditional capital budgeting problem. But it is a unique one for several reasons that executives and boards must appreciate.

First, acquirers pay everything up front—the full market value of the target's shares plus a premium—before they even get to "touch the wheel." There are no dry runs, no trial and error, and unlike other capital investments, like R&D—there is no way to stop or divert the funding, other than divesting. Most important, the cost-of-capital clock on all that capital starts ticking from the beginning. So, delays will be costly. There are no do-overs.

Second, when acquirers pay a premium, they are taking on an already existing performance problem and creating a brand new one—one that never existed, and no one ever expected for those already existing assets, people, and technologies. In other words, acquirers have two performance problems: 1) they must deliver all the profitable growth and performance the market *already* expects from both the acquirer and the target, and 2) meet the even higher targets implied by the acquisition premium. Achieving those new performance requirements typically requires an enhanced set of capabilities, and competitors will not sit idly by while acquirers attempt to generate synergies at their expense. Putting together two profitable, well-managed businesses does not magically create strategic gains because competitors are ever present, and customers may not value the new offers.

That yields a clear definition of measurable synergies: *Performance gains over stand-alone expectations*. Putting together the up-front premium with the brand new performance problem, we have a straightforward view of the value created for the acquirer, the net present value (NPV) for a transaction:

NPV = Present Value (Synergies) – Premium

That is, assuming you don't ruin the businesses and can deliver all the stand-alone growth value already expected of the target (and your company), you create value only if you can achieve at least a cost-of-capital return on the premium. Executives paying a premium commit themselves to delivering more than the market expects from the current strategic plans of both companies.

Third, once acquirers begin intensive integration—so essential to generating the required synergies they have promised—they will have jacked up the costs of exiting and unwinding a failing deal. Closing a world HQ, merging IT systems, integrating sales forces, and reducing headcount is expensive and time-consuming to reverse. And in the process, acquirers may run the risk of taking their eyes off competitors or losing their ability to respond to changes in their competitive environment or evolving customer needs.

What's more, not only can shareholders readily diversify on their own, without paying a premium, but paying a higher premium does not necessarily yield a higher return or more synergies—in other words, the payoffs are not a function of the size of the bet.

The characteristics of deals that make them unique, taken together, form the three parts of what Mark has called the "synergy trap." Executives must do the hard work to avoid the following:

1. **Failure to understand the performance trajectory already priced into the shares of both stand-alone companies.** The result: Acquirers often mistake "synergies" with performance improvements already expected by investors. Synergies are improvements over that base-case trajectory—savings or profitable growth that can only be achieved as a result of the deal ("if but for the deal"). Confusing synergies with that base case will haunt you and your employees throughout the entire process.

2. **Failure to consider synergies in both competitive and financial terms.** If competitors can easily replicate the "advantages" of the combined company, then synergies are unlikely. They aren't just advantages because you say it is so; your customers have to agree. Achieving synergies means competing more efficiently and through a more differentiated and defendable position. Moreover, synergies don't come for free—there may be significant one-

time costs and ongoing costs to achieve the benefits. We call this the "synergy-matching principle" because you have to match the benefits with the costs to achieve them. Those one-time and new ongoing costs are, in effect, additions to the premium.

3. **Failure to understand the performance promises built into paying an up-front premium.** When you pay a premium, you are signing up for a new performance challenge that didn't exist before and no one expected—over already existing expectations. Acquirers must fully understand both the promises they are making and the capabilities, resources, and discipline required to realize those new required performance improvements. Remember, the cost-of-capital clock is ticking on all of that new capital from Day 1, whether or not you are ready to deliver.

The result is simple from a shareholder-value perspective. Think of it like an economic balance sheet. When you make a bid for the equity of a target, you will be issuing cash or shares to the shareholders of that company. If you issue cash or shares in an amount greater than the economic or present value of the assets under *your* ownership (without fully realizing the synergies), you have merely transferred value from your shareholders to the shareholders of the target—right from the beginning. This is how the economic balance sheet of your company stays balanced. It is the NPV of the acquisition decision—the expected present value of the benefits less the premium paid—that markets attempt to assess. That's what it means when sophisticated capitalists bid down the price of an acquirer while the price of the target goes up from the offer of a premium.

Because they fail to understand the traps and anticipate those complexities, acquiring companies tend to predictably overpay—by a lot. Faulty analysis is often baked into the calculations that companies use to evaluate the deal. The advisers make it look so easy. They price the target company as a stand-alone. Then they add in the form the synergies will take by putting the two companies together: a boost in revenue growth, lower cost of capital, efficiency gains through scale—and voilà! Out comes the right price and off they go to integrate the companies.

But so many errors can creep into an acquirer's M&A process, if they even have one, that oftentimes those synergies don't exist or are greatly exaggerated in a valuation model, on a deal that may not have been the right target from the get-go. The result: Without a disciplined process, target valuations converge to how other acquisitions are getting priced. And that's where the potential for value destruction begins.

The Solution

But here's the thing: It isn't that *all* acquisitions are bad, it's that poorly conceived or executed acquisitions are bad. Executives *can* generate valuable growth through significant investments in M&A. But it does mean that executives must understand why acquisitions are unique and risky—and begin to treat capital as luxurious. CEOs must answer the question whether they and their senior teams have done the proper strategic homework, careful valuation with specific synergies, and post-deal planning that might earn them the right to spend that luxurious capital.

Winning the acquisition game requires a lot of work and informed discipline—with myriad complexities ranging from considering valuation issues, competitor reactions, employee expectations and uncertainty, investor and employee communications through to the design of the new organization. This is the root of why so many companies fail and why investors are so skeptical.

There is an art and science to getting M&A right. We plan to guide you through how to develop and execute an acquisition strategy that avoids the pitfalls that so many companies fall into, how to properly communicate the performance promises you are making when you pay a premium, how to realize those promised synergies, how to manage change and build a new culture, and how to create and sustain long-term shareholder value.

We've learned the answers to these questions the hard way—through research, innovation, and hard-won experience. Between us, we have over 50 years of experience with M&A, from multibillion-dollar acquisitions to carve-outs and everything in between. We've been behind the scenes helping companies with crafting their M&A strategy, conducting diligence that tests the deal thesis, preparing for Announcement Day, and assisting with merger integration.

We wrote this book to help companies that are planning to use M&A as part of their growth strategy. It should help executives prepare and understand the intricacies of incorporating M&A into strategy, from developing a list of their most important potential deals to understanding the overall process and how to make success more likely—and deliver on the promises they make to their shareholders, employees, and customers. At the same time, it's also for the working managers on whose shoulders falls the responsibility of conducting diligence and synergy planning, and making the merger work and deliver on the promised results—oftentimes even when they first learn about it on Announcement Day.

The Synergy Solution offers an integrated view of the issues surrounding M&A. It provides background to those considering M&A, teaching which issues they have to consider, how to analyze them, and how to execute effectively. It also shows those who have already started the process of M&A how to maximize their chance of success.

The following five fundamental premises have guided our thinking and should be the touchstones for senior management and boards when considering M&A as a component of a successful growth strategy. They will become more salient as we proceed through our journey.

1. Successful acquisitions must both enable a company to beat competitors *and* reward investors.

2. Successful corporate growth processes must enable a company to find good opportunities and avoid bad ones *at the same time.*

3. Prepared acquirers (what we call "always on" companies) are not necessarily active acquirers—they can be patient because they know what they want.

4. A good PMI will not save a bad deal, but a bad PMI can ruin a good one (i.e., strategically sound and realistically priced).

5. Investors are smart and vigilant—that is, they can smell a poorly considered transaction right from announcement, and they will track results.

The Chapters

The Synergy Solution proposes a unique cascade that takes the reader from pre-announcement strategy through understanding the acquisition premium, how to understand the performance promises made to investors, Announcement Day, and on to how to execute on the promises made to investors. (See figure 1-2.)

In other words, *The Synergy Solution* encompasses the entirety of the process in a comprehensive methodology appropriate for multiple levels of the firm. It will give you the tools to distinguish smart acquisitions from poorly considered ones, effectively communicate the economics to multiple stakeholders, and execute and ultimately deliver value.

FIGURE 1-2

The M&A cascade

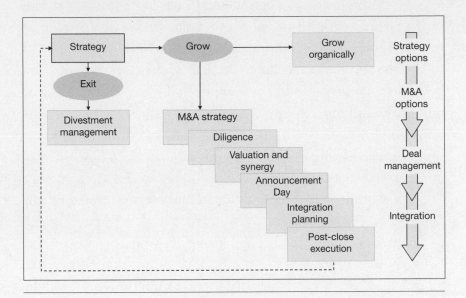

We've organized the book around a series of questions that speak to each stage of the process, beginning with "Am I a Prepared Acquirer?," the subject of chapter 2. It argues that most companies are reactive—responding to deals that appear before them—rather than proactively developing a priority watch list of their most important deals. The chapter lays out the case for why and how companies should and can prepare, including strategy and governance, and helps set up the logic for the rest of the book.

Chapter 3 asks, "Does It Makes Sense?," exploring three kinds of due diligence: financial, commercial, and operational. While diligence often is treated as a necessary evil—or even as a mere review of audited financials—this chapter argues that a robust, insight-driven diligence process that's rooted in your investment thesis will not only help you value the potential deal and identify potential integration hurdles, but can also suggest when to walk away.

Chapter 4 is all about the implications of the valuation and asks, "How Much Do I Need?" It shows a theoretically correct and direct approach to valuation and synergy that's based on the well-accepted concept of economic value added (EVA) to first examine both the acquirer and target as stand-alone companies— to understand the performance trajectory already expected by investors. We then use the new capital allocated in the form of paying the full market value of the target's shares (while assuming the debt) *plus* the acquisition premium, to show the annual improvements being promised by the acquirer, and how the premium translates into required improvements in after-tax net operating profit—the synergies; calculations that investors can and will do themselves.

Chapter 5 asks, "Will They Have Reason to Cheer?" on Announcement Day. Investor reactions set a tone that will impact all stakeholders. When material M&A transactions are brought to the market, they are often professionally staged and treated as a celebration for the senior executives of both the acquirer and target. But acquirers must treat Announcement Day less like a celebration and, instead, like a carefully orchestrated presentation, one with the clearly established goal of communicating the deal's value to all stakeholders.

Chapters 6 and 7 form a pair to address pre-close planning. They focus on how to avoid the mess that can come from poor planning, and how to capitalize on the deal momentum to rally the troops, energize customers, and lay the foundation for results to report to investors. Chapter 6, "How Will I Deliver on My Vision and Promises? Part I" shows how to realize the promise of your deal strategy during pre-close integration management. It focuses especially on the role of the Integration Management Office (IMO), a temporary structure that manages integration, both top down and bottom up.

Chapter 7, "How Will I Deliver on My Vision and Promises? Part II" examines the workstreams at the heart of integration and how to get ready for Day 1. Here, we focus on the cross-functional workstreams that are typical of the vast majority of pre-Day 1 integration structures and overseen by the IMO: organization design, synergy planning, communications and employee experience, and Day 1 readiness.[12]

Chapter 8 asks, "Will My Dreams Become Reality?" and focuses on the core job of the post-close execution team: to transition from the pre-close workstreams with the aim of getting the integrated businesses to business as usual as quickly as possible and well on their way to realizing synergy targets. The longer post-close execution takes, the less likely management is able to deliver on the value detailed in the original deal thesis. In an unforgiving market, this can lead not only to adjustments in earnings expectations, but also to management losing the ability to achieve the financial results achieved prior to close.

Chapter 9, "Can the Board Avoid the Synergy Trap?" offers several tools that can help boards spot those deals that are likely to result in negative market reactions. It also provides the board with a common framework that will drive more informed discussions about potential material deals. The tools will help close the gap between what management believes and what investors are likely to perceive *before* the market does. Without those tools, the board will be unable to answer the fundamental question: *How will this transaction affect our share price and why?*

Finally, chapter 10, "Getting M&A Right," brings the book to a close by reviewing the M&A cascade. If you make a mistake in M&A, you'll not only see a drop in your share price on Announcement Day, but you'll be stuck with the acquisition for years of pain before you grudgingly divest. By working through *The Synergy Solution*, you can avoid that ugly fate and transform into being a prepared acquirer who can realize the value of M&A done right.

CHAPTER 2

Am I a Prepared Acquirer?

M&A Strategy and Governance

Successful M&A begins with becoming a prepared acquirer—focusing on an "always on" watch list of the most important deals and making M&A strategy a part of a company's larger strategic aspirations and priorities. Prepared acquirers make difficult choices to establish a thoughtful agenda for their luxurious capital and pursue acquisitions based on a coherent strategy of how to compete and win in their chosen markets—and delight customers in ways not easily replicated by competitors.

Most companies, though, don't have an M&A strategy—they don't know what they want. Instead, they are *reactors*. Executive teams have kicked around lots of ideas for growth and M&A, but they aren't aligned around what the goals of their M&A program should be. They haven't thought through the deals they believe are the most important for their businesses, nor have they confronted a universe of other deals they may have no business even examining in the first place. They have few priorities.

Consider the hypothetical case of a company we'll call Homeland Technologies, a rapid-growth company that competes in the government IT services business. Founded in 1975, Homeland went public in 2011 with revenue of roughly $500M. Through internal growth and several small acquisitions, Homeland has successfully grown to $2B in revenue with respectable shareholder returns. Now, Homeland CEO Chas Ferguson is preparing to announce he intends to double revenues within three years and has asked an investment banker to bring him prospective acquisitions that will enable him to meet that goal. The board has given the thumbs up for Ferguson to begin conducting due diligence on deals brought to the company.

Is there anything wrong with this familiar picture? While motivated by the best of intentions, Homeland and its board are unwittingly about to join the growing ranks of other reactor companies—companies that make the often fatal mistake of outsourcing their inorganic growth strategy to investment bankers or other external parties, and merely react to available deals.

Unless it gets extraordinarily lucky, Homeland, like the vast majority of reactors, will likely execute one or more transactions—major capital investments—that disappoint investors as they send clear signals to sell rather than buy their shares at announcement.

Such mistakes are most common during merger waves, when inexperienced companies rapidly enter the acquisition game or companies with experience look for more or larger deals and radically change their risk profiles. That's how we get a wave shape. Companies can be driving toward M&A simply because so many other companies in their industry have started pursuing deals, and their banker warns them about being left without a dancing partner. (See the sidebar, "Great Myths of Reactor Behavior.") No one wants a *Wall Street Journal* reporter to write, "The world was changing and Charlie just sat there," but that pressure rarely yields a good result. Lacking a well-developed growth thesis, these unprepared companies engineer their own failures as they become part of the merger bandwagon.

Even worse, when reactors bid but don't close a deal or two, and the news gets out on their failed attempts, they feel even more

Great Myths of Reactor Behavior

Merger waves bring with them powerful myths that help support many reactive and unfortunate decisions. The following is an all-star lineup from the last few decades. Board members in particular should hold shareholders' pockets tightly when hearing any of the following:

- "Initial market reactions don't matter, we're in this for the long term. The stock price of acquirers always drops on announcement of a deal." Well, not on *good* ones. Negative market reactions are bad news—they are the investors' perceptions of what the company has communicated to the marketplace.

- "The financials looked fine on paper, but we didn't manage the cultures right." This excuse for past deals gone bad has become so powerful that "culture" often gets blamed for everything that goes wrong. Many deals that ultimately fail were *predictably* failures and managing cultures well rarely rescues a deal with bad economics.

- "Good deals must be accretive to earnings." There is little correlation between accretion or dilution and the stock market's assessment of deals.[a] Stock price is earnings per share (EPS) times price-to-earnings (P/E) ratio and a short-term increase in EPS can easily be offset by a drop in the P/E ratio—a proxy for expectations of long-term profitable growth.

- "If we don't do this deal, we'll be the last man standing without a dancing partner." Committing capital to an acquisition through fear of having nothing left to buy is never a good bet for your shareholders. This logic is a signal to all of a lack of preparation.

(continued)

> • "It will cost us much more money and time to build it from scratch." That may be true, but it might not be the right business or investment in the first place.
>
> a. David Harding and Phyllis Yale, "Discipline and the Dilutive Deal," *Harvard Business Review*, July 2002, https://hbr.org/2002/07/discipline-and-the-dilutive-deal.

compelled to close something. Sellers *really* love those reactors. Their largest strategic choices get made for them.

Prepared acquirers are the antithesis of reactor companies. These companies have developed a disciplined process that allows them to find good opportunities and avoid predictably poor ones, thereby enabling them to accomplish the chief objectives of successful corporate development—beating competitors and rewarding investors. They establish an agenda for M&A capital through an orchestrated process of strategic choices. They have many options.

Becoming a prepared acquirer is the main focus of this chapter. But, first, let's continue to shine a spotlight on reactors because it's through understanding the problems reactors create for themselves that we can uncover insights and solutions.

The Reactor Condition: Playing Not to Lose

Reactors predictably drive up pre-deal costs and risks and will have significantly reduced expected value from their deals. In an important sense, reactors are anti-strategic.

Reactors typically outsource—that is, hand over—their largest capital investment decisions to third parties who effectively drive a reactor's growth strategy by bringing them deals to consider. They have given up their power of choice—they don't have options. They kick around a lot of ideas that don't yield clear milestones or priorities. Without those priorities, reactors can't create or maintain an active deal pipeline. As a result, every potential deal that is presented to them is likely to be important to some executive, meaning that the process becomes political and not strategic. Since the CEO can't explain the, say, 20 most important deals they want to pursue over the next 12–18 months, they don't have an M&A strategy.

Instead of agreed portfolio priorities or capability needs driving their search for targets, reactors work backward—from an available deal that determines their strategic priorities. That is, reactors have deals chasing a strategy instead of strategy chasing deals. Rather than consider on an ongoing basis the total universe of options, reactors tend to focus exclusively on the deal at hand.

Viewed in isolation, a deal might look attractive, but compared with other potential M&A candidates, it could likely be a poor fit. This is a little like marrying the first seemingly compatible person you ever took out on a date: It could work—but the odds are against it. And the mistake often compounds itself. Enamored with the deal in front of them, reactors often fall prey to a confirmation bias—management may ignore or explain away negative information that emerges and search for positive evidence they are doing the right thing, even in a thorough evaluation of the candidate.

In negotiation terms, it is difficult for reactors to walk away from a deal because there is no better alternative to walk away to. A deal without a BATNA—a "best alternative to a negotiated agreement"—makes it far easier for a reactor to get caught up in the deal frenzy, racing to sign a deal, with full support of their advisers and confirmation bias, because there are no alternatives under consideration. The result: Without discipline and alternatives, internal target valuations converge to how other comparable acquisitions are getting priced, with the focus being on what the reactor *must* pay to get the deal done as opposed to how much it *should* pay for the deal at hand. Overpayment and the winner's curse become predictable.

Reactors also fail to consider potential operating model and integration issues that may affect the ease of actually realizing the value they are paying for. Some deals are going to be tougher and more complex to integrate than others. But because reactors look at deals sequentially, they miss the opportunity to differentiate deals that may more plausibly create value. Even worse, as reactors are forced into a compressed time frame to do diligence, they typically close a deal with few details of the operating strategy of how the target businesses will be managed. So not only do they run the risk of exaggerated claims of synergies—unable to justify the premium—they greatly increase the risk of damaging the growth value embedded in the target's stand-alone business as they try to achieve synergies that are unlikely to occur.

Acquiring the wrong company will just create a new set of operational problems beyond the ones that already exist for both companies as stand-alone firms. Little wonder that bad buyers often become good targets themselves. Evidence also suggests that wealth gains from corporate spin-offs may result from the correction of prior M&A mistakes.[1]

What's more, when reactors trap themselves into reacting to deal pitches from outsiders or by jumping into auctions, they waste precious time and resources that could have been devoted to finding more suitable opportunities in the first place. That's because management must conduct extensive and expensive due diligence for merger opportunities that present themselves, even though many should never have made it to the table. Careful due diligence may help avoid bad deals, but it doesn't help a company find the right ones.

Here's the crux of it: Reactors spend most of their time in diligence on deals that emerge trying to avoid false positives (accepting deals that should have been rejected) and thus drive up their risk of false negatives (rejecting a whole universe of other deals that might have been better). When a company reacts to a single opportunity, it has implicitly ruled out other potentially better alternatives that were not even considered. They trap themselves in a constant game of playing not to lose and, ironically, increase their risk of losing. They have great difficulty explaining to their board why they rejected other opportunities.

Becoming Prepared: Playing to Win

Successful M&A and corporate development require much more than simply attempting to avoid economically unsound deals. Prepared acquirers have a process that enables them to avoid bad deals and at the same time find the value-creating ones. It means the ability to reduce the risk of both false positives as well as false negatives.

Prepared "always on" acquirers play to win instead of only playing not to lose. They fully use their power of choice to bring strategic integrity to M&A by developing a thoughtful agenda for M&A capital. Although they may use external advisers to help them better understand a changing industry landscape, they don't outsource their strategies. Prepared acquirers treat capital like it is luxurious—expensive to touch and best treated with care. Most important, prepared acquirers have an identifiable M&A strategy. They know what they want and how they will create value.

Playing to win means putting in place a strategic process that allows you to answer the following five questions:

1. What is the role of M&A in our company's growth?

2. What companies or divisions do we want to buy, and why?

3. Which do we *not* want to buy?

4. Which do we not want our *competitors* to buy?

5. What deals are we going to do after this one, whether or not we close?

Senior teams should be able to project their appetite for deals to their business leaders. They know if M&A is going to make up 10 percent of their growth or 30 percent or more. They will be able to discuss with their boards the most important targets they are monitoring over the next 12–18 months (or a shorter horizon in rapidly evolving markets) and be able to describe a universe of targets that would be of little or no interest—and why—so they don't waste time or money on those if they were to become available. They will have also considered the deals their competitors might do that could impact their businesses as the competitor attempts to generate synergies at their expense. Before they would jump into an auction, just because their competitor is doing so, they would need to value just how much they would be impacted before they open the bank vault to do a defensive deal. Moreover, whether or not they close a particular deal, acquirers that are playing to win have a view on what deals might come next.

These five questions beg a series of other questions and force leadership teams to have conversations and debates, among themselves and with their board, and conduct analysis to get on the same page and establish priorities. It also helps to avoid—or at least dampen—internal politics. This is a point worth pausing on. Reactive acquirers can get tripped up by internal politics because a deal lacking a strategy will inevitably have an internal champion who feels strongly about "winning" the deal. Without any priorities or criteria to say whether this deal is a good one or not, that internal champion can push their deal through their management team—a team that doesn't share a common understanding of what role M&A plays in the company's growth or other deals that should be under consideration.

Prepared acquirers don't look at deals in isolation. They think about portfolios of assets that the deals on their watch list represent, and how those portfolios can be assembled over time to grow their existing core businesses or create new, advantaged businesses based on their organic capabilities. In other words, companies that play to win have prioritized the most promising *pathways* along which they search for the most important assets in the market. Pathways might be focused on certain products, services, and customer segments, end-market applications, emerging technologies, or different approaches to serving specific customers in ways competitors will have difficulty replicating.

Imagine our Homeland CEO Chas Ferguson was presented with a list of 100 deals, some related to the core, some in adjacent spaces, and some new businesses that might be part of Homeland's future. If Chas were to look deeply into the list, like a Rorschach test of sorts, he would see many different strategic pathways. For Homeland, that might mean prioritizing major government customer segments like the Department of Defense, Central Intelligence Agency, or Federal Bureau of Investigation, or certain businesses to prioritize in Homeland's portfolio of government IT services like secure infrastructure or military systems engineering (we illustrate this later).

Perhaps no company illustrates development of pathways better than Amazon.

Amazon: Creating Pathways for Acquisitions

Amazon's humble beginnings as an early internet book retailer run out of Jeff Bezos's garage bely the strategic ambitions that made the company the successful behemoth it is today—one that would be barely recognizable to anyone traveling into the future from 1994. While Amazon still sells books, it has expanded into a wide range of seemingly unrelated areas. Through more than 150 transactions (87 full acquisitions), including nearly $20B spent on its top 10 deals, M&A has played a central role in the development of several strategic pathways from e-commerce to the Kindle to Amazon Web Services (AWS) to grocery to Alexa and the connected home.[2]

From its earliest days, Amazon has invested in companies that, on their surface, didn't seem core to its business but offered potential pathways for future growth. For instance, Amazon acquired a 35 percent stake in Homegrocer.com in 1999 to test the waters in food, but it wasn't until 2017 that Amazon was fully credited with its commitment to grocery and food retailing, buying Whole Foods for $13.7B. Wall Street analysts often failed to understand this approach: An analyst from Piper Jaffray, for example, commented that endeavors such as AWS were a distraction to profitability.[3]

Some of these forays have yielded full-fledged products or business lines such as the Kindle and AWS. Others served as beachheads into developing technologies or markets, such as artificial intelligence (AI) (e.g., TSO Logic), home automation products (e.g., Echo and Ring), healthcare, media, or retail investments (e.g., India's Aditya Birla and Witzig).

An aptitude for learning and a penchant for highly strategic acquisitions have enabled Amazon to penetrate and lead many business and consumer categories—and for journalist Brad Stone to call it "the everything store." Amazon's original business model of selling books online laid the foundation for its hyper-scalable platform of bringing buyers and sellers together. Since the late 1990s, it has broadened its product focus from books to an extended portfolio of retail goods, supported by both organic growth (e.g., operating other e-commerce platforms such as CDNow) and M&A (e.g., Back to Basics Toys for hard-to-find toys, Woot for electronics and household goods, Quidsi for baby and childcare, Zappos for footwear, and Shopbop for apparel).

Going beyond adding new categories, Amazon embraced its platform, initially as a two-sided online exchange, enrolling external vendors by providing them with a self-serve merchant platform and giving them access to its millions of existing customers who, in return, benefited from access to a wealth of new vendors. These new vendors quickly went beyond the initial rare and out-of-print books categories Amazon had acquired through Bibliofind and Exchange.com, which were closer to its original core business of bookselling.

From there, Amazon has expanded along many pathways— not always successfully but always using a highly strategic lens for acquisitions. Amazon had a blueprint for extension into peripheral segments, sometimes taking a stake in adjacent markets that would bear fruit several years after initial acquisitions and investments.

The development of Kindle, for example, can be traced back to 2004 when Jeff Bezos and Steve Kessel assembled a team of veteran hardware, software, and computing engineers to create the secret Lab126 "skunkworks." Through acquisitions complementary to their hardware development, especially Mobipocket, an ebook publishing platform accompanied by e-reader software for handheld devices, the Kindle launched barely three years later. The Kindle, beyond just innovation, allowed Amazon to enhance the network effect of its platform, and indeed Amazon customers who owned a Kindle spent over 55 percent more per year ($1,233 vs. $790) than customers who did not own one.[4]

Guiding principles

Amazon's approach to M&A is rooted in several key guiding principles. It first identifies business models and pathways with growth potential and then assesses what capabilities are required to successfully enter those areas. It then looks for companies with the necessary capabilities and assesses its targets based on specific criteria. This means that Amazon is always evaluating dozens of targets rather than being fixated on one deal or being reactive to deals that others are bringing to it.

This is a key point: Amazon has made M&A strategy a core part of its overall growth strategy. Whether through full acquisitions or minority stakes in companies where it sees potential,

Amazon M&A is focused on supporting and relentlessly exploiting its core capabilities of customer experience, lower cost structure, and lower costs for seemingly unlimited choices.

This approach—a *customer-centric* business model with specific capability needs driving the search for deals that will complement Amazon's portfolio of existing assets while making a portfolio of bets on the future—has resulted in a dramatic transformation of the company over 25 years from an online book retailer to a multi-sided online marketplace (customers, merchants, and financing sources for merchants and customers) to a top-tier player in a multitude of distinct, yet related, pathways including cloud services, food ecosystems, and connected homes.

One can see these principles at play, along a clear pathway, in Amazon's development of Alexa, Amazon's virtual assistant, introduced in 2014 alongside the Echo line of smart speakers. Lab126, Amazon's internal skunkworks, started the development of the Echo in 2010. Alexa, its main interface, is a voice-activated assistant. To develop it, Amazon had to augment Lab126's hardware with AI capabilities to enable functions such as text-to-speech, voice recognition, and natural language processing.

Amazon bought Yap in 2011 (a speech-to-text company that provided expertise in translating the spoken word into written language), Evi in 2013 (a UK AI company with software that could process and respond to users' spoken requests), and Ivona in 2013 (a Polish company with text-to-speech technology that enabled Echo to generate natural voice). As *Wired* reported, "Initially, Amazon planned to leverage Evi's technology to build an artificial speech-based book reader. This narrow vision later evolved into an idea to create a new platform that would be powered by a combination of Amazon Web Services (AWS), speech recognition, and high-quality speech synthesis and would be tied to an affordable piece of dedicated hardware, ultimately producing the Alexa-powered Amazon Echo Smart Speaker, which launched in late 2014."[5]

The Echo offered an entry point into homes everywhere and has allowed Amazon to establish itself as a strong competitor to Apple in home automation—which rapidly became the connected home ecosystem—with a suite of products coming from various acquisitions. Amazon acquired Blink in 2017 (security cameras), Ring in 2018 (intelligent doorbells), and Eero in 2019 (mesh Wi-Fi routers).

Our brief example of Amazon shows how M&A strategy, if done right, allows acquirers to strengthen and extend their business models and leapfrog organic growth scenarios. More important, M&A is an ongoing effort of establishing priorities and making strategic choices of what to develop organically versus what to acquire. That requires being fully aware of the landscape of companies and capabilities in the market and pursuing those assets that will allow the acquirer to delight customers in ways not easily replicated by competitors. Amazon made clear choices of its pathways and the deals it wanted, regularly reviewing a universe of options.

The upshot: Successful M&A is rarely a one-shot effort. Prepared "always on" acquirers can afford to be patient, and don't necessarily need to be active, because they know the landscape and they know what they want and why.

It takes a tremendous amount of work and time discovering and prioritizing deal candidates, but it yields so many benefits. As one *Fortune* 50 executive told us: "The more you look, the more you find; the more you look, the more you learn; the more you look, the more you test your strategies."

The good news: You don't have to be as impressive as Jeff Bezos and Amazon, but the company's impressive use of acquisitions to expand beyond its core business and fundamentally transform itself—from online bookseller to AWS and the connected home—should give you a sense of what a clear, "always on" M&A strategy looks like, and how totally different it looks and feels compared to being a reactor.

From Reactor to "Always On"

It is no coincidence that the most successful acquirers are also the most disciplined. Before making a deal, experienced acquirers such as Disney, PepsiCo, Ecolab, and Amazon satisfy themselves that their strategic alternatives and acquisition opportunities have been carefully explored and their potential for creating value quantified. They understand which of their businesses should be developed organically, which should be sold, and which would benefit from growth through acquisition. They are often the most credible buyers, able to pay the most, because they know what they are looking for and how they will integrate the acquired assets. Ultimately, valuable growth through M&A is an outcome of overall corporate and business priorities and strategy through a regular and relentless pursuit of a portfolio of the most important deals.

Few companies fall into the category of Amazon regarding acquisition experience. But inexperience is no excuse to be a reactor. To avoid becoming a casualty of merger mania, every company that seeks growth through acquisition must first look itself in the mirror to determine whether it is a reactor or an "always on" prepared acquirer. Companies that want to become prepared before beginning or ramping up their acquisition strategy must see the process as a transformation—a dynamic state change. It requires an ongoing process of alignment, learning, and execution in the market as companies play to win in M&A.

That transformation process, regardless of experience, involves four major steps toward answering the questions we outlined earlier on playing to win:

1. Self and competitor M&A assessment

2. Aligning the top team on strategic pathways and priorities

3. Developing a master list of potential acquisitions across chosen pathways

4. Strategic screening and detailed profiling of a priority watch list

Self and competitor M&A assessment

Because superior performers are typically judged by their investor returns, M&A strategy development begins with an evaluation of how the market values a company and what the company has led investors to believe. That means ultimately understanding their current operations value and future growth value (we cover this in detail in chapter 4), and the growth trajectory implied by their market value and investor expectations. If there is a gap between that and their organic growth trajectory, M&A may play a role in closing that gap. Corporate-level growth expectations can be de-averaged to business-unit level and used to highlight gaps—and advantages—and prioritize the role that M&A might play across those business units.

Some pathways and specific deals along those pathways may be far better than others in delivering management's aspirations and investors' expectations. Because capital is expensive, this kind of evaluation should be table stakes for business units to earn the right to grow through M&A.

It's also important to set the stage by evaluating competitors' strategic intent. M&A strategy is a three-dimensional chess match that includes not only your own competencies and growth plans, but also the strategic intent competitors are signaling from their past deals. There's often a lot to learn from examining the M&A deals your competitors have done over the last several years, in terms of geographies, capabilities, size, product or service offerings, and targeted customer segments. Call it "competitor signaling"—their past behavior will often foreshadow which acquisition targets may be next on their priority lists. Armed with that information, a prepared acquirer will have a better view of how the industry is evolving relative to what competitors are signaling in the market with their largest investment decisions and how their competitors are trying to win. It also may highlight the cases where the acquirer and some of its competitors are likely going to battle over the same transaction.

Figure 2-1 shows what an acquirer can learn by looking at the pattern of competitor deals and by plotting its own deals, the signals it is sending to its competitors and investors about what might come next. Ultimately, Homeland—our example here—needs to make choices on where it wants to play in M&A. Preparing a similar chart sets the stage for the choices that an acquirer will need to make as it establishes priorities (e.g., customer focus, capabilities, businesses, geographies, and so on).

Aligning the top team on strategic pathways and priorities

Before considering any acquisition opportunity, senior management and boards of directors must agree on important strategic choices that set the direction of the businesses. These include realistic growth aspirations and the most profitable growth opportunities in light of how competition in the industry and unmet customer needs are evolving. Management must decide which customer segments, end markets, respective geographies, and so on they want to serve, with which products, and how they intend to do so in ways competitors cannot easily replicate.

Such an analysis calls for assessing the company's competitive strengths and weaknesses as well as setting priorities for what capabilities will be required to win in their targeted markets. Executives must consider what they have led investors to believe about their growth prospects and their strategies and investments to achieve them. Major capital investments such as acquisitions often leave investors puzzled about what the company is trying to accomplish beyond merely getting bigger.

A real danger is that without alignment among the top team, individual members can champion a deal for purely political reasons. Without a common understanding of what role an acquisi-

Homeland Technologies M&A strategy

		Air Force	Army	DIA	DISA	OSD	Navy	NGA	NRO	NSA	CIA	DHS	DoS	NASA
SYSTEMS ENGINEERING	Independent verification													
	Research and development													
	Testing and evaluation		■											
	Systems engineering services		■											
INFORMATION TECHNOLOGY	Web technologies													
	Enterprise messaging /groupware									■				
	Application development													
	Knowledge management													
	Enterprise system management													
	Systems integration solutions													
SECURE SYSTEMS AND INFRASTRUCTURE	Personnel security investigative services		■									■		
	Networking monitoring and analysis		■						■		■			
	Computer forensics and analysis								■					
	Secrecy and security architectures									■				
	Information assurance				■						■			
	Critical infrastructure safeguards										■			
	Security/software engineering				■									
	Communication system and infra. support													
	SIGINT systems life cycle engineering													
	Intelligence operations support									■				
	Strategic and tactical intelligence systems									■				
	Counterintelligence operations													
		Air Force	Army	DIA	DISA	OSD	Navy	NGA	NRO	NSA	CIA	DHS	DoS	NASA
					DEPARTMENT OF DEFENSE									

Note: Government agencies and offices are abbreviated.

tion is going to play, a passionate investment pitch from someone looking to increase their profile or expand their part of the business can drive the process forward—again, often with disappointing results.

Most boards and management teams complain they spend little time discussing where they want their business to be over the long term. A common frustration among directors is that they spend too much time talking about current and recent past issues instead of focusing on future growth. These short-term issues are important, but they can keep the board and management from setting and regularly updating a forward-looking vision and strategy.

Without that vision, it's hard to answer the question of whether to achieve growth targets organically or through acquisition, or some balance of the two. There is no substitute for regular discussions between the board and senior management on this issue. This process helps identify the rationale for acquisitions— especially priority pathways—and initial criteria for screening potential candidates along those pathways. If an acquisition shows up out of the blue, then *at least* there will be a strategic context to decide whether it is worth any time to evaluate it. An examination of the successes and failures of past acquisitions gives an invaluable backdrop for discussing industry evolution and strategy adjustments to make for the future.

Business leaders will all have their favorite adjacent pathways to their core business, and those all need to be debated and tested. Acquirers must be aware that *today's adjacency is tomorrow's core*. That might sound obvious, but it is a cautionary note. Although adjacencies may be attractive areas for growth, an acquirer might be opening the door to a whole new set of competitors that will not sit idly by as the acquirer attempts to generate synergies at their expense.

Quaker's move in 1993 to buy Snapple is a classic case. Once Quaker announced it was going to turn Snapple into a greater threat in the ambient beverage segment, it meant Quaker would have to wrestle shelf space away from Coke and Pepsi. Nearly overnight, Coke and Pepsi announced marketing campaigns greater than the entire Snapple marketing budget. The best way to avoid such a rude awakening is to anticipate competitor reactions, which lies at the heart of any M&A strategy.

Amazon too faced the challenge of determining the universe of pathways where it would face new competitors: from selling other consumer goods to an e-reader to retail grocery to web services. While Amazon has displayed patience and a willingness to invest capital (both through M&A as well as R&D) to enter then-adjacent now-core markets, an obsession with its customers has guided its strategic decisions over the long term. Amazon leadership has been steadfast in its belief that unrelenting customer obsession in whichever markets it serves gives it a sustainable competitive advantage. This has proven largely true and has enabled Amazon to lead categories and keep formidable companies at bay, for example in web services where AWS holds a commanding market share lead over Microsoft, IBM, and others. As Bezos said, "If we can keep our competitors focused on us while we stay focused on the customer, ultimately we'll turn out all right."[6]

Further, failing to have clear and agreed M&A strategy priorities instead of "many ideas for growth" up front will create difficult questions about "strategy" during diligence, when it will be challenging to develop clear hypotheses you are trying to test in the market. It is not uncommon for those stuck with the task of diligence to ask how that deal ever got to that stage.

Developing a master list across chosen pathways

Casting a wide net, management should then generate a master list of acquisition candidates in its priority core or adjacent industry spaces where it has decided it wants to grow and compete.

The purpose is to leave no stone unturned and to learn along the way. The goal is to know all relevant players so well that it's difficult for an outsider to bring an opportunity management has not already considered in some way.

Once all major players begin appearing on subsequent searches and few new businesses emerge, management can be confident of a solid initial list. The next step is to consider the high-level information that will later force choices—to sort the list and make it meaningful. At this stage, only the most relevant information needs to be collected on these companies: size, geography, and whether public, private, or subsidiary of a larger parent. As the process proceeds, more and more relevant information will be collected for those companies that remain under consideration.

This is not a one-shot process. Over time, competitors may buy companies on the list, emerging companies will appear, and rapid growth companies doing deals may become a peer competitor right in front of your eyes. If you have never done this before, you are likely going to be amazed with all the potential targets that exist in your priority markets. As you stare at the list, before you even start to screen you will see clusters of opportunities that you probably haven't ever considered. This is all part of the learning process that sets up the need for choices on how you will screen those potential targets. Those clusters are different M&A strategies along the pathway you are about to screen.

A note on pathways. As you search and build your master lists, it will become quickly apparent that if you haven't prioritized the parts of your core or potential adjacencies to explore, you will have a mess of potentially thousands of potential targets across multiple pathways. There's no harm in populating multiple pathways with players to see just how many different M&A strategies exist within and across those pathways, but it's far better to establish your priorities early or you will face several predictable problems. A look back at many unsuccessful M&A programs shows scattered unintegrated deals, signaling that the senior team wasn't aligned on an M&A strategy.

It's vital to recognize that *pathways* are not *screening criteria*. In other words, most companies will have multiple pathways they can pursue in core, adjacent, and new business, but making the difficult choices of where you want to play and what advantages you have, or need, to compete should come before you start looking for and differentiating among a universe of targets.

Both pathways and specific screening criteria represent strategic choices. But if you mix them up and start screening a bunch of targets before you have prioritized broad strategic pathways in your core business or potential adjacencies, the pathway question will inevitably emerge later. If you find someone asking what your strategy is for a proposed target during screening—"Hey, what was the strategy here?"—it's a pretty good sign that you have a target in search of strategy, *any strategy*, rather than a clearly delineated strategy that the team understands and can articulate.

Confusing pathways with screening criteria will later lead to the question of whether the work has been done to establish strategic priorities. We call this common issue "pay me now or pay me later." That is, if you don't make the tough choices early, then you will end up debating deals that represent entirely different strategies later on. Or worse, without that prioritization, you can expect to be back in that political process where more powerful executives push their favorite deals that may not be in the best interests of the company.

Strategic screening and selection of a watch list

Once the universe of opportunities is identified, prepared acquirers must develop strategic screens of increasing detail to narrow the list of candidates. While M&A strategy helps develop prioritized pathways for growth, target screening filters the deal universe within those pathways to help generate portfolios of priority candidates.

This is hardly a mechanical exercise. Gone are the days when the state of the art was to take a list of, say, 100 specialty chemical companies and then "come up" with nine screening criteria—ranging from size and geography to whether the targets had any unwanted businesses, each of which would be assigned a weight based on its perceived importance. Then a junior analyst would score every deal on that list on a scale of 1 to 10, across each of the nine weighted criteria. And boom, the short list would emerge.

The problem is, of course, if the weights or scores were changed just a little, you would get a different list. The lesson, and it's a big one, is that this is no way to do screening. One never knows all the things one will need to know to choose criteria—strategic choices—up front, especially if one has never been through the exercise. Screening is essentially an orchestrated process of making strategic and operational choices, and the depth of those choices gets finer grained as the list gets smaller.

Executives often find this the most challenging part of the process because it involves implementing a whole set of tough choices about the assets they believe they need to compete and grow. Let's admit it: Choice is hard because it shuts down seemingly attractive options. Management may debate what those strategic priorities are along chosen pathways. But the screens are actually important strategic choices that can help senior management and the board understand why a particular priority target was identified in the first place—and why others did not make the cut. Screening out bad fits—while identifying good ones—based on agreed-upon criteria is what this process is all about.

Initial screens may be based on size or geography consistent with the broad strategic needs of the business; subsequent deeper-dive screens might concern specific product lines, specific customers, R&D and manufacturing capability, facility locations, and management experience. Designing these criteria forces executives to revisit and refine their strategic priorities. Executives are often surprised about how much they learn about the landscape from working through the process across a universe of targets. Additionally, this effort helps minimize the risk of doing the wrong deals by preventing unsuitable candidates from even being considered.

Later in this screening process, as more detailed profiles have been completed on remaining candidates, the ease or difficulty of post-merger integration becomes a more important part of the discussion. Then, potential transition risks such as culture fit, outstanding labor or supplier contracts, geographic or customer concentration, distribution gaps, and management depth can be identified to differentiate deals and identify those opportunities most likely to create value. It is virtually impossible to conduct a sophisticated financial analysis of synergy potential—including probability estimates and timing of expected synergies—without evaluating integration risks and opportunities early on. Prepared acquirers begin these considerations during the screening process. Different transactions will have different integration issues that directly affect due diligence and valuation, and, ultimately, whether a candidate should remain under consideration.

Bankers are great at bringing prospective deals that appear to be attractive based on market growth or target growth. Such targets may appear attractive but are often not plausible for an acquirer because they don't fit with the agreed-upon strategic needs of the business or might be extremely complex to integrate. This distinction is important as you get to later phases of fine-grained screening to differentiate the best-fit deals.

The product of this exercise is a watch list of the most attractive and plausible acquisition candidates, subject to further diligence, with detailed profiles of each candidate. Even with the smaller watch list, each target will still represent a slightly different strategy offering varying advantages and opportunities.

The watch list can also be grouped by transaction strategy—larger platform deals followed by smaller tuck-ins on the list or just the opposite. Creating a watch list also offers the opportunity to easily cultivate and refresh the pipeline and broader M&A program as the competitive environment shifts, potential disruptors emerge, and other deals get done in the industry.

At times, the process will require significant discussion and heated debate, but there is no substitute for guiding what the company is searching for and what is competitively meaningful. In the end, management will have a much better view of its competitive landscape, what it needs to create value for customers, and the true priorities of its businesses. Moreover, this process will allow senior management to develop and communicate more sensible, credible acquisition stories to the board, investors, and employees. It should be obvious by now that reactors looking at one deal at a time cannot compare options.

Reaping the Benefits

Becoming a prepared acquirer—one that is "always on"—is less about executing a project and more about going through a transformation. Being "always on" means that you'll develop a better pipeline of priority targets as part of your M&A strategy. It will allow you to save significant resources by not focusing on inappropriate deals. You will drive your own M&A process and timeline rather than being driven by someone else's (e.g., seller or competitor) timing, meaning you'll be less likely to be rushed to close. You'll know which auctions are most important and which should be avoided—and why. You can raise diligence and integration issues before valuation and negotiation even begin. You can use this landscape education process to reassess growth pathways and alternative transactions. You'll also build credibility with the board and efficiently move targets through the pipeline.

And, finally, you will construct a better, more robust investment thesis that will be tested during due diligence (see chapter 3).

Even the most experienced acquirers, who may have dozens of people supporting them throughout the business units, typically complete only 10 to 20 percent of the deals in their pipelines. And many targets might not be readily available for sale. That low conversion percentage underscores the importance of being "always on" with plenty of smart alternatives and a full pipeline. You'll also end up with a portfolio of desired assets that represent deliberate strategies rather than looking at a deal in isolation.

In other words, you'll be playing to win in M&A instead of playing not to lose.

Management teams that go through the process we have outlined do not have to be *active* acquirers. They can afford to be patient because they have well-developed alternatives. They can negotiate with multiple parties on their watch list and seek the best values as they learn more about those candidates. After the stock market implosions in 2000–2002 and 2008–2009, these companies were in an excellent position to shop for valuable deals.

Routinely observing this process will also enable management to track what deals have been done by competitors and better consider the signals competitors are sending about their own growth objectives and how they intend to compete. Because they have a clear watch list of competitively important targets, management will also know those deals competitors might do or attempt to do that will, in fact, require an immediate response.

Becoming a prepared acquirer requires effort at multiple levels of an organization—but the effort is sure to help the people working at each level meet their responsibilities more successfully (see below, "A Note on M&A Process Governance"). Most important, an aligned "always on" management team is the lifeblood of a successful corporate development process, one that will give investors strong reasons to buy shares on deal announcements and will grow shareholder returns over the long run.

Directors who insist that a documented strategic M&A process be in place well before any opportunities are presented to them can avoid merely being the last hurdle on the CEO's path to announcing a major transaction—and can thereby shoulder their fiduciary duties far more credibly. The business and corporate development executives who devise and implement the M&A process can be satisfied that any deals they do will be much more likely to succeed. Shareholders, meanwhile, can be glad their company has gotten a lot smarter about how to move ahead in a complex and fast-changing business.

Real M&A strategy is about creating value versus doing deals. It's also a landscape education exercise that forces you to rethink your strategies. It's a top-team alignment exercise that drives regular discussions about strategic priorities. And it adds to the tapestry of management credibility with investors, employees, and the board.

A Note on M&A Process Governance

Even with a dynamic watchlist of several priority targets, would-be acquirers are unlikely to get those deals done if they don't have rules and practices that govern the entire M&A life cycle. Without formal governance, powerful executives can force through deals detrimental to the company. Others may have their deals killed by overly large committees with conflicting incentives before they even have a chance to present their case. Inconsistent procedures and metrics will cause confusion. Business unit executives may simply stop bringing deals knowing that their efforts will be wasted.

Like any governance process, the ideal is to know the scope of each stage of the M&A cascade, who must be in the room for each stage, a process for convening those stakeholders, required knowledge transfer during and between each stage, clear decision rights and accountability, and logical and stable criteria for those decisions.

The imperative is to establish an effective organization and specific procedures with capable leadership. Together, these will support an M&A process that everyone can follow and is repeatable: "This is the way we do deals." Successful acquirers have well-developed M&A playbooks that all players follow.

M&A strategy, for example, begins with the CEO, the senior executive team, corporate development and business unit leadership, and the board. Together, they address the role of M&A in overall corporate strategy, which aligns executive leadership around issues like appetite for risk and the appropriate degree and purpose of M&A for growth. That guidance sets the foundation for determining priority pathways, at both the corporate and business levels, and, later, initial criteria for screening acquisition targets and the development of the deal pipeline—which will likely involve additional subject-matter experts from the businesses as business cases are developed for specific deals.

Each subsequent stage must rely on the analysis of the stage before. New stakeholders will build on the work of those who were involved earlier. Between each pre-deal stage are clear decision gates, with criteria for moving forward or ending the exploration of the deal.

Acquirers will need to decide the appropriate level of centralization of M&A-related activities. What are the specific roles and responsibilities of management at corporate versus the business units? Who owns the deal model? What are the reporting relationships during each stage? What competencies and level of talent are required? Which stages will require external support and who gets to decide?

The M&A process itself requires specific procedures and decision rights that cover the complete span and timing of activities. What issues must be addressed in the deal thesis? When and from whom are approvals required before proceeding to the next stage? What knowledge transfer is required between stages and which players need to become involved while maintaining confidentiality? When must leadership interface with the board and on what issues?

While many of these issues and questions might seem basic, we would characterize them instead as fundamental. By having a clear process and well-defined roles and responsibilities consistent with agreed objectives for M&A strategy, companies can monitor competitor M&A activity and sustain an active deal pipeline that is refreshed regularly. Ownership and accountability at each stage of the process, along with agreed evaluation criteria rooted in an M&A growth thesis, will help acquirers avoid falling prey to political games and allow them to drive toward closing the most important deals and creating value: one of the outcomes of being "always on."

CHAPTER 3

Does It Makes Sense?

Financial, Commercial, and Operational Due Diligence

Sellers—unsurprisingly—present buyers with rosy pictures of their future revenues and margins, and for good reason: A significant portion of most companies' shareholder value is based on future growth expectations. Acquirers must take on the fact the future is filled with uncertainty for both the stability of the current business and profitable revenue growth.

As a consequence, acquirers must perform due diligence on both the current business and its stand-alone future growth potential because they will pay for both—plus a premium. Remember, when acquirers play this game, they pay an up-front premium for some distribution of potential outcomes—the synergies that will make the newly merged entity more efficient internally and grow faster and more profitably in the marketplace as a result of the deal ("if but for the deal"). In addition, to satisfy investors, acquirers must earn a cost-of-capital return on all of that luxurious capital that they're investing.

The analyses performed during the diligence process are intended to get under the hood of the target and identify financial, commercial, and operational issues, as well as critical red flags. Proper diligence helps develop reasonable assumptions and inputs used in the valuation model as well as an early view of integration issues that will need to be managed to realize the value of the deal. Ultimately, diligence tests the investment thesis of the deal—its value creation logic and how that value will be captured. It should help make the case that you will present to your board, and ultimately to your investors.

In our experience, while successful acquirers rarely lament deals they walk away from that would have resulted in paying too much, they hate to lose a deal to someone else because they missed valuable opportunities that could have been illuminated during diligence. Our approach is intended to improve the sensibility of the offer price, increase confidence in the maximum bid, and minimize downside risk.

Prepared acquirers benefit as they perform diligence regularly on their watch list deals, because they are able to learn a lot, over time, about the landscape of players, executive talent, market trends, and changing customer demands—beyond a particular deal at hand—and incorporate those findings in improving their overall businesses and ongoing corporate development efforts. Reactors, by contrast, force themselves into compressed time frames as a target emerges for a bid, so they are under even more pressure to get this right. This chapter will be helpful for both.

Often, the diligence process is described as useful in making the acquirer "comfortable." A truly thorough strategic due diligence process helps acquirers develop the confidence they need to proceed with the deal—or to walk away. It will help determine whether a potential deal offers the profitable growth and value worth paying for and avoid the trap of confusing existing revenue or cost improvement trajectories in stand-alone valuations with would-be synergies. Diligence provides support for the strategic vision, and for the operating model and integration design of the new combined company. It challenges the assumptions coming from acquirer and target executives and those of their advisers pushing the deal, and forces an explicit view of what must be true to defend why the deal is indeed strategic and why and how it is worth the capital that will be required.

While financial due diligence (FDD) looks backward to gain a more accurate view of the baseline of the state of the business by removing accounting distortions, commercial due diligence (CDD) and operational due diligence (ODD) look forward and examine the stability of the current business and the likelihood of growth in revenues or improvements in the cost profile, respectively. The three meet in the present to create a three-dimensional picture of the target—a picture of how the target has performed in the past, its ability to maintain today's business performance in the future, its potential for future growth, and possible cost and revenue synergies under new ownership.

There are, of course, important technical and operational tax issues that should also be explored—and could be the subject of several chapters on their own. Tax diligence for strategic buyers will attempt to uncover skeletons in the closet such as potential legacy tax risks that the buyer might be inheriting and how that would need to be priced in the deal.[1] Pre-closing tax diligence also focuses on structuring to capture value in the post-closing combined enterprise, which could include opportunities for tax efficiencies from certain legal entity rationalization, integrating and realigning supply chains, or establishing a more favorable intellectual property footprint.

In short, FDD, CDD, and ODD serve to test the business case required to support the price of the deal. The upshot: Post-merger meetings are the wrong time and place to build that case.

Financial Due Diligence: Looking Harder at the Numbers

FDD focuses on providing an alternative view of the target's business than what may be reflected in audited financials. That may require peeling back the onion and unwinding some accounting rules—rules that may be perfectly reasonable to use in service of the target's day-to-day business but that don't represent actual business trends (e.g., one-time events, changes in accounting policies, and out-of-period adjustments). Recognizing items that are non-recurring or non-cash, or not core to the business, can help an acquirer assess the quality of earnings (QoE), typically earnings before interest, taxes, depreciation, and amortization (EBITDA), for an indicative and normalized business-focused picture of the target.

Undistorting historical sales, operating expense trends, and working capital and capital expenditures (CAPEX) needs will establish a more accurate starting point, or baseline, and allow an acquirer to clearly evaluate key assumptions used in target management's forecast, which in turn can be used to build more reliable and testable forecasts of revenue and EBITDA.

Without proper FDD, the nuances of financial accounting can be missed, limiting an acquirer from developing a normalized operational understanding of the business and a consistent and credible starting point for other diligence workstreams. For example, if an acquirer were to overstate the stand-alone EBITDA baseline of the target, it could deliver an overvalued win from a deal multiple applied to the wrong base case and a new, combined firm that's unable to meet the growth and synergy forecasts of the deal thesis.

Although company financials are audited and certified, landmines may hide below the surface. Financial accounting contains judgments, including estimation of reserves and when and how revenue is recognized, creating a significant impact on reported profits. An audit's purpose is to provide assurance that management has presented a view of a company's financial performance consistent with generally accepted accounting principles (GAAP), but audited financials don't identify significant issues likely to be of interest to an acquirer. While the audit is about certifying numbers, an FDD says *why* the numbers are what they are. Audits *verify* results, while FDD *explains* results.

Think of it this way: The process of buying a company is not unlike buying a house. You can walk away, attempt to adjust your price, or identify issues where you might want to make contractual adjustments.

FDD can also help to inform acquirers what exposures they are signing up for that they might not otherwise know—because it's not the seller's job to reveal everything they know (and sellers may not know everything regardless). Potential exposures may be triggered by a transaction and include the upcoming renewal of a collective bargaining agreement, change in control provisions in employment or lease agreements, or higher levels of required funding for regulated pension schemes, and acquirers had better know about those before they become a sad surprise.

Because FDD can uncover some irregularities and a greater understanding of the financial performance of the target, it may also provide ammunition for negotiations after the initial offer. For example, trends in historical financial performance may be inconsistent with the target's rosy projections. That also sets the proper stage for the forward-looking tests of future revenues and costs in CDD and ODD, respectively.

FDD may mean different things to different people. But at its core, FDD focuses on answering three major questions:

1. Do we have conviction in the numbers—are they correct?

2. What is the "normalized" profit and loss (P&L) and balance sheet?

3. What do those diligence-adjusted numbers tell us?

Are the numbers correct?

While the scope of FDD will never provide assurance on the operating results and financial position like an audit, acquirers often take comfort in the fact that another set of skilled eyes have been through the detailed financials. It is not uncommon for experienced diligence teams to uncover accounting errors or management estimates that push the boundaries. Additionally, audits often operate with a materiality threshold where known or likely misstatements are not corrected because they are below that threshold. While the management team and auditor have determined these errors to be immaterial, in a transaction context an acquirer might take a different view.

What is the "normalized" profit and loss and balance sheet?

It's one thing to have confidence that the numbers are accurate but another to know what they say about the current state of the business. The key insight behind FDD is to "normalize" earnings—to take out extraordinary earnings (revenues or expenses), sometimes unwind accounting rules, and better represent the baseline of the business for forecasting. FDD provides a perspective on "core" recurring operations of the target and ultimately informs your confidence in recurring revenues (believability and repeatability) and the forecast for growth.

For example, are earnings impacted by the target's revenue recognition practices versus their peers, their estimates with regard to recorded reserves, or expense capitalization policies? Has management been overly aggressive or taken an alternate approach compared to the industry?

Understanding the trends and what is happening in the core business is important, but acquirers may have to cut through a lot of accounting noise. As one active acquirer told us, "We spend a lot of time unwinding the accounting rules. Accounting rules can get you further away from cash, and sometimes it's best to bring earnings closer to cash to give us a sense of what's happening in the underlying operations."

Although there are many types of adjustments, acquirers must be aware of the following major adjustments that make up the vast majority of FDD.

Out-of-period adjustments. These might include true-ups or changes in estimates to reserves from one year to the next that can distort the P&L when you make the subsequent adjustment. In that way, FDD provides you the ability to present the financial statements with the benefit of hindsight and apply a consistent accounting approach, removing the potentially lumpy impact for changes in estimates or policies from prior periods.[2]

For example, suppose the target had to record a large bad debt reserve in 2016 but it turns out the receivable was collected in 2018. In this situation 2016 would be overburdened with a bad debt expense and 2018 earnings would benefit from the reversal of that reserve simply by the collection of a receivable. FDD gives you the ability to look through the impact of these out-of-period changes.

Or suppose you have a potential patent litigation exposure that requires you to record an expense on your P&L and a $10M liability on the balance sheet. If you win the case in a subsequent year, you'll reverse that liability and will have a positive impact on the P&L of $10M just because you won the case. If you don't take these out-of-period adjustments into account, you'll likely misunderstand the trends.

One-time revenues and one-time expenses. These might include one-time customer sales where, for example, the company "won" a new large customer because a competitor had a fire and the target was able to sell products to them at an artificially high price—but such revenue is not recurring once the competitor's production comes back online. Even worse, after adjusting for the one-time sale, a closer look might reveal that the target's backlog is weak: actual customer renewals are down, and the target doesn't have a backlog to fill growth projections or replace key customer losses—and the trend is actually negative rather than positive.

On the other hand, companies can incur one-time expenses that are either not core to their operations or abnormal. If a company undergoes a restructuring, they will record expenses to establish restructuring reserves, so an acquirer needs to strip those out if they want to evaluate the normalized expense profile. Other typical one-time expenses are large litigation expenses, unusual losses, transaction costs related to debt or equity raises, M&A transaction costs, or one-time bonuses.

Including those one-time expenses might artificially depress the bid price, just as including the one-time revenues might result in a higher valuation and the bid being too high.

Non-cash adjustments. This category of adjustments is used to put certain P&L line items on a cash basis. There are two general reasons you may want to evaluate certain P&L items on a cash basis. First, as you determine your free cash flows (FCFs) for debt service there may be meaningful differences between GAAP-reported operating results and cash flows that you want to understand. Certain non-cash adjustments are allowed in debt covenants, and an acquirer would want to make sure those are understood early to optimize available leverage. Second, the cash flows from operations may be a better indicator of growth trends.

Common non-cash adjustments include stock-based compensation, goodwill impairments, unrealized gains and losses, recorded booked versus cash rent expense or differences due to the deferral of revenue recognition. By removing these non-cash items, you not only have a clearer picture of the cash flows, you may also have a better picture for operating ratios or growth trends. For example, by evaluating revenue on a cash basis as if it were paid up front, where accounting rules require you to defer its recognition, you may have a better sense for sales growth and momentum, particularly in high-growth companies.

In situations where EPS dilution might be important (for public companies), non-cash charges may burden EPS, often called "EPS drag." Suppose you were going to pay $100M for a business where the fair value of net tangible assets is $75M and the

$25M left over gets recorded as $15M to goodwill (that will ulti-mately go through an impairment test) and $10M to intangibles with a 10-year life. Over a 10-year life, $1M per year would hit the P&L as amortization expense and result in an EPS drag that has nothing to do with the baseline of business operations, which might drive a lower bid than justified. That would also be the case for a target that had done deals and was amortizing items from those deals—an acquirer would want to look at the state of the target's business without those accounting charges, like a business that had not done deals.

Pro-forma and run-rate adjustments. Pro-forma and run-rate adjust-ments attempt to adjust the earnings (i.e., EBITDA) to better rep-resent the target's earning potential given significant material changes going on in the business.

For instance, a pro-forma adjustment might include adjusting EBITDA for the impact from a recent acquisition. Suppose a target had done a bolt-on acquisition only five months ago; an acquirer would want to present the target as if they owned the bolt-on all along. If the EBITDA of that recent acquisition were $25M during the seven months prior to the acquisition, an acquirer would add this to the target's reported numbers so that they were evaluating a full year of earning potential.

Run-rate adjustments are sometimes more controversial but can be effective tools to evaluate the earning potential of an enter-prise. Let's say the target is in the business of operating physi-cian clinics. On average, each clinic earns $500,000 in EBITDA after three years of operations. Newer clinics take time to mature, and a greenfield clinic that opened one year ago is only earning $150,000 in EBITDA. A run-rate adjustment will present the dif-ference between the $150,000 and the run rate of $500,000. So, embedded in reported EBITDA is $150,000, but we could give credit as if the clinic has reached its ultimate run rate of $500,000. This is a judgment call; if we were to do that, we would want to be sure we are not applying a valuation multiple that would double count the expected growth.

Technology companies have trended toward subscription revenue models over the past decade. As a result, there has been a greater emphasis on analyzing the recurring revenue of these subscription-based businesses to understand their current monthly recurring revenue (MRR). During diligence significant effort should be put into analyzing customer churn and retention to assess the stability of MRR for these types of businesses. Properly evaluating MRR, the amount of predictable revenue a company expects to earn each month, allows acquirers to understand monthly trends and growth momentum. Additionally, acquirers may choose to make a run-rate adjustment for fast-growing businesses where the recent MRR would indicate a higher revenue base than the recorded revenue during the last 12 months.

CAPEX and working capital adjustments. Companies require CAPEX for maintenance, just to keep the lights on, and for growth, to build the new factories. The target may have had a one-time capital project that is not ongoing or has deferred CAPEX, and their factories may be in bad shape. Evaluating the historic CAPEX for either non-recurring or deferred maintenance is important as you consider FCFs, so you only include those required cash investments in your forecasts.

Examining and adjusting working capital will allow an acquirer a better understanding of trends in net working capital (NWC) such as seasonality and cyclicality driven by customer and vendor trends (faster payments demands, customers taking longer to pay, or higher inventory levels to facilitate on-time delivery) or develop a plan to reduce NWC and extract cash during the acquirer's ownership, and effectively improve balance sheet performance.

The evaluation of optimized NWC is a frequent component of FDD. Suppose a high-performing benchmark for NWC balance would say the company could operate with $90M of NWC and the target currently has $100M. If you can reduce NWC by $10M through better inventory management or improving cash collection on receivables, you now have $10M in cash you can either take out of the business and pay as a dividend or reinvest in new capital projects, reducing new investment—effectively reducing the total cost of the deal. Alternatively, because you believe you can decrease invested capital (lower NWC), then you will have increased FCF and economic profit (because you have the same operating profit at a lower capital charge; more on this in chapter 4)—effectively allowing you to pay more, if necessary.

The evaluation of NWC also allows an acquirer to define and quantify a normalized NWC "target" when there is a purchase price adjustment mechanism for NWC. That represents an acquirer's point of view on the amount of NWC required to be delivered with the transaction by the seller. Should the NWC delivered at the closing be an amount higher or lower, the adjustment mechanism would lead to an adjustment in the purchase price.

What do the numbers tell us?

The diligence-adjusted numbers allow a business-oriented view of current operations. Acquirers must make sure they are starting in a good place before they attempt to forecast the future. With properly normalized numbers, they reduce the chance they compound mistakes in their valuation model.

For example, suppose the non-normalized numbers suggest margins of 40 percent and historic annual revenue growth of 6 percent, but the normalized numbers suggest margins of 47 percent, because of non-recurring one-time expenses, but growth of only 3 percent. Both of those adjustments will have significant impact on the valuation and forecasts of the future.

And if both the revenue growth and margins are overly rosy, the acquirer will likely miss the forecast it paid for in all subsequent years and will have overvalued the target's stand-alone value right from the beginning.

Pulling all of this together, FDD informs a go or no-go decision, the ultimate value you'd be willing to pay, how you mark up a purchase agreement with the types of protections you want to incorporate, the lender package for underwriting the debt, and the underwriting process for insurance protections.[3]

This is the key point: You must understand that you are buying the future. The reason that you want to strip out one-time or out-of-the-ordinary events and recast earnings is because you need a true picture of the business today to help forecast the future. Without proper FDD, you can miss the nuances of financial accounting, limiting an acquirer from developing the operational understanding needed to create accurate forecasts of future revenues and profits. FDD allows you to start with accurate numbers. You want the trend to be your friend.

Commercial Due Diligence: All the Answers Are in the Market

CDD is the natural follow-on to M&A strategy—using market intelligence and analytics to test the investment thesis of a deal. It answers the question of whether the deal's growth strategy will likely create value. CDD tests the validity of the acquirer's beliefs of the target's revenue line (price × quantity) as a stand-alone business (recurring revenue and future growth), and the revenue enhancement opportunities the acquirer imagines through synergy. Proper CDD serves to validate the major assumptions around the market opportunity, the target's position in the market, and the likelihood the acquirer can deliver all that it is assuming in the valuation.

Done carefully, CDD yields defendable inputs for the valuation model as well as early inputs to integration planning for the improved go-to-market strategy and potential revenue synergies. It may also slow down the "Wow! Grab it! acquisition locomotive" if the acquirer learns the target's prospects are not as favorable as initially imagined.[4] It's here that acquirers test the elements of the investment thesis over which they may have little control: changing customer preferences, competitors, and headwinds and tailwinds from market trends. Since all valuations begin with the revenue line, ignoring diligence on the commercial opportunity can spell disaster for a valuation. Acquirers who rush or forgo a careful CDD because they fully believe they know their business miss the last chance to stress test the strategy they are about to pay for.

CDD forces acquirers to face the realities of the market, customers, and the target's capabilities and position relative to competitors, and how those realities will influence the revenue line in their valuation assumptions. An acquirer may not want to face those realities, but they have to test their assumptions to protect against bias—bias that can creep in from the target's numbers and assumptions, optimistic new go-to-market strategies, or from internal pressure to get the deal done. As we like to say, *All the answers are in the market*.

Testing claims and beliefs lie at the heart of CDD—claims made by the target's management reflected in a management presentation, or what they have guided investors to believe about the stability of their business and prospects for growth. Moreover, CDD tests the acquirer's beliefs about how they will create additional value in the market in combination with the target. Does the acquirer fully understand the market and the target's ability to capture more of the market or to produce better margins (through pricing and product offering) than they have today? Are they defining the market or estimating its size correctly? Are the target's growth projections plausible? How is the target positioned for growth relative to its closest peers? And, ultimately, can the acquirer and target create more value together than apart because they can serve customers in ways they couldn't before, and in ways not easily replicated?

Answering those questions means identifying and testing key assumptions in the target management's business case and the plausibility of the acquirer's forecasts—often in a frightfully short period of time, especially for acquirers stuck in auctions. CDD also can unearth and evaluate previously unrecognized issues and risks to deal success that will have to be mitigated.

Elements of commercial due diligence

Performing CDD requires three major baskets of work that provide a view of the commercial prospects of the target and opportunities for the merged entity:

1. Market analysis of size, growth, and trends

2. Competitive positioning of the target and customer behavior and preferences

3. Revenue enhancement opportunities

Market analysis offers insights on the addressable versus true serviceable market size and growth potential, emerging technologies and competitors, new strategies and business models evolving in the market, changing government regulations, and stability of margins.

Positioning and customer analysis, largely through primary research, unveils customer and non-customer key purchase criteria and behaviors, how the target is positioned relative to its peers across relevant competitive dimensions and how that has changed over time, switching dynamics, willingness to pay, the value of brands, channel strength and evolution, and the stickiness of its customer relationships. (See the sidebar, "How to Get All the Answers: Primary Research.")

How to Get All the Answers: Primary Research

While secondary research—that is, buying reports—is an obvious way of getting some commercial information, those same generic reports of varied quality are available to everyone else, so they're unlikely to be a source of advantage. The key to unlocking the market's secrets is primary research—the secret sauce for CDD. Talking with a diverse group of market participants will reveal important insights about the target's business. Effective primary research yields insights for the analytical work on serviceable and addressable market size, competitive positioning, switching dynamics, recurring revenues, market share, go-to-market strategy, and growth prospects.

In our experience, a primary research program involves three parts: hypothesis development, interview and survey design, and execution and synthesis.

Hypothesis Development

Because there is tremendous ground to cover, developing testable hypotheses helps provide direction on to whom you will speak, what groups you may need to survey, and the questions you need to ask. Some acquirers may be acquiring in their core markets and may have a strong command of the market dynamics. For them, the scope of their CDD may be understanding the stability of the target's customer base. Some acquirers may be entering into new markets, geographies, or other adjacencies that require a more thorough evaluation of the market and the target's positioning. Hypotheses should not be a laundry list of items, but rather items that are material to the presumed valuation of the company. For example, typical hypotheses to be tested are "The target believes it will outpace market growth by X percent over

(continued)

the next five years" or "The target believes its leadership position is defendable for product Y."

Interview and Survey Design

Interview questions are designed to test your hypotheses—and are refined throughout the program. Surveys are designed to quickly reach much larger, targeted populations, and obtain quantitative and more granular insights.

It is important to determine the types of people who can *meaningfully* answer the questions relevant to the deal. These will typically include current customers (the actual decision-makers), customers who switched or decided not to purchase from the target, future potential customers, channel partners, competitors, the target's current and past employees, and industry experts. As interviews continue and you learn more, you'll be able to refine your questions and focus on the most important issues that need validation and make the best use of your time.

Execution and Synthesis

Execution begins with sourcing and reaching the most important potential candidates. Options for sourcing candidates include the acquirer's network of contacts, direct facilitation by the target's management team to arrange interviews with key customers, third-party meeting organizers, and targeted blinded outreach by third-party diligence advisers. Acquirers use surveys (or shopper intercept techniques for consumers) to reach much larger customer and non-customer audiences to get statistically significant insights on the hypotheses being tested.

It's important to get hard numbers or validation of existing numbers (estimates of market size and trends) from the interviews and quotable commentary on market dynamics, competitive differentiation, and customer perception of the target's products. Without being misleading, you are trying to learn information you otherwise couldn't get through secondary resources. Skilled interviewers will build a rapport and ebb and flow with the conversation versus rigidly reading off an interview guide.

Primary research interviews should create a platform for customers, non-customers, and other market participants to voice their thoughts as opposed to simple answers to pre-set questions. Deal teams should leverage the customer outreach the company has already done in the brand management of their products and services and avoid the "no one ever asked me" problem. Interviews and surveys should provide enough information to either confirm or refine the original thesis or to strongly raise red flags of a problem.

Done well, the first two baskets of analysis will yield significant data and insights so relevant to assessing whether the acquirer can generate revenue enhancement opportunities (the third basket) and create new value for customers with the target. Are there opportunities to improve the go-to-market strategy of the target? Are there potential revenue synergies because the integration will yield better geographic coverage, cross sells, or new offerings that address unmet customer needs that competitors can't easily replicate and for which customers are willing to pay?

One final point: No matter how well you know the market as part of your business-as-usual, many companies don't actively reassess their markets through ongoing research. Even if they do, if they are not fully reaching out to all relevant parts of the market for answers (current customers, lost customers, potential customers, and competitors), their research can actually reinforce biases they have about their customers, products, and markets, and their own advantage.

Re-evaluating the market and how things have changed is a great opportunity to understand changing customer preferences, technology evolution, and emerging players who can serve customers better or differently. Smart acquirers test their understanding of the pace of change of the commercial aspects of the opportunity even if they've been operating in the industry for a long period of time. Technological changes, for example, might be on the horizon that could reshape the marketplace. Amazon's disruption of incumbent retail giants through strong digital, direct-to-customer, and customer intimacy and analytics capabilities is a classic warning for companies not keeping abreast of the market and their presumed advantages.

Major insights from commercial due diligence

The market in which the target operates is—like all markets— often rapidly changing and evolving. CDD is focused on revealing the realities of those markets and insights on how the target operates and competes within them: market size and growth, product satisfaction and distribution capability, competitive positioning, and the stickiness of customer relationships. Taken together, they provide an assessment of the stand-alone value of the target, and a better sense of how you might go to market differently with existing or new offerings. We'll examine these each in turn.

Market size and growth. Accurate sizing of the market—the total size for sure, but, more important, the parts of the market the target can actually serve today with current capabilities and how fast it is growing—uncovers important inputs to strategy and value.

The only way to understand the target's trend in market share is to first understand the size of the market the target can serve today—its serviceable market. While that might seem self-evident, targets often stress the total addressable market—the one that *might* be served with new (or better) capabilities or market access, rather than the *actual* serviceable market. In other words, sellers will typically promote a larger market size than the company can service through existing products and geographical distribution. They may very often promote a compound annual growth rate (CAGR) of their total addressable market that may be far higher than the CAGR of the market segments they can serve today.

Let's consider two examples: First, we were engaged to evaluate a Hispanic foods company with a solid revenue base, but the target trumpeted the $90B Hispanic foods market and unlimited opportunities for growth. We peeled away the layers of the market they actually served: the 15 US states they actually operated in, the specific ethnicities they viewed as their customers (Dominican, Puerto Rican, and Cuban), and the food categories where they were most advantaged (e.g., frozen food varieties). The target loved to say that the overall market was a $90B opportunity. But our analysis revealed that it was really a $5B–$6B opportunity, a far smaller serviceable market than the target claimed.

Second, we worked on behalf of a large industrial client, evaluating size and growth of the global backup power generation set (genset) market. Based on initial reports the client believed a market opportunity of $15B+ existed. However, refining the market specifics by fuel type (e.g., diesel), commercial end markets, and power output revealed the addressable market was under $7B, or roughly 55 percent less than original estimates. Further, regional specific analysis revealed different expected growth profiles by region and end market with, for example, data center and telecom customers driving the most significant growth within Asia Pacific.

Why is any of that important? Market sizing estimates are used to determine what share of the target's current serviceable market it really has—its market share. The market share of its serviceable market will typically be larger than the market share of the target's addressable market (with additional capabilities or market access). Do you think that targets are more likely to overstate or understate their market share? It turns out that targets will often understate their share or overstate the size of the market, so it appears like there is more headroom for growth. These types of discoveries expose a potentially inflated view of the target's growth potential, resulting in a higher valuation than is justified.

Understanding the actual serviceable market also offers a view of the target's market share dynamics overtime—how has it been changing? If the target has been gaining or losing share, you need to understand why. And if the target's projected growth rate is greater than that of its serviceable market, you need to understand from whom they expect to take share. That will help drive both the strategy and integration hypotheses and valuation of the deal. That also leads to considerations regarding whether or not the new combination of capabilities and market access will yield a larger serviceable market or expand the size of the market that can be addressed.

Product satisfaction and distribution capability. Evaluating whether the target has products that customers value and why, and their ability to scale distribution is fundamental. Almost anything else can be fixed, but if customers perceive their products as inferior or don't value the brand, it's a real problem. Do the target's products or services deliver on customers preferences and specific purchasing criteria better than competitor offerings, and are they willing to continue paying for them? Does the target have sufficient current distribution capability to serve the growth in its markets? Customer satisfaction and distribution capability may sound obvious, but they are phenomenally important and often overshadowed by other issues like marketing, advertising, or lack of qualified sales reps that can be more easily remedied.

Improving product advantage or attractiveness and demand in the face of competition and creating and building distribution capability is costly, takes a lot of time, and carries huge execution risk. That said, the acquirer may have strong distribution capabilities that could be a source of significant synergies when paired with the target's products.

Competitive position and the evolving landscape. Examining the target's competitive position reveals the customer segments and geographies it serves successfully (and those it doesn't) and its customer value propositions relative to its competitors—where does it play and why does it win? That means also understanding the positioning of target's peers—how they contrast with the target and how the target differentiates its offerings. The target's positioning, as well as the acquirer's, directly influences an acquirer's ability to defend and take share and achieve potential revenue growth from the combination.

Competitive position is dynamic. Position can be deliberately chosen and where the target has worked to build advantage, delighting customers with more of what they want (better than competitors) at prices they are willing to pay. Or, it can be where the target finds itself because of competitive forces, technology changes, and changing customer needs and preferences over time that it didn't anticipate or address. In other words, the target can have strong growing positions in certain segments or geographies, and yet weakening positions in others. Done correctly, this analysis will create an animated view of positioning changes over time.

We were engaged by a client investigating the world's largest global manufacturer of an industrial product with a variety of uses, from household and personal care to pharmaceutical applications. In recent years, the target exited the lowest-margin segments but did not innovate in the highest-margin segments such as pharmaceuticals. Over time they found themselves stuck in the middle. And it was getting worse: They were being attacked by the lower-end competitors in the US market and from Chinese competitors in Europe and Asia, and were constrained from the high-growth, high-margin segments globally because of a lack of R&D investments. In short, they had become horribly positioned, attacked on all fronts. Most acquirers would have walked away from an impending disaster. Although the target was poorly positioned, through extensive primary research, we learned that many of its more than 1,000 industrial customers had long-standing relationships and, more important, they wanted the target to survive to maintain price competition in the market. Without that primary research the acquirer would not have fully understood what additional role they played for customers.

Acquirers may find that the target is addressing the needs of customers better than competitors at more attractive price points, which means it's reasonable that they can continue to execute on their current commercial strategy. On the other hand, acquirers may discover that the target is not positioned to address key customer segments, which means the target's ability to achieve projected growth requires some serious investment and attention, or complementary capabilities and market access from the acquirer.

Acquirers should be prepared to debate prospects for the target with respect to its global peers—and how that context may change over the next several years under the acquirer's ownership. It's important to recognize that some elements may be largely out of the acquirer's control but are crucial to understand for evaluating the current position and the growth potential of the target.

Stickiness of target's customer relationships. An important part of evaluating recurring revenues and the target's growth potential is assessing the tenure and growth it has had with its major customers. Even if a target is poorly positioned and will likely struggle with growth, it may have a saving grace. It may have strong "sticky" relationships with its customers that took years to develop. And those customers may want to make sure the target survives to maintain price discipline in the market, as was the case for our industrial goods target we just described. Customer stickiness—the stability and growth of customer relationships—

is the lifeblood of recurring revenues and the platform for future growth, and for cross-selling new offerings after the deal has closed.

There are several drivers of stickiness. Customers may value the brand, service levels or quality, or their relationships with the sales force, and may be price inelastic. Then again, even if they might consider switching, the process of switching might be lengthy and costly, especially for industrial customers, and the benefits of switching unclear. Understanding switching dynamics, especially the cost to switch, ease of switching, and under what conditions customers would switch—is a vital part of assessing the stability of the business and the platform for growth.

That said, customer stickiness can cut both ways: Sticky relationships may help you maintain share but at the same time make it hard to take share from competitors. On one hand, customer relationships that are less sticky may yield opportunities to take share given the right market offerings or raise red flags for vulnerabilities that need to be addressed. On the other hand, if customers won't leave a competitor, for example, your serviceable and addressable markets may be even harder to capture than you thought.[5]

Understanding non-customers (those who have switched and those who have never been customers) is just as important because it helps the acquirer understand segments of the market the target has not addressed, or at least not successfully. That will inform the size of the actual serviceable market, offer a deeper assessment of stickiness, indicate why customers shop for alternatives, and uncover why and how certain competitors are doing better. (On how technology can support CDD, see the sidebar, "The Role of Data Analytics in Commercial Due Diligence.")

Insights gathered from those four areas—sizing the market and growth potential, understanding product satisfaction and distribution capability, evaluating competitive positioning and the

The Role of Data Analytics in Commercial Due Diligence

Data analytics can offer benefits for CDD from the enormous amounts of data that exist across customer purchasing behavior, price and volume trends, social media sentiment, geospatial mapping, and other data. AI tools and approaches such as natural language processing (NLP) and machine learning enable better and faster insights and predictions in ways that were not possible before.

The initial use of data analytics involved trying to get to an answer faster. It is now focused on generating a deeper understanding of customer behavior and demand drivers impacting current and future product revenues by finding connections and statistical correlations that otherwise might have gone unnoticed.

For example, analysis of social media postings and product reviews using NLP can help articulate what users are saying publicly. That can help explain customer behavior and key purchasing criteria and their impact on past sales of specific products or services, along with providing insights on future behavior and demand faster and with a broader lens than customer surveys alone.

Machine learning can predict future price and volume trends of a given product or service based on statistical analysis of anonymized credit card data with concurrent external factors or events. Geospatial analysis can help construct a localized picture of market penetration and competitive pressures, in retail or healthcare for instance, by using customer concentration, provider locations, and local socioeconomic data from the US Census Bureau.

When robust analytics enables us to find proxies for customer behavior and competitive positioning to develop informed commercial hypotheses up front, acquirers can use more targeted primary research to test those hypotheses that matter.

evolving landscape, and testing customer stickiness and switching dynamics—are all inputs into how you might go to market differently post-merger, yielding a 360-degree fact base that allows for considering improvements in the target's go-to-market strategy and an initial integration strategy. Further, with that fact base discovered in the market by CDD, acquirers can identify revenue enhancement opportunities from combining with the assets of the target.

Potential revenue synergies from merging the two companies are ultimately the result of a change in go-to-market strategies. Revenue synergies can be evaluated from several potential sources: cross-selling, leveraging sales infrastructures across geographies, offering customers on both sides new integrated bundles they couldn't buy before, or innovating new products or services. In the pre-deal phase, clean rooms can be essential to share information deemed competitively sensitive (more on clean rooms in chapter 6). Each source of synergy will have associated costs, so the analysis must be linked to ODD and cost to achieve.

Acquirers should consider the answers to the following important questions: How does the target's product portfolio complement current offerings of the acquirer? Can the acquirer or target now penetrate customer segments or geographies either has struggled with? Are there untapped opportunities in core and adjacent markets from different applications of existing products? What ongoing problems can we solve for customers because of the combination that will enhance stickiness? How can the acquirer better address changing or unmet customer needs through new or more compelling offerings?

CDD paints a dynamic picture of the target, how it's perceived by customers, the size of its serviceable and potentially addressable markets, its current positioning, and opportunities for growth and revenue synergies. In summary, CDD validates the stability of target's current business and its growth potential based on what's known today and reveals what challenges or opportunities are on the horizon.

Operational Due Diligence: Are the Cost Synergies Real?

ODD is an overall holistic inspection of the target's operations, and the first layer of testing the potential transformation—from current state to future state—required to realize value from the transaction and help "pay for the deal."

Why bother? Because acquirers not only purchase the target's cash flow, products or services, market presence, and customer relationships; they also acquire the target's operating model and upstream and downstream inputs to production and distribution that drive the cost structure. They also inherit any already planned cost-reduction programs the target says it has in place—yeah, you could just take their word for it.

ODD spans the problems of the efficiency and scalability of the current operating model, cost-synergy capture (size, timing, and complexities of achieving cost synergies), and an assessment of the effectiveness of the target's ongoing operational programs. That includes assessing the current efficiency of a target's selling, general, and administrative (SG&A) expenses, cost of goods sold (COGS), and operations strategy. ODD can also uncover operational issues that might threaten the business case and challenge the valuation of the deal.

But here, we're going to focus on capturing cost synergies. Acquirers typically rely on high-level, top-down assumptions, from benchmarks or their advisers, to identify the cost synergies that are then built into valuations. The target's bankers will regularly present a "magic 10 percent" as a top-down cost-synergy target. They'll have limited support for the assertion. It is especially important to differentiate whether potential cost reductions are from synergies as a result of the deal or from the target's claims of an ongoing cost transformation process that has yet to be realized.

Yet those same acquirers are often surprised when assumed post-deal operational improvements aren't as significant as planned, or take longer and are costlier than expected to realize. Further, failing to realize expected cost synergies can easily cause delayed attention to customers and revenue-enhancement programs, opening the door to competitor actions and derailing revenue synergies.

ODD also includes areas like HR and IT. While these are important because the acquirer will want to fully understand the costs and complexity of issues such as the transformation related to payroll and other information systems changes or harmonizing benefits plans, we won't go into detail here because of their technical complexity.

Practical elements of operational due diligence

ODD focused on cost synergies involves three major analyses that allow a view of the go-forward cost structure of the target and opportunities for the merged entity:

1. Cost and headcount baselining and benchmarking of acquirer's and target's core operations (and true stand-alone costs for divisional carve-outs)

2. Plausibility of target's stated ongoing cost-reduction programs

3. Bottom-up synergy analysis including one-time costs, potential interdependencies, and timing of synergies

ODD requires a high degree of cooperation and interaction between the acquirer and the target. Access to data—the target's as well as the acquirer's internal data—is at the heart of ODD. Acquirers often assume that gaining access to their own internal data will be easier than it actually is, which can slow analyses that require information from both companies. Procurement data, product prices, detailed functional cost and headcount breakdowns, and other internal data are typically required to build the functional baselines central to performing thorough ODD and assessing potential synergies.

At the same time, because rapid access to target data is so critical before the deal, establishing a quick, simple, and trackable data request process will help the acquirer avoid delays. Prioritizing requested data enables the target's management to focus their time on providing the most important data first. The diligence team should stay coordinated to avoid multiple data requests for the same data from the target.

Establishing a baseline and performing bottom-up analyses of cost (and revenue) synergies often involve accessing sensitive target company information such as supplier pricing for potential procurement savings or employee salaries, hire dates, and termination policies for possible labor savings; or pricing and customer information for potential cross-selling initiatives on the revenue side. Management teams can manage confidentiality concerns related to this information using clean rooms and avoid potential anti-trust issues (more on this in chapter 6). Because confidentiality is essential, the acquirer's diligence team should be small with as few functional leads "under the tent" during initial negotiations as possible. Where it is not practical to have representatives from each function, external advisers can help fill expertise gaps. In any case, bringing leaders under the tent as diligence progresses must be coordinated so that their knowledge or inputs are obtained.

Experienced acquirers look not only for cost synergies from the integration of current-state businesses during diligence but also larger transformation opportunities that can impact value. "Transforming while you transact" might include offshoring non-core business operations, leveraging robotic process automation (RPA), using centers of excellence for high-volume, low-value transactions, or migrating to a digital cloud-based IT infrastructure.

Top-down and bottom-up

Without bottom-up ODD—which begins with assuming there are zero synergies and builds up from there—it will be unclear where or how synergies can be delivered, what the run rate of synergies is, and what the one-time and ongoing costs to achieve the synergies are. Acquirers will miss the opportunity to consider operational-fit risks with the target, along with the timing and complexities of realizing synergies, creating operational blind spots missed in a top-down view. This is especially true when buying a division. (See below, "Operational Due Diligence for Carve-Outs.") Without understanding supplier relationships and contracts and the cost structure (labor and non-labor) of the overall operating model during ODD, acquirers push that work into the integration phases after promises to shareholders have been made and without testing hypotheses of what the acquirer will actually do with the business.

It's not that top-down ODD is useless. In fact, it is the starting point. It's important to develop initial synergy targets based on a review of the acquirer's and target's P&Ls against industry benchmarks and have a clear picture of the headcount, by function, on both sides. It also helps to validate estimates based on industry deal data or past experience. Although it is a useful starting point, it's not enough.

Acquirers often gloss over cost reductions that are perceived as easy to achieve—the top-down magic 10 percent. But this oversight can have huge ramifications on realized value and management credibility if those synergies do not occur or are delayed. As a result, unexpected and needless delays in realizing synergies—so-called value leakage—can become costly to investors and cause confusion for employees who have to deliver them.

Why? The story is a familiar one. Post-signing, when an acquirer needs to quickly launch critical integration planning around geography, headcount, and functional alignment, the executive team belatedly realizes that projected cost reductions have not been fully tested and related decisions have not been made. What often happens next? Integration teams are forced to perform the bottom-up diligence that should have taken place pre-signing, and the resulting integration slowdown causes confusion and angst in the workforce. Questions then surface about the credibility of the deal's true value or, even worse, the deal's overall investment thesis.

Synergy-capture ODD offers something more. It's a bottom-up approach that puts management's skin in the game early on to identify where specific cost reductions may be achieved, or where there may be potential for dis-synergies that will need to be netted against the benefits. For example, closing one corporate HQ may generate substantial savings, but will require leasing some additional, more expensive floor space at the remaining HQ. Such diligence can help provide—or test—important inputs to valuations and drive early alignment around the new operating model for the combined businesses. You may arrive at the same magic 10 percent, but you'll know why and how those savings will be achieved, and how much it will cost to deliver them.

Often, bottom-up cost-synergy diligence with sufficient data from both companies will yield different results from top-down analysis. Understanding what drives the variance by function between the two methods can yield important insights to help prioritize where to improve performance, achieve synergies, and build an initial integration roadmap, by function, with early identification of interdependencies.

Synergy-capture diligence by the numbers

Bottom-up synergy-capture diligence involves five major steps: create consistent cost and functional baselines; segment and prioritize synergy opportunities; quantify specific benefits, costs, and owners of each opportunity; develop the new financial model;

and create a synergy-capture roadmap by function with initial identification of sequencing and interdependencies.

1. **Create consistent cost and functional baselines.** The acquirer's diligence team should begin by gathering P&L data from recent financial statements, and the data room, for both companies to view the total pie and normalize the statements by removing one-time, non-recurring costs. The team can use this information to create a consistent baseline that maps headcount and cost pools from the combined P&L to specific functional areas such as finance, HR, and marketing. This is where it is vital both to understand any target cost-reduction initiatives so they can be assessed and removed from the forward-looking baseline and to identify complexities and interdependencies created by the target's ongoing programs (e.g., an ongoing ERP cloud migration effort).

2. **Segment and prioritize synergy opportunities.** Team members should make initial hypotheses about synergies that can be realized quickly, such as full-time-equivalent (FTE) rationalization, corporate insurance, public company costs and audit fees, and management overhead. Also important are hypotheses about synergies that will require additional information, such as IT and customer relationship management (CRM) consolidation, supply chain and logistics efficiencies, and corporate facilities and customer service site rationalization.

3. **Quantify specific synergy opportunities and cost to achieve by functional area.** Through detailed interviews with executives and functional leaders, the acquirer should next identify redundancies across all functional support areas for synergies. This helps to build the new organization from the ground up, identifying responsible parties

who are signing up for the plan. Other parts of this step are determining the costs to achieve synergies, such as severance pay, lease termination and vendor sunsetting fees, and other one-time exit costs, as well as any potential increases in ongoing costs as a result of the merger. Clean rooms will be required for sharing competitively sensitive information. Acquirers will also seek to identify additional overhead cost pools that may have been missed in initial assumptions. (Of course, the more data the target reveals in the data room, the better.)

4. **Develop the new financial model and explain variances from initial assumptions.** The acquirer team can use the bottom-up cost-reduction and cost-to-achieve estimates to develop a new financial model and resulting P&L to present to the board of directors as part of the deal package. The model should identify and explain all variances—both positive and negative—from the initial top-down analysis.

5. **Create a synergy-capture integration roadmap.** An integration roadmap is an initial view of how the new organization should operate to achieve the deal's intended business results. Developing this roadmap—with milestones, dependencies, and potential bottlenecks—is a critical step that will guide the organization later in its pre-close planning. While the combined organization's end-state vision likely will evolve as new information is assimilated during the transaction, an initial roadmap provides a valuable frame of reference for focusing the entire organization on results and prioritizing the areas that will require the most attention.

By following these steps, acquirers should be able to surpass mere top-down cost-reduction assumptions, whether they are provided by bankers or based on past industry experience. It forces the assessment of the plausibility of the target's cost-reduction programs so that synergies are not double counted with reductions already expected, and that interdependencies with those programs are considered. This process also encourages relevant management involvement, input, and personal commitment from the outset. It stress tests inputs to the valuation according to size, timing, and investment required to achieve specific cost-reduction targets, and is designed to generate a flexible financial model to accommodate multiple scenarios and new information as it is revealed.

Because responsible functional parties are identified along with specific synergy initiatives, senior management can focus much earlier on the new end-state operating model, serving customers, and preserving and growing revenue—the lifeblood of any acquisition.

A robust bottom-up ODD cost-synergy process not only positions the acquirer to size cost-synergy opportunities, but also allows it to consider the relationship and tensions between cost and revenue synergies where improving margins through cost reductions might cut too deep to support revenue synergy expectations.

It also means that the acquirer's functional leads will be invested, since they've voiced their inputs (even if they need to be prodded). They'll also have a better sense of the time and resources that will be required and complexities they may need to manage in the combined organization. The objective is to minimize value leakage after the deal is signed.

Thorough ODD will also help you jump-start the development of an integration roadmap and avoid downstream confusion as you embark on structuring your integration strategy and sign-to-close planning, and your go-forward operating model (we discuss these in chapters 6 and 7). Finally, ODD is another great opportunity to glean insights that might benefit the current operations of the acquirer, even if you don't do the deal.

Operational due diligence for carve-outs

Buying a division of a seller creates even more complex problems of understanding the true run-rate costs of the division, separation costs, and supporting structures that will or will not come along with the business: direct costs, allocated and unallocated costs, and the need for transition services agreements (TSAs) that will have to be negotiated with the seller before and after signing while integration planning for the division is progressing from sign to close. Consequently, carve-outs add another layer of risk and complexity to integration because acquirers must ensure the business continuity of the division while it is separated, and understand the total cost base before they can estimate opportunities for improvement through synergies.

Acquirers must understand what they are receiving from the parent—for example, customer-facing front office staff (sales force and customer service) and back office support (IT, finance, HR, legal). You might say, why do I care about all that if I'm going to integrate the division into my systems anyway? Well, say you are buying a division with 30,000 employees—do you have sufficient capacity to provide all the necessary HR support with your existing HR information system (HRIS) and your current executive talent? Or, if the division is in 17 global locations and with 17 different tax structures in 17 jurisdictions with 17 different currencies, you may need a far more robust financial planning and analysis (FP&A) and treasury system than you have today. Those considerations will matter as the acquirer considers how it will integrate and operate the business.

Once acquirers know what they are getting, they will need to determine the total cost required to support the division as a stand-alone—direct, allocated, and unallocated costs. *Direct costs* are those directly attributed to and embedded in the division (e.g., division finance, IT, legal, HR business partners, manufacturing, supply chain and logistics, sales and marketing) and captured in the division P&L. *Allocated costs* that hit the division P&L are charges for shared services provided by the parent such as corporate FP&A, treasury management, corporate IT and legal, audit, and regulatory compliance—but what is being allocated may include costs not required to run the business or, on the other hand, might be understated, resulting in a higher valuation than warranted. Acquirers need to make their own assessment. *Unallocated costs*, which are typically related to global brand support or corporate HQ, are costs for services that the division has received from the parent but may not be charged. Acquirers will need to understand that total cost picture along with the degree to which they will integrate the division before they can estimate potential synergies.

Acquirers also must estimate the one-time costs required to separate the target from the parent, which will include breaking existing contracts such as an Oracle enterprise resource planning (ERP) system with the parent, and data separation from the parent ERP (division customers, employees, financial, and regulatory filings) that has to be logically and physically separated and then moved to the new medium. All of these are in addition to the typical integration one-time costs—IT, rebranding, facilities buildout, signage, and severance payments.

The complexity and risks of the transaction will be driven by how entrenched the proposed carve-out is within its parent. In general, the higher the level of integration and dependence on parent corporate functions or other business units, the more complex the carve-out. We have found that the higher the dependency, the higher the risk of underestimating the costs and time required to separate and integrate to achieve the required functionality.

Hard dependencies will include intellectual property, comingled IT and ERP systems, facility colocation, and shared talent pools, but there can be softer dependencies such as master procurement terms with suppliers, sales contracts through the parent, and tax advantages or revenues from transfer pricing regimes based on existing legal entity structures. This is where TSAs may be required to maintain business continuity to enable the separation while it is being integrated into the acquirer. Acquirers will need to determine the cost and the time those TSAs are required, while the sellers providing those TSAs work to end them quickly because they are not in the business of providing service to another company to run their former business.

Once one-time and run-rate costs, complexities, and issues for business continuity have been addressed, acquirers can then assess how to integrate the assets they are buying and the opportunities for improvement and synergies with the acquirer's business. That may involve changing the go-to-market strategy in subscale markets or scale benefits from being a much larger parent than the previous parent in areas such as purchasing, facility overlap, and duplicative supply chain components (e.g., transportation, warehouses).

We have also observed a strong "agency conflict" among leaders of the division being sold. Many of these individuals have a strong affinity and attachment to the parent enterprise and feel conflicted about their future role. Qualitative evaluations, including the assessment of talent, their cultural identity, and compatibility with the acquiring organization, also need to be considered because critical talent might be at risk.

Conclusion

When CDD, ODD, and FDD come together, they can generate truly better insights. Each piece helps paint a total picture—but only if you put those pieces together. Acquirers can use what they learn during diligence as feedback to their original investment thesis and valuation, and to the larger growth strategy. These diligence processes will also help with pre-close planning—informing the future integration and value capture plan.

We will see in chapter 4 that diligence maps neatly onto what we will call "current operations value" and "future growth value," and onto the improvements in performance required to justify the premium and the total price of the deal.

CHAPTER 4

How Much Do I Need?

Valuation and Synergy

Valuation remains a cornerstone of any discussion of M&A. Nobody intends to overpay for a deal, yet the evidence continues to challenge the results from typical valuation approaches, especially discounted cash flow (DCF). Of course, DCF is rooted in finance theory and applications. Properly used, it forces enumeration of specific beliefs about the future and the business case for a deal.

But DCF can be improperly used and can lead to predictable problems. We propose a sanity check for what acquirers are assuming when they make a bid and what they are promising to deliver when the deal closes—whatever the value they arrive at. Once an acquirer closes a deal, they have fixed the price of the target, and the only price that will fluctuate is the acquirer's, starting right at announcement based on the offer price. Investors are smart and will react immediately based on what they are told.

Let's start with a typical example that we will return to later in the chapter.

In a recent mega-deal, the acquirer offered a $10B premium and $500M of pre-tax cost synergies. But they neglected to provide a timetable for when the synergies would be fully realized (or even when they would begin) or a plan for realizing them. In a flash—more or less—investors multiplied the $10B premium by their cost of capital of around 8 percent. That simple calculation revealed that the acquirer needed a ramp up of improvements—over and above what the two companies would have achieved on their own—that would be worth the cost-of-capital return on the $10B premium. The lack of a plan with sufficient synergies telegraphed that there was no way the acquirer could achieve this, and their share price immediately fell by billions—the majority of the premium—right on Announcement Day.[1]

We know you may have hated your finance classes, but investors do these calculations in seconds without being privy to your detailed valuations. As a consequence, it's imperative that you know what you are promising, especially when you offer a significant premium.

The valuation should be the ultimate business plan that drives the integration strategy. Instead, it is often a confusing mess of assumptions. Acquirers need a better and more direct approach to understanding the values of their current operations and future growth already expected for both companies and the additional periodic performance required from synergies to justify the premium paid.

In this chapter we present a theoretically correct and direct approach, based on the well-accepted concept of economic value added (EVA), to first examine both the acquirer and target as stand-alone companies to understand the performance trajectory already expected by investors. Then we use the new capital allocated in the form of paying the full market value of the target's shares (while assuming the debt) plus the acquisition premium to show the annual improvements being promised by the acquirer and how that promise translates into improvements in net operating profit after tax (NOPAT). Paying a premium creates required synergies and the new business performance problem that will be driven by the integration strategy and, just as important, that will set the stage for sensible board and investor communications.

You are probably saying, "Please, not another chapter on how to use DCF to properly value a company." After all, a quick search on Amazon shows that there are over 75 books on DCF valuation written during the last 30 years. Anyone who has studied at a business school has learned capital budgeting to judge whether a stream of cash flows will deliver a required rate of return on the necessary capital investments.

Virtually everyone can tell you that valuation of a company requires assumptions about free cash flows (FCFs) over time, growth rates, the weighted average cost of capital (WACC), and the terminal value (TV)—with growth rates in perpetuity—to build a DCF valuation model.

Our approach here is not to teach valuation. Rather, we want to use DCF as a familiar and popular tool to set the stage for DCF's mirror image, so to speak: the EVA approach. We will show how using the EVA approach is straightforward and a simple way of illuminating the required performance improvements an acquirer is promising when buying a company at a premium. Our approach is a sanity check of sorts, where we take the outcome of a DCF, or any valuation process, and translate that price into required synergies or performance improvements beyond what either firm was expected to accomplish independently. In other words, we want a simple way of understanding the promise implicitly made by the acquirer's management to its own shareholders in its willingness to pay a premium to the target's shareholders.

This chapter is somewhat technical—not onerously so, but technical nonetheless. But it's worth it. We'll carefully work through the math because it's necessary to achieve the right conceptual framework for understanding what investors will expect at a given deal price and the tools to better communicate the synergy plan with those investors. We're boiling down a lot of financial wisdom here, but these concepts and the tools will help to stress test a deal's valuations, and, more important, to understand the promise to shareholders.

Discounted Cash Flow

DCF valuation is a mainstay of M&A, and valuation in general, because it has several important advantages. DCF forces a consideration of the components that drive FCFs: revenues, operating costs, cash taxes, and investments in working capital and fixed assets (reflected in CAPEX)—investments that will support the projected growth of the merger. DCF is flexible and can easily accommodate changing assumptions as an acquirer thinks through scenarios of the future. The methodology also forces a consideration of the WACC, or the risk class of the assets under consideration.

DCF valuation is also, implicitly, a business plan—a story. It is your year-by-year belief of the growth and margins achievable for the businesses along with periodic investments that will be required to facilitate the strategic vision. You have to remember that your whole merger plan is based on promises—promises about future performance to stakeholders, including shareholders and employees. And if you don't understand or haven't thought through the business plan supporting those promises, then you will likely be challenged when it comes time to explain the logic of the deal.

Valuing a target using DCF essentially comprises two valuations: 1) the stand-alone value of the target—which means assessing the value of current business(es) plus the growth value of the business(es), *like any value investor would*; and 2) the amount and timing of the anticipated synergies—operating gains above stand-alone expectations—along with the one-time and ongoing costs to achieve those synergies. Thus, acquirers are building two business plans: the base case of the stand-alone value of the target and the overlay of all the net synergy benefits on top given the up-front investment of the premium.

When acquirers negotiate with targets, any upward or downward changes in price implicitly means assumptions about the inputs in the DCF model must be changing—a slightly lower WACC, a little bit more revenue growth in the fifth or sixth year, or a little bit lower investment in working capital to support the growth, and so on. That is all fine as long as those changes in assumptions are plausible.

"Multiples" approaches to valuing deals, such as enterprise value (EV)/EBITDA or EV/sales, are often viewed as more objective than DCF because they are based on the value of relevant comparables.[2] The DCF, in contrast, can be affected by "beauty is in the eye of the beholder" subjectivity. That said, any value based on an average market-based multiple implies a stream of cash flows that would have to discount back to that number. Of course, those approaches are subject to their own problems, like using the wrong multiple.

In practice, investment bankers follow a seemingly rigorous process and triangulate on value by looking at various EV or P/E multiples of comparable public companies ("compcos"), multiples for precedent or comparable acquisitions ("compaqs"), and the DCF. They then show a "football field" with a range of assumptions for each approach and determine the most "appropriate" range of values given by the three techniques. (See figure 4-1.)

But here's the thing: The seller's bankers are doing the same thing—except they don't really care as much about the DCF valuation, although they'll do one too. The seller and especially their board want a "fairness opinion" that shows they are realizing an appropriate or "fair" price for the company. Ultimately, they will want a premium that is based on how precedent transactions have been recently valued and how comparable companies, often at their 52-week highs, have been valued. Of course,

FIGURE 4-1

Football field illustration

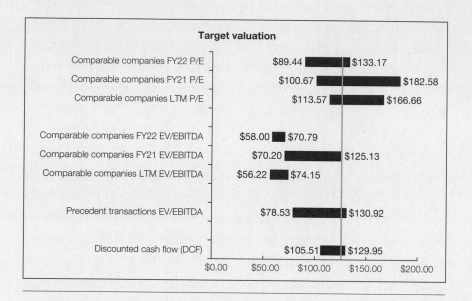

Target valuation

Comparable companies FY22 P/E	$89.44 ▮ $133.17
Comparable companies FY21 P/E	$100.67 ▮ $182.58
Comparable companies LTM P/E	$113.57 ▮ $166.66
Comparable companies FY22 EV/EBITDA	$58.00 ▮ $70.79
Comparable companies FY21 EV/EBITDA	$70.20 ▮ $125.13
Comparable companies LTM EV/EBITDA	$56.22 ▮ $74.15
Precedent transactions EV/EBITDA	$78.53 ▮ $130.92
Discounted cash flow (DCF)	$105.51 ▮ $129.95

$0.00 $50.00 $100.00 $150.00 $200.00

that is the anchor for negotiations, because if they were to sell for less, directors of the seller will be sued for not getting a "fair" price.

Thanks largely to the landmark 1985 case *Smith* v. *Van Gorkom*, which holds that officers and directors of a public company could be held personally liable for not making an informed decision about the appropriate selling price of a company, fairness opinions for sellers are practically mandated. In ruling against Van Gorkom and the directors of Trans Union, the Delaware Supreme Court found that, even though Trans Union shareholders would receive a 50 percent premium, the directors were grossly negligent because they did not properly inform themselves about the intrinsic value of the company. In what was a boon for investment banks, fairness opinions—and the market-based multiples of compcos and precedent transactions—effectively now largely determine what an acquirer will have to pay to do a deal.[3]

An Invitation for Mischief

Given the long-run disappointing evidence of the performance of major deals, often through overpaying, together with the well-accepted DCF approach to valuing deals, it begs the question of what has gone wrong. A plausible answer is that DCF is the perfect tool to support market-multiple approaches to value. In other words, DCF is an invitation for mischief and the perfect model for the tail—that is, *what you have to pay*—to wag the dog.

How? Because DCF valuation is seductively simple to use and incredibly sensitive to small changes in the variables in the model. Those changes can be pushed into an inflated terminal value at the end of the forecast period, especially for synergies. Not only that, but for a CEO dead set on doing a deal, it is so easy to bury optimistic assumptions about future revenue growth, margin sustainability, or investment requirements—and mix up synergies with already existing growth expectations—that only the most sophisticated analysts with a deep understanding of the businesses would be able to see where the bodies are buried. We've also learned that synergies pushed into later years lose their urgency and are easily forgotten.

For example, consider the following stream of FCFs with a 5 percent growth rate (table 4-1). For simplicity, we use a five-year model with a TV based on a "perpetuity with growth" or $TV_5 = FCF_6/(c-g)$, where c is the cost of capital and g is the projected growth rate of the FCFs. We show a range of costs of capital and $c-g$ spreads that can drive a wide range of valuations. At a 7 percent cost of capital, for example, just nudging the perpetual growth rate from 2 percent to 3 percent (or a $c-g$ spread from 0.05 to 0.04) yields a valuation of $2,861.3M, up from $2,383.6M, for an increase of 20 percent, which might be used to justify a higher premium.

TABLE 4-1

DCF valuation sensitivity analysis

TOTAL FREE CASH FLOW TO FIRM ($M)

2020A	2021	2022	2023	2024	2025	2026
100.0	105.0	110.3	115.8	121.6	127.6	134.0

SENSITIVITY ANALYSIS

		VALUE OF TARGET			
c − g spread		0.02	0.03	0.04	0.05
Terminal value		6,700	4,467	3,350	2,680
Cost of capital	9%	4,802.4	3,350.8	2,625.0	**2,189.5**
	8%	5,020.1	3,500.0	2,740.0	2,283.9
	7%	5,250.0	3,657.6	2,861.3	2,383.6
	6%	5,493.0	3,824.0	2,989.5	2,488.8
	5%	**5,750.0**	4,000.0	3,125.0	2,600.0

Of course, it *is* difficult to make forecasts five or 10 years into the future; projections by their nature are risky, and that is where the pitfalls lie. Common red flags are when an acquirer inserts unrealistic operating margin improvements or understates CAPEX to support all the wonderful new revenue growth that will result from the strategy of a deal. That often shows up in the model as significant increases in earnings before interest and taxes (EBIT) without the required investments. The result: a much higher valuation because FCF is overstated forever in perpetuity, buried in an inflated terminal value. That is how easy it is for the tail to wag the dog.

In the M&A context, markets have already done a valuation of the target, and your company, for that matter. So, the trouble often stems from the acquirer's assumptions about operating gains over already existing growth expectations—the synergies. Your banker will tell you the premium that will be required to do the deal, and so even the most prepared acquirers must be cautious of plugging numbers into a model. At the end of day, the premium you pay signs you up for a future business case. If you pay—that is, invest—all that luxurious capital up front and don't deliver on that business case, you will have let down your shareholders and your employees.

That is exactly why DCF can be an invitation for mischief—because it is so easy and seductively simple to bury assumptions that drive wild swings in "value" and support virtually any price required to please the seller and get the deal done. At the minimum, acquirers should not mix up synergy assumptions with the value and growth expectations of the stand-alone business of the target—or of the acquirer. That is a real invitation for mischief and the resulting predictable overpayment.

Now, we are not saying not to use DCF—far from it. DCF is widely accepted and theoretically correct and yields the *most* you should be willing to pay for an asset to yield a cost-of-capital return on that investment. Used properly and with realistic discipline about the prospects for the target under your ownership, DCF is an effective way of valuing assets so that you don't overpay for a series of free cash flows over a specific forecast period. DCF is at its core a business plan that shows how much cash is available to investors after making required investments in working capital and fixed assets to drive the growth plans.

Here's the crux of the matter: When you are building a DCF valuation model, the numbers you put in the model are assumptions, but when you buy the company those numbers become promises.

There is another way, an equivalent mirror image of DCF, if you will, of showing what you are indeed promising when you pay a given amount for an acquisition—a simple way of converting a value given by a discounted series of free cash flows to an equivalent series of periodic benefits relative to the cost of capital each period. We want a way to take that value (or a range of values) from a DCF, cut through the clutter of all assumptions, and recast that value into a stream of yearly performance increases that are measurable and trackable, and reflect the promises an acquirer is making by doing a deal at a given price.

What Are You Promising?

As Warren Buffett once famously wrote about M&A, "Investors can always buy toads at the going price for toads. If investors instead bankroll princesses who wish to pay double for the right to kiss the toad, those kisses better pack some real dynamite." His point is so clear: Since investors can diversify on their own, without paying a premium, synergies must be thought of as improvements as a result of the merger—"if but for the deal." Paying a premium only raises the operating performance bar (perhaps Mr. Buffett said it better). This is as true for the acquisitions of private companies or carve-outs of divisions as it is for public targets, except that acquirers won't have a public market valuation (they'll have to do that themselves).[4]

Thus, operating gains over stand-alone expectations—the synergies—must be performance improvements over what was already expected. Illuminating synergy expectations in addition to already existing expectations requires an approach that separates value into its *known* and *expectational* components. The result is a forward-looking view of just how much the bar is being raised. That approach should be able to dissect the total value of a company into the value of the current business without improvements, the current expectations of improvements in the stand-alone businesses, and the additional improvements required to fully justify the price, and the premium, you are about to pay.

Although DCF accommodates a business plan, even when done with discipline—and in deals, with a full understanding of how the integration of the target will yield benefits—it suffers an important shortcoming especially for deals: the major input, the FCFs, do not provide a reliable measure of *periodic* economic

Calculation of Economic Value Added

Revenues

− Operating Expenses

= Operating Profit (EBIT)

× (1 − tax rate)

= NOPAT

− Capital Charge (Invested Capital × WACC)

= EVA

operating performance. That's because, by definition, FCF subtracts the entire cost of an investment in the year in which it occurs rather than spreading the cost of the investment over the life of the asset that has been acquired with a capital charge. In other words, DCF, and FCFs specifically, don't offer an obvious lens to express whether acquirers are creating economic value each period with the capital they are committing or have committed to a deal.

That shortcoming of FCF as a measure of periodic value creation can be avoided by using the concept of EVA. EVA is calculated as NOPAT minus a capital charge equal to invested capital for the period times the WACC. (See the sidebar, "Calculation of Economic Value Added.") Unlike FCF, EVA effectively capitalizes instead of expensing much corporate investment, and then holds management accountable for that capital by assigning the capital charge we just described. EVA is based on the idea of economic profit where value is created when a company covers not only its operating costs but also the cost of capital—the return expected by investors.[5]

Fortunately, EVA offers a different but equivalent lens for FCF because the present value of the cost of a new investment is the same for EVA and FCF. The present value of the deprecation expense and capital charge for EVA is exactly equal to the initial investment cost for FCF. The present value of future FCF is equal to the present value of future EVA *plus* beginning capital. (We need to add back beginning capital to recover the EVA charge on beginning capital—a charge that does not affect FCF.) Recasting market value based on the idea of EVA as economic profit, or the value created by invested capital, can be summarized as follows:

Market Value = Invested Capital + Present Value of Future EVAs

EVA is especially useful for performance measurement and evaluation because it allows us to dissect a company's market value into its *known* and *expectational* components. We can do this by breaking the present value of all future EVAs into two pieces: 1) the present value of maintaining the company's current EVA (its perpetuity value), which we know; and 2) the present value of the *expected* EVA improvements above current EVA— that are maintained.

Don't worry, we're not introducing some crazy new idea of valuation. In fact, *both* of these approaches—DCF and EVA—were developed and proved equivalent in the same famous 1961 *Journal of Business* article "Dividend Policy, Growth, and the Valuation of Shares," by Nobel Prize winners Franco Modigliani and Merton Miller. Modigliani and Miller—affectionately known as M&M—were giants in academic finance, and their famous Equations 11 and 12 are well studied by students of finance. Equation 11 is the DCF model and Equation 12 is what they termed the "investment opportunities approach" (IOA), which laid the groundwork for the EVA approach. In fact, M&M thought this approach was the most natural from the standpoint of an investor considering an acquisition because it offers a view of value based on whether the return on new investments would exceed their cost of capital (see appendix B).[6]

M&M's Equation 12 yields a practical expression in the context of EVA. Incorporating beginning capital and both components of EVA (NOPAT and the capital charge) into M&M's IOA equation implies the following fundamental EVA equation, which breaks total market value into its known and expectational components.[7] (For additional details on the EVA equation, see appendix C.)

$$\text{Market Value}_0 = \text{Cap}_0 + \frac{\text{EVA}_0}{c} + \frac{1+c}{c} \times \sum_{t=1}^{\infty} \frac{\Delta \text{EVA}_t}{(1+c)^t}$$

Where Market Value$_0$ is a company's total market value today (equity plus debt); Cap$_0$ is beginning book capital (or total assets minus non-interest bearing current liabilities); c is the required cost-of-capital return, or the WACC; EVA$_0$ is beginning EVA (NOPAT$_0$ − Cap$_{-1}$ × c) or prior year's NOPAT minus the prior year's capital charge; and ΔEVA$_t$ is investors' expectation, today, of EVA *improvement* in year t. Notice that is exactly where we started the discussion, except we have broken market value into what we can measure today and the expectations of improvements in the future.

The sum of the first two terms, beginning capital and the present value of constant current EVA (capitalized current EVA, its perpetuity value), can be thought of as "current operations value" (COV). The remainder of the expression, the third term, can be thought of as "future growth value" (FGV). We express FGV as the capitalized present value of expected annual EVA *improvements*—improvements that will yield a cost-of-capital return on the growth value investors are awarding the company today. We capitalize the present value of expected improvements because we assume that each improvement is maintained in perpetuity. Restating our earlier market value expression, we now have:

Market Value = Beginning Invested Capital + Capitalized Current EVA + Capitalized Present Value of Future EVA Improvements

So, market value today can be expressed as performance we know today and improvements expected in the future, or

Market Value = Current Operations Value + Future Growth Value

Since investors expect a cost-of-capital return on the total market value of a company, then they expect a cost-of-capital return on COV *and* a cost-of-capital return on FGV because they are buying both. Merely maintaining current economic performance, or current EVA, and offering no EVA improvements, will only deliver enough NOPAT to provide a cost-of-capital return on COV but no return at all on FGV. The bottom line: FGV implies investors expect improvements in EVA.

For example, let's say you are buying a company with a market value of $2B with beginning invested capital of $1B, a recurring stream of NOPAT of $120M, and a 10 percent WACC and current EVA of $20M. For simplicity, we assume no changes in capital from the prior year. We have:

$$\$2B = Cap_0 + \text{Capitalized Current } EVA_0 + \text{Capitalized Present Value of Future EVA Improvements}$$

$$\$2B = \$1B + \$20M/0.1 + \$800M$$

$$\$2B = \$1.2B + \$800M$$

In this example, our COV is $1.2B and FGV is $800M. Maintaining current EVA of $20M ($120M – capital charge of $100M) will only deliver enough NOPAT to yield a cost-of-capital return on COV.[8] The company will need to generate EVA improvements (ΔEVA) sufficient to justify the $800M of FGV it is currently being awarded by the market. There are many ways to achieve that value.

For example, at the extreme, if you could deliver increased performance of $80M of EVA improvement in the current year, perhaps through a major cost reduction effort, and maintain that forever, then you could certainly justify growth value beyond the value of current operations today. From our EVA equation above, and using a simplified notation, we have:

$$\text{Market Value}_0 = \text{Cap}_0 + \text{EVA}_0/c + ((1+c)/c) \times \Sigma \; \Delta\text{EVA}_t \, /(1+c)^t$$

FGV is the third term of the market value equation:

$$\text{FGV} = ((1+c)/c) \times \Sigma \; \Delta\text{EVA}_t \, /(1+c)^t$$

With a one-time improvement, the FGV expression would reduce to:

$$\text{FGV} = ((1+c)/c) \, (\Delta\text{EVA}_1/(1+c)) \text{ and } \Delta\text{EVA}_1 = c \times \text{FGV}$$

So, with FGV of \$800M and WACC of 10 percent, required ΔEVA_1 for the one-time improvement will be:

$$\Delta\text{EVA}_1 = 0.1 \, (\$800\text{M}) = \$80\text{M or,}$$

$$\$800\text{M} = 11 \, (\$80\text{M}/1.1) \text{ or a spike of } \$80\text{M of } \Delta\text{EVA that}$$
$$\text{is maintained}$$

That one-time change would represent a huge increase in performance, which is probably unrealistic in one year. While that would be an extraordinary accomplishment, if EVA weren't expected to grow from there, you would have effectively converted FGV to COV (it becomes next period's current EVA), and you would have become a no-growth company, from a value perspective. Of course, if that level of performance increase was a signal of a bright future, then investors would surely bid up the price of your shares, awarding you with significant growth value.

Now, let's take the FGV portion of above and assume that instead of a one-time increase in EVA, you could achieve a stream of *equal* annual EVA improvements, in perpetuity, which when capitalized is equivalent to the one-time spike. Here, we'll assume that FGV remains constant. Using our FGV expression:

$$FGV = ((1 + c)/c) \times \Sigma \; \Delta EVA_t \; /(1 + c)^t$$

With equal annual EVA improvements in perpetuity, the FGV expression reduces to:

$$FGV = ((1 + c)/c) \; (\Delta EVA/c) \text{ and } \Delta EVA = (c \times FGV)/((1 + c)/c)$$

Using FGV of \$800M and WACC of 10 percent from our example, required perpetual annual ΔEVA will be:

$$\Delta EVA = 0.1 \; (\$800M)/(1.1/0.1) = \$7.27M \text{ or,}$$

$$\$800M = 11 \; (\$7.27M/0.1) \text{ or } \$7.27M \text{ of annual EVA}$$
$$\text{improvements in perpetuity}$$

So, equal annual EVA improvements of \$7.27M in perpetuity would equate to a 10 percent WACC return on \$800M in FGV.[9] If growth expectations remain the same, we would have constant FGV of \$800M and COV would increase each period as would the market value. The major takeaway is that when investors are expecting valuable growth, they are willing to pay for FGV. However, if you don't deliver or can't maintain those expectations, your share price will suffer accordingly.

What Happens When You Pay a Premium?

What happens when you offer to pay a premium for our target company? Let's say a 40 percent premium, or \$800M for our \$2B company. What have you done? You have added, immediately, $800M, directly to the FGV of the target, which was already $800M, for a new grand total of $1.6B in FGV.

We started with $2B = $1.2B + $800M, but with your offer of a 40 percent premium, we now have:

$$\$2.8B = \$1.2B + \$800M + \$800M$$

The target still has $1.2B of COV but *you have doubled FGV*. Are you starting to get the picture?

That is what you are setting up for investors when you pay a premium. Paying a premium establishes a brand-new business performance problem that never existed, and no one ever expected. In the example above, you are essentially doubling the required improvements in performance to earn a cost-of-capital return on FGV from the total investment. In this simple example, for either of our ΔEVA approaches above the required ΔEVA will double.

Once you acquire the target with the $800M premium, you have fixed the price of the target. The target's value won't fluctuate in value anymore. The only share price that will fluctuate is yours—based on the expected return you can generate with all that luxurious new capital. You will need an additional cost-of-capital return, just to break even. Failing to demonstrate a path to do that will likely lead shareholders—and other stakeholders—to question and perhaps doubt the logic of the deal and the offer price, right from announcement. Merely achieving expected stand-alone improvements, a cost-of-capital return on current FGV, but not realizing sufficient synergies on top of that is a recipe for trouble.

Because the offer of a premium is a surprise to investors (and a pleasant surprise to the sellers), equal annual improvements over time in perpetuity are likely not going to be very satisfying and will probably try their patience. Even if you have a long track record, a significant premium for performance not expected before is still a shock. And just telling investors you will double what they expected before won't work. The good news: Our EVA equation handles that with ease.

Let's focus on the $800M premium and consider a ΔEVA ramp up of required synergies. From our FGV expression:

$$FGV = ((1+c)/c) \times \Sigma \; \Delta EVA_t \, /(1+c)^t$$

So, a three-year ramp up starting in year 1 would mean:

$$FGV = ((1+c)/c) \; [(\Delta EVA_1/(1+c)) + (\Delta EVA_2/(1+c)^2) + (\Delta EVA_3/(1+c)^3)]$$

Where one solution in this case with a three-year ramp up would be:

$$\$800M = 11 \; [(\$20M/1.1) + (\$30M/1.21) + (\$39.6M/1.33)]$$

In other words, an increase of $20M in the first year, an additional $30M increase in the second year, and additional $39.6M increase over that in the third year—so we have a run rate of EVA improvements over current EVA of roughly $90M per year by the end of year 3 that is maintained. There are lots of combinations you could offer, but the sooner the better.

You might recognize this as the familiar synergy ramp up typically observed in successful deal communications. Imagine what happens when you don't offer an aggressive plan to deliver synergies. A ramp up effectively shows a path to justifying or "paying off" the premium. Once the full run rate is achieved after year 3, you will have converted that FGV from the premium into COV. Presumably, investors will take that confidence as a signal that there will be ongoing profitable growth as a result of the many long-term strategic benefits of the deal and be willing to pay for additional growth value—that is, that the "synergies" will continue to grow.

If we assume that your company (or another acquirer) has stand-alone required ΔEVA in perpetuity of $10M, we get the schedule shown in table 4-2, which illustrates the EVA improvements required for the stand-alone companies along with a three-year ΔEVA ramp up needed to justify the $800M premium, for the next five years (and beyond).

The increase in FGV and implied increase in ΔEVA in this example translates to huge percentage increases in required performance. If investors believe that such gains aren't possible, then your share price will fall right on Announcement Day, to adjust for the proper growth value. On the other hand, if you project a confident story with numbers they can follow, and the deal is really strategic, you will likely be rewarded with additional growth value, and a higher share price, as is the case with successful acquisitions. (We address investor communications in chapter 5.)

Thus far, we have developed something important and useful: a rapid and valid method of taking the premium "justified" by the DCF or any other valuation technique and translating it to a sensible ramp up of synergies—ΔEVAs—that

TABLE 4-2

Required EVA improvements with an $800M premium ($M)

	Year 1	Year 2	Year 3	Year 4	Year 5
Stand-alone acquirer	10	20	30	40	50
Stand-alone target	7.27	14.54	21.81	29.08	36.35
Total stand-alone	17.27	34.54	51.81	69.08	86.35
Add for premium	20	50	90	90	90

will offer a cost-of-capital return on the premium. It is a sanity check that you understand what you are promising based on your valuation.

On that note, let's revisit what ΔEVA means in the context of synergies to make this tangible. Since ΔEVA must be $\Delta(NOPAT - Cap \times c)$ or $(\Delta NOPAT - \Delta Cap \times c)$, if we assume for simplicity there aren't any significant increases in invested capital post deal, then that reduces to changes in NOPAT—which could be compared to the NOPAT assumptions in the original DCF valuation. That said, any additional capital investments and any additions to the premium, such as one-time cost to achieve synergies, will require commensurate improvements in NOPAT.

Now, suppose you tell your investors there might be a delay in getting a cost-of-capital return on the new growth value—the premium—you have just created by giving the target's shareholders their windfall. How might your investors respond?

Delay: What Do Investors Hear?

Remember from chapter 1 when you wanted to buy that apartment in New York City? Well, you go through with it, but you need a mortgage to pay the entire value that includes that 50 percent premium ($500,000) you are paying over market value. So, you agree to pay $300,000 as a down payment and approach your local bank and go through the necessary paperwork to secure your $1.2M loan. You feel ambitious so you take a 10-year mortgage with a 5 percent interest rate on the loan. For the bank to earn its 5 percent for the life of the loan you will need to pay $12,728 per month for 10 years. Now, imagine, you are at the closing and there are many new people around the table—the sellers, the lawyers, the brokers on both sides, and of course your banker.

Now, just before you sign on the dotted line, you lean over to your banker and tell them, "Uhm, I may miss a few payments," just before you sign the loan agreement.

"What?" asks your banker.

"Yeah," you say in return. "And not only that, I don't know exactly when I'm going to start paying. The only thing I know for sure is that I'm going to miss a fair number of payments."

"Oh, boy," mumbles your banker. "How many payments do you think you might miss?"

And you reply, "It could be 24 or even 36 months," you say, but add emphatically, "Trust me, I'm good for it."

That is what paying a premium sounds like to investors, when you tell them you are going to pay more than anyone else in the world is willing to pay for a company and you are not going to realize a return on all that new capital—the synergies—until some vague time in the future. You are taking out a mortgage for your shareholders that they didn't need to buy shares of the target on their own, and they will expect you to get a return on all that new capital. You can expect investors to be suspicious if you can't communicate a sensible plan, or if you signal you have none. That's the recipe for a typical negative market reaction. Offering a premium means you will need to show significant improvements early on, or your market value will decline to reflect the appropriate FGV.

Putting It All Together: Homeland Technologies Makes an Offer for Affurr Industries

Chas Ferguson—the CEO of Homeland Technologies, whom we introduced in chapter 2—proceeded with his quest for potential deals that might rapidly increase the size of Homeland and build shareholder value in the process. His bankers brought him several deals and he focused on Affurr Industries, for which he performed FDD, CDD, and ODD, and Affurr Industries seemed like a perfect fit—at a 40 percent premium.

When you buy another company, you don't just pay a premium, you also immediately write up the invested capital of the target to the total market value, and we have to account for that. In other words, when you buy a company at the premium, you need to generate a cost-of-capital return on the COV and FGV of the target (because you have written up the capital on the combined balance sheet when you pay full market value of the target's shares and assume the debt) plus a cost-of-capital return on the premium.

To do that we can look at both acquirer and target as stand-alone companies, and then put them together as a new company, with a new amount of invested capital, a new WACC for the combined company, and a new COV and FGV. We can then show the required EVA improvements for each company pre-acquisition and how those required EVA improvements change as a result of the deal. For simplicity, we assume the new WACC is a weighted average, based on market values, of the pre-deal WACCs of both companies.[10]

First, for both the acquirer and target, begin with total market value (equity market cap plus debt). Then determine the beginning invested capital (total assets minus non-interest-bearing current liabilities (NIBCLs)) for each company. Next calculate current EVA (prior year NOPAT − (prior year beginning capital × WACC)) and capitalize current EVA at the respective WACC. Per our EVA equation, adding beginning capital plus capitalized current EVA yields COV. Finally, total market value minus COV gives us FGV—the capitalized present value of future EVA improvements expected by investors.[11]

Let's examine Homeland and Affurr Industries as two independent companies and take this step by step, starting with the fact sheet in table 4-3 (values in $M).

Let's look at each company separately so we can determine what investors are expecting from each company as a stand-

TABLE 4-3

Homeland Technologies and Affurr Industries fact sheet ($M)

Metric	Homeland Technologies	Affurr Industries
Equity market cap	3,500	2,000
+ Debt	1,500	0
= Total market value	5,000	2,000
Total assets	2,100	1,050
– NIBCLs	100	50
= Beginning capital	2,000	1,000
Prior year beginning capital	2,000	1,000
Beginning NOPAT	390	120
WACC	10%	10%
Premium		800

TABLE 4-4

Homeland Technologies COV and FGV ($M)

	Homeland Technologies	COV	FGV
Market value	5,000		
Capital	2,000		
Capitalized current EVA (190/.1)	1,900	3,900	
Capitalized PV of expected EVA improvements			1,100

alone. Table 4-4 relates to Homeland Technologies, where Current EVA = NOPAT – Capital Charge, or $390 - (2000 \times 0.1) = \$190M$. We have FGV of $1,100M so our perpetual $\Delta EVA = (1,100 \times c)/((1+c)/c)$, or $1,100(0.1)/11 = \Delta\$10M$ every year.

TABLE 4-5

Affurr Industries COV and FGV ($M)

	Affurr Industries	COV	FGV
Market value	2,000		
Capital	1,000		
Capitalized current EVA (20/.1)	200	1,200	
Capitalized PV of expected EVA improvements			800

Table 4-5 relates to Affurr Industries, where current EVA = NOPAT − Capital Charge, or $120 - (1{,}000 \times 0.1) = \$20M$. We have FGV of $800M so our perpetual $\Delta EVA = (800 \times c)/((1 + c)/c)$, or $800(0.1)/11 = \Delta\$7.27M$, just like we showed earlier.

Now for what you've all been waiting for: putting the two companies together in six easy steps:

1. **Calculate total market value of combined entity:** Pre-Announcement Market Value of Buyer + Pre-Announcement Market Value of Target + Premium

2. **Capital of combined entity:** Beginning Capital of Acquirer + Market Value of Target + Premium

3. **Calculate new capitalized current EVA:** [Combined Prior Year NOPAT − ((Prior Year Beginning Invested Capital of Acquirer + Market Value of Target + Premium) × New WACC)] / New WACC

4. **Calculate new COV:** Capital of Combined Entity + New Capitalized Current EVA

5. **Calculate new FGV:** Total Market Value of Combined Entity − New COV

6. **Calculate required EVA improvement:** (New FGV × New WACC) / ((1 + New WACC)/New WACC)

Step 3 is important. We are restating current EVA as if the acquirer had all the new capital—the total investment in the target and the target's debt—on its balance sheet before the deal announcement (i.e., our pro-forma base year). That is why we add the acquirer's prior year beginning capital plus the total market value of the target plus the premium to calculate the capital charge for current EVA—effectively the new starting point we use to restate FGV and the improvements required in the future. Our method allows an easy comparison of the stand-alone ΔEVA expectations before the deal with the combined required changes as a result of the deal.[12]

Table 4-6 puts the two companies together without the premium.

TABLE 4-6

Homeland Technologies/Affurr Industries COV and FGV ($M)

	Homeland Technologies/ Affurr Industries	COV	FGV
Market value	7,000		
Capital	4,000		
Capitalized current EVA (110/.1)	1,100	5,100	
Capitalized PV of expected EVA improvements			1,900

Let's walk through the calculations:

1. New Market Value = $5,000 + 2,000 = 7,000$

2. New Capital = $2,000 + 2,000$ (because you've written up the target's capital to market value)

3a. New NOPAT = $390 + 120 = 510$

3b. New Capital Charge = $(2,000 + 2,000) \times 0.1 = 400$

3c. New Current EVA = NOPAT – Capital Charge = $510 - 400 = 110$

3d. New Capitalized Current EVA = 110/0.1 = 1,100

4. New COV = 4,000 + 1,100 = 5100

5. New FGV = 7,000 – 5,100 = 1,900

6. New ΔEVA = 1,900 (0.1)/11 = Δ\$17.27M every year in perpetuity

You'll notice a few things that illustrate the mechanics: We now have lower capitalized current EVA, but we have more invested capital because Homeland bought the target at its market value; the new COV is just the sum of the independent COVs. So the new FGV is also the sum of the independent FGVs, and the total required EVA improvements remain the same.[13]

Table 4-7 adds the 40 percent premium of \$800M, and voilà!

TABLE 4-7

Homeland Technologies/Affurr Industries COV and FGV with an \$800M premium (\$M)

	Homeland Technologies/ Affurr Industries	COV	FGV
Market value	7,800		
Capital	4,800		
Capitalized current EVA (30/.1)	300	5,100	
Capitalized PV of expected EVA improvements			2,700

Let's again walk through the calculations:

1. New Market Value = 5,000 + 2,800 = 7,800 (adding the premium)

2. New Capital = 2,000 + 2,800 (because you've written up the target's capital to market value plus the premium)

3a. New NOPAT = 390 + 120 = 510

3b. New Capital Charge $= (2,000 + 2,800) \times 0.1 = 480$

3c. New Current EVA = NOPAT – Capital
Charge $= 510 - 480 = 30$

3d. New Capitalized Current EVA $= 30/0.1 = 300$

 4. New COV $= 4,800 + 300 = 5,100$

 5. New FGV $= 7,800 - 5,100 = 2,700$

 6. New ΔEVA $= 2,700 \ (0.1)/11 = \Delta\$24.54M$ every year in
perpetuity[14]

New Homeland's combined COV is still the same and FGV
has increased by the amount of the premium. Like before, we
have lower capitalized current EVA, but we have more capital,
and the premium is simply a direct addition to combined FGV.

The new ΔEVA of \$24.54M increases by the amount of the
premium \$800M times its required cost-of-capital return on the
premium ($\$800M \times (0.1)$) divided by ($(1+c)/c$) (or 11), which
yields a perpetual annual increase of \$7.27M over the indepen-
dent stand-alone expectations of both companies.

Here's the big thing: Although this is a simplified example, taking the dollar premium times $c/((1+c)/c)$, where c is the WACC,
gives us a rapid calculation of required ΔEVA with equal annual
improvements in perpetuity. We can of course convert that to a
ramp up that will be more satisfying to investors, as we showed
in the earlier schedule (see table 4-2). *And investors can also do
that in seconds.*

A few important notes: As we discussed earlier, these are
expected increases in EVA (NOPAT minus the capital charge),
so if there aren't major additions to capital, then we are talking
about changes in NOPAT. Because NOPAT is by definition after-
tax, we would need to gross up that number to the pre-tax synergy number (given an effective tax rate), which is improvement
in EBIT we would typically offer at announcement. NOPAT

changes can take the form of faster growth or better profitability. And we could easily develop a table of different growth or profitability improvements that would yield the required result. Finally, because DCF and EVA are equivalent, we can compare the EBIT or NOPAT changes from our approach against the NOPAT changes in the DCF.

Revisiting Our Mega-Deal: Future Industries Makes an Offer for Cabbãge Corp

Now let's work through the mega-deal example we introduced at the beginning of the chapter. We can now disclose that Future Industries, a large and rapidly growing technology player, made an offer for Cabbãge Corp, a large company that has developed innovative applications at the intersection of technology and healthcare. Table 4-8 shows the fact sheet.

TABLE 4-8

Future Industries and Cabbãge Corp fact sheet ($M)

Metric	Future Industries	Cabbãge Corp
Equity market cap	38,902.28	34,565.80
+ Debt	2,022.13	11,233.44
= Total market value	40,924.41	45,799.24
Total assets	42,425.41	44,471.97
− NIBCLs	8,827.05	13,781.15
= Beginning capital	33,598.36	30,690.82
Prior year beginning capital	32,009.84	29,888.60
Beginning NOPAT	1,889.34	3,151.33
WACC	8.00%	7.60%
Premium		10,000.00

Consistent with our approach for Homeland and Affurr, let's look at each company separately so we can understand investor expectations for each company as stand-alone enterprises.[15] (See table 4-9 for Future Industries and table 4-10 for Cabbãge Corp.)

TABLE 4-9

Future Industries COV and FGV and Perpetual ΔEVA ($M)

	Future Industries	COV	FGV
Market value	40,924.41		
Capital	33,598.36		
Capitalized current EVA (−671.45/.08)	(8,393.13)	25,205.23	
Capitalized PV of expected EVA improvements			15,719.18
Perpetual ΔEVA to justify FGV			93.15

TABLE 4-10

Cabbãge Corp COV and FGV ($M)

	Cabbãge Corp	COV	FGV
Market value	45,799.24		
Capital	30,690.82		
Capitalized current EVA (879.80/.076)	11,576.32	42,267.14	
Capitalized PV of expected EVA improvements			3,532.10
Perpetual ΔEVA to justify FGV			18.96

Now, we follow our method and combine the two companies to form the new Future Industries, along with the $10B premium Future is offering for Cabbãge Corp. We also calculate the new WACC based on the market values of both companies plus the premium, which is 7.77 percent.[16] Table 4-11 shows the COV, FGV, and perpetual annual EVA improvements required to justify the FGV of the new Future Industries and Cabbãge Corp combination.

TABLE 4-11

Future Industries/Cabbãge Corp COV and FGV ($M)

	Future Industries/Cabbãge Corp	COV	FGV
Market value	96,723.65		
Capital	89,397.60		
Capitalized current EVA (−1,782.10/.0777)	(22,935.65)	66,461.95	
Capitalized PV of expected EVA improvements			30,261.70
Perpetual ΔEVA to justify FGV			169.53

Let's again walk through the six steps of calculations:

1. New Market Value = 40,924.41 + 45,799.24 + 10,000 = 96,723.65 (adding the premium)

2. New Capital = 33,598.36 + 45,799.24 + 10,000 = 89,397.60 (because you've written up the target's capital to market value plus the premium)

3a. New NOPAT = 1,889.34 + 3,151.33 = 5,040.67

3b. New Capital Charge = (32,009.84 + 45,799.24 + 10,000) × 0.0777 = 6,822.77

3c. New Current EVA = NOPAT − Capital Charge = 5,040.67 − 6,822.77 = −1,782.10

3d. New Capitalized Current EVA = −1,782.10/0.0777 = −22,935.65

4. New COV = 89,397.60 + −22,935.65 = 66,461.95

5. New FGV = 96,723.65 − 66,461.95 = 30,261.70

6. New ΔEVA = 30,261.70 (0.0777)/(1.0777/0.0777) = Δ\$169.53M every year in perpetuity

We can now easily compare the combined pre-deal stand-alone annual EVA improvement expectations of both companies with the new expectations for annual improvements, given that Future is paying the full market value for the shares of Cabbãge (and assuming the debt) *plus* a \$10B premium. Table 4-12 shows that Future is promising a perpetual increase in annual EVA improvements of \$57.42M, or a whopping increase of over 50 percent every year in perpetuity. We also show an easy approximation to our method by just taking the \$10B premium on its own as a direct increase in FGV and calculating the perpetual annual increase in EVA improvements, using our new WACC, and our formula for perpetual ΔEVA.[17]

Let's pause for a moment, because this is very important and the crux our journey. If we just directly take the \$10B premium as new FGV and multiply by $c/((1+c)/c)$, we arrive at \$56.02M of required perpetual annual EVA improvements, which is very close to working through the whole method.[18]

TABLE 4-12

Future Industries/Cabbãge Corp ΔEVA calculation results (\$M)

ΔEVA calculation results

Expectations of ΔEVA combined pre-deal	112.11
Expectations of ΔEVA in new company post-deal	169.53
Expectations of ΔEVA driven up using our method	57.42
Direct premium calculation	56.02

In other words, performing a sanity check for any DCF or multiples-based valuation is simple to do.

Now, making this more realistic for what you will need to announce, we can convert perpetual equal annual improvements and show a three-year ramp up of required synergies expressed as EVA improvements. We are essentially converting that FGV into COV by the end of the three years, which is likely far more satisfying for investors. And remember, because EVA is based on NOPAT, these are after-tax results. Recall our formula earlier in the chapter for a three-year ramp up:

$$FGV = ((1 + c)/c) \ [(\Delta EVA_1/(1 + c)) + (\Delta EVA_2/(1 + c)^2) + (\Delta EVA_3/(1 + c)^3)]$$

Using the $10B premium as FGV at a 7.77 percent WACC with an illustrative 25 percent, 35 percent, and 40 percent path to value, and a level P&L run rate after three years, gives us the figures in table 4-13.

Because these are EVA improvements, without significant additions of capital, they are changes in NOPAT.[19] That would translate to an after-tax P&L impact of $194M in the first year, $487M ($194M + $293M) in the second year, and a level run rate of $848M ($194M + $293M + $361M) in the third year maintained going forward.[20]

TABLE 4-13

Future Industries/Cabbãge Corp 3-year ramp up of ΔEVA ($M)

3-year ramp up of ΔEVA

Year	ΔEVA required	ΔEVA run-rate
1	194.25	194.25
2	293.08	487.33
3	360.97	848.30

However, if the new Future Industries were to delay realizing synergies until the third year (with no synergies realized in the first two years), this would blow up to $902M in after-tax improvements required all in the third year and maintained—not even close to the $361M increase of after-tax synergies required after three years, with a reasonable ramp up. You might also notice that the $902M in after-tax synergies is not even close to the $500M in *pre-tax* synergies (or $360M after tax with a 28% effective tax rate) that Future announced at the beginning of the chapter, *with no timetable for delivery*. When you don't offer a timetable, investors don't know what to think other than *you don't have a plan*. Little wonder our buyer lost the majority of the premium right on Announcement Day.[21]

The big finale is—wait for it—anybody can do these calculations before making an offer. If the results are not consistent with the after-tax, or equivalent pre-tax synergies you are about to promise the markets, "Houston, you may have a problem."

Conclusion

The math is clear, but let's reiterate the chapter's main points. Paying a premium for an acquisition requires a business plan to support the up-front investment. DCF valuation—although widely used—is sensitive to small changes buried in future assumptions, especially for synergies, and presents the potential for the tail to wag the dog to justify the price and premium you have to pay to get the deal done. Notably, DCF *assumptions* pre-announcement become *promises* embedded in the offer price of the deal—the acquirer is on the hook to achieve them. Once you fix the price of the target and pay for the deal, the only price that will fluctuate is yours, not the target's.[22]

Any delay in achieving those improvements will prove costly. Investors don't like it when you tell them you can't pay the "mortgage" for a while. Investors are smart: They know you can't just flip a switch and turn on synergies some time in the future. As a consequence, any deal must include some ramp up of synergies at announcement that does two things: 1) gives investors confidence you have a plan, and 2) yields a cost-of-capital return on the premium paid.

Future growth value, or FGV, implies EVA improvements, and any premium paid only raises the bar. Translating the premium to a ramp up of EVA and NOPAT improvements is a sanity check of the output of a DCF valuation that justifies a premium—and investors can do that calculation in seconds. Assuming no significant increase or decrease in invested capital, and the associated capital charge, EVA changes become changes in NOPAT—but, of course, any increases in invested capital will require a commensurate increase in NOPAT to compensate for the additional capital charge.

Remember, this process is not only a test of the valuation of the target; it's implicitly a review of the business plan of the deal—a story to be told to the board, to employees, and to investors. If expectations aren't met, the acquirer's stock price will drop. Announcement Day, the subject of the next chapter, is the day when all of these elements come together, and must be treated as seriously as every other part of the M&A process.

CHAPTER 5

Will They Have Reason to Cheer?

Announcement Day

Sure, there are some synergies here. I don't know where they are yet. To say that now would be an idiot's game.

—Barry Diller at the announcement of QVC's
   proposed acquisition of CBS, 1994

Announcement Day is often treated like a party. And why not? There's often good reason to celebrate. The boards of both companies have approved the transaction. The acquirer's board has reviewed the strategy, scrutinized the valuation, and presumably given substantial thought to high-level aspects of the integration. It has the blessing of investment bankers and lawyers on both sides, who have confirmed that the deal is in the best interest of each company.[1]

Often, though, this focus on celebration increases the likelihood of poorly considered communication to key stakeholders, especially investors. And if acquirers stumble on Announcement Day, they will give investors reasons to sell. It doesn't matter whether it's a lack of preparation, or the strategy of the deal is unclear, or the acquirer can't defend the price, the method of payment or the premium, or investors can't track the synergies—what investors hear is that management doesn't have a plan, and they react accordingly.[2]

As we saw in the study we presented in chapter 1, market reactions to M&A announcements, positive or negative, are essentially an initial forecast by investors of the value of the deal for the acquirer based on the new information that management has revealed. Substantial evidence, including our study, points to the importance of investor reactions. Gregg Jarrell, former chief economist of the US Securities and Exchange Commission, summarized the literature, "The evidence we have suggests that the initial market response is a fairly reliable predictor of how the deals are going to turn out." That's consistent with our study that if a deal gets a bad reception, it's more likely than not that the acquirer's share price will continue to perform poorly (especially for stock deals).[3]

Yet dealmakers and students of deal making alike have treated M&A communications as an afterthought. This is a huge mistake. Announcement Day represents a pivotal moment in the life of a deal and investor reactions set a powerful tone. Multiple stakeholders and observers will immediately evaluate and interrogate the investor presentation and other communications for whether the deal—perhaps the largest capital investment ever made by the acquirer—has any strategic logic and if it is worth the price.

And shareholders are not nameless and faceless: they are very often a company's own employees. When a deal is met with a drop of 5 percent or 10 percent or more in the acquirer's share price, not only do employees—the folks who will have to make the deal work—lose a significant portion of their pension assets, but their morale also suffers accordingly, even before the critical tasks of integration and delivering promised synergies begin. The best ones will start searching for new jobs. That, in turn, damages the tapestry of management credibility and makes it more difficult to cultivate the confidence of other stakeholders about the economic soundness of the deal.[4]

Consequently, communications strategy on Announcement Day can make the difference between success and failure on everything from securing shareholder approval to meshing the cultures of two distinct organizations. It is most definitely not just about putting on a "show." Remember, though, investors are smart and vigilant—they will rapidly see through claims that don't make sense—and slick press releases and conferences calls won't save a deal with bad economics.

Designing Announcement Day communication requires that both the acquirer and target consider, then address, the full world of stakeholders who will become aware of the deal when the press release is issued. Leaders from each company should anticipate jam-packed, down-to-the-minute schedules that will put them in front of investors, media, employees, customers, suppliers, and others all in a single day. When leaders overlook or mishandle messaging to any individual or group, the consequences are often immediate and long-lasting, including rumormongering and mudslinging on social media and lost productivity that may impact your customers' experience. Even when your plan is perfectly executed and your message is strong, your stakeholders are likely to have a heightened receptivity to phone calls from competitors who are looking to recruit them away.

Principles of Announcement Day

Announcement Day is an incredible moment when the disciplines of strategy, corporate finance, communications, competitor behavior, and human behavior all come together. It can immediately affect the value of the acquirer. It is the inflection point of the M&A cascade.

Three important functions

Preparing for Announcement Day serves three important functions.

First, well-conceived M&A communications during diligence can serve as a litmus test of the deal logic for acquirer executives—where they can think like an investor—well before Announcement Day itself. Think of it as the last stop in diligence. Does the deal give investors more reasons to buy than sell? Second, press releases, investor presentations, conference calls, and interviews will provide investors with fodder for their own diligence. Third, culture starts at announcement. The words leaders use matter to employees on both sides, so communications must be thoughtful and intentional. Don't say you are buying for the best of both companies when you don't mean it. Leaders are setting a tone—and expectations—for how things will work.

Although employees and shareholders—and customers and suppliers for that matter—may not have a perfect alignment of interests, they certainly do have a lot in common. All sides have to deal with uncertainty and doubt and all want to know the logic of the strategy behind the deal, the CEO's plan, "what's in it for me" (WIIFM), and if the new executive team has the experience—and stomach—to manage the new organization if something goes wrong.

How should a company prepare a sound M&A communications strategy? By taking the process seriously: Don't prepare the weekend before your announcement. Develop a story for important stakeholders, presenting them with the same logic that convinced *you* that the deal is worth doing, where the synergies lie, and how you'll achieve them. Finally, make sure that you anticipate what your critics will say and the questions that will come at you during the announcement. This will require you to view the deal from the outside in. But each of these three functions will prove worth the effort because they will get you in front of the market's reaction.

Get started early

Companies must put themselves in the shoes of investors long before transactions are brought to the board. Communications experts should be brought in as early as possible to understand the transaction and strategic benefits so they can begin crafting the communications package. A merger rollout is akin to a political campaign, with detailed schedules, timetables, and risk factors—and plans for responding to opponents. Too often, this process gets underway too late.

Discuss in detail the deal assumptions, specific benefits and synergies, worst-case scenarios, and execution timetable

The marriage partners must think long and hard about their message and the forum for delivering it to their key constituencies, including shareholders and analysts, bankers, employees, media, and customers, and frequently, unions, regulators, government officials, strategic partners, and rating agencies.

Moreover, materials should explain clearly and logically why the transaction's business case is value-enhancing. If the deal is dilutive to EPS in the short term but makes strategic sense long term, there had better be compelling economics for profitable growth. Investors and employees especially must be convinced that the company is capable of delivering on its promises and that they will be better off if the deal is completed. If the deal is truly strategic, you will also need to describe why you needed to pay the premium to do it.

Prepare an exhaustive question and answer document in advance for potential critics

The press release, the investor presentation, letters to various constituencies, and other documents will emerge during Announcement Day preparations. The Q&A document attempts to ask and respond to all the tough questions that investors, analysts, and the media will likely ask on the morning of the announcement. If the deal team can't convincingly answer the 40 or so questions crafted by the communications team, that will not augur well for the transaction. (These are similar to the questions that an engaged board should ask before they approve the deal. For more detail on the board's role, see chapter 9.)

In fact, asking tough questions may force the deal team to think about details they may not have carefully considered, such as:

- What are the major sources of cost savings?

- Where will layoffs take place?

- What plants will be closed?

- What is the timetable?

- What are the revenue implications?

- Are there operating model changes for the businesses?

- Who will lead the integration process?

Managers should avoid carelessly using buzzwords like "convergence" and "synergies," which, together with an excessive acquisition premium and without a plan, send a clear message to investors: *Sell*.

Essential Tests of the Investor Presentation

Preparing the investor presentation is ultimately a forcing mechanism to test the credibility of the economic and operational claims of the deal—the last stop in diligence. M&A communications must signal that senior management fully understands what it is proposing and promising—and that it can follow through.

Chas Ferguson—the CEO of Homeland Technologies, whom we introduced in chapter 2—is preparing to announce the acquisition of Affurr Industries, another major federal IT company. Chas knows he is paying a large premium for a large deal, but he believes that he has a solid strategic logic that will obviously offer significant valuable opportunities for Homeland. He has been reviewing other investor presentations and is struggling with what to consider.

But Chas's head of investors relations, Allison Demmings, assures Chas that she and her team, with the help of outside advisers, have prepared a fantastic investor presentation—detailed, informative, respectful. Allison's presentation reviews the industry mega-trends, the size of the deal and how Homeland will pay for it, how the deal makes the combined company number 1 or number 2 in all their business market shares, and a large number for cost synergies that will be fully realized by the end of the third year. It also includes a detailed review of proforma financials and how the deal will be accretive to earnings.

On the surface, Allison's investor presentation appears to offer a lot of information. But it will have to go farther—much farther—to pass the essential tests of investor presentations. Three questions take paramount importance when you're explaining an acquisition to investors and other stakeholders.

1. Is there a credible case with defendable and trackable synergy targets that can be accomplished by the acquirer, and monitored over time by investors?

2. Does the story help reduce uncertainty and give direction to the organization so employees can effectively deliver?

3. Does the presentation convincingly link post-merger integration plans to the economics of the transaction?

1. Do you have a credible case with defendable and trackable synergy targets that you can deliver and that investors can monitor over time?

The story that you're telling—the strategic logic—must address why the company can beat existing expectations, as reflected in the pre-announcement share price, and do so in ways not easily replicated by competitors. This logic must be accompanied by reasonable operating targets that can be easily understood, tracked, and monitored.

Forecasting overly optimistic gains from would-be synergies without explaining how or when they will be realized sends a red flag to investors. You might as well say nothing rather than make bold predictions that obviously can't be assessed or tracked.

More important, investors simply do not believe one big fat synergy number—the kind that's so often given in investor presentations. Why? Because they can't track it or assess the logic of how specific gains will add up to the total. But they can and will expect to track details. When management cannot give credible guidance that investors can track, it fails this first crucial test and comes across as seriously misguided. Stating one big number with nothing to track signals there is no plan.

Consider the case of a large technology company that announced its largest-ever acquisition of a rival, an all-stock deal at a 25 percent premium. On announcement, management announced a whopping $2.5B of cost synergies, most of the savings based in headcount reductions but without any guidance at all about which businesses those reductions would come from or when they would happen. They also announced that their combined revenues would be down by 10 percent in the first year. Their amorphous statement that they would achieve those synergies sometime "over the following two years" is not guidance. Markets hate that.

The result? Their share price dropped so much on announcement that the target was worth less at the end of Announcement

Day than at the beginning, more than erasing the 25 percent premium offered to the seller in this all-stock deal.

Less obvious, and potentially more damaging, is forgetting about your own growth story and announcing, without sufficient explanation, a radical change in direction to what you have been delivering. Investors have been attracted to your strategy because they regard you as expert in your business. Telling them that you're going to acquire another company and head off in a new direction—without showing them how and why—is inviting disaster.

Consider the classic case of Conseco, a financial services company that led the S&P 1500 in total shareholder returns over a 15-year period, with a 39 percent average annual return to shareholders. Conseco had a long track record of focused acquisitions, buying over 40 regional life and health insurance companies, immediately taking costs out the back office, and integrating the acquisitions into Conseco's back office systems in Carmel, Indiana. Conseco tracked these companies and, from experience, understood how much it could predictably take out of costs, how long it would take, and how much it could pay to do it and deliver superior returns to shareholders.

Just as important, investors grew comfortable with Conseco's strategy and were rewarded with increasing growth value in the shares year over year. They believed that such a successful strategy would continue.

But in 1998 Conseco announced its largest deal ever, offering $7.6B for sub-prime mobile-home lender Green Tree Financial at an 83 percent premium in an all-stock deal. Conseco CEO Steve Hilbert attempted to present the acquisition of Green Tree as "strategic" by asserting that the company had a successful track record and that the acquisition gave Conseco a position in a growing part of the financial services market. He also asserted that the deal was not driven by cost savings, as Conseco's past deals virtually always had been. Instead, synergies would come from revenue increases from cross-selling.

Conseco's shares dropped by more than 20 percent on announcement and were down 50 percent within a year. The company filed for Chapter 11 bankruptcy protection just a few years later. Not only was the deal a radical change in strategy, but it also gave investors nothing to track. Investors won't believe the deal is strategic, with lots of benefits, just because you say it's so.[5]

In contrast, when Nexstar Media Group announced its $6.4B (with assumed debt) all-cash acquisition of Tribune Media in December 2018, its investor presentation clearly spelled out the strategic, financial, and operational rationale, along with plans to better compete within the rapidly transforming media industry by "delivering a nationally integrated, comprehensive, and competitive offering across all our markets."

Nexstar effectively shaped investor expectations for the new organization, and clearly spelled out the breakdown of the trackable $160M synergy target—$20M for Corporate Overhead (duplicate expenses), $65M Station and Digital Group Expense Reduction (station expenses, support services, revenue migration from third-party vendors), $75M Net Retransmission Revenue from Tribune programming (margin uplift by applying Nexstar rates to Tribune subscriber counts)—all projected to occur in the first year following the completion of the transaction, along with planned divestitures (estimated at $1B, based on Federal Communications Commission ownership rules). Perry Sook, Nexstar's CEO, also stressed the company's ability to generate projected synergies based on the success of achieving promised synergies in recent deals.[6]

Investors responded by bidding up Nexstar's shares by 11 percent (nearly $400M) in the 48 hours following announcement. Nexstar then went on to outperform its peer index by 14 percent in the first year after announcement with a 38 percent total shareholder return.

Providing investors with trackable details of the deal is vital to earning—and maintaining—their trust and confidence. Further, those acquirers with strong acquisition track records of delivering on their promises have a real advantage. Acquirers announcing their first material deal to public markets with significant synergy promises, along with high premiums, or a transaction with a radically different deal thesis than in the past, will have to be even more clear and convincing in their presentation— particularly for all-stock deals that are typically met with skepticism.[7]

2. Does your story help reduce uncertainty and give direction to the organization so employees can effectively deliver?

Uncertainty is one of the unavoidable facts of life in M&A— especially for employees, who are the ones who have to execute the plan. But major M&A announcements that inject unnecessary uncertainty are even more disruptive, compounding the already unsettling effects of integration planning. Such announcements will not only cause employees to question the deal logic but will also prompt many of them to aggressively consider other career options.

Employees will want to know quickly and honestly how they will be affected. So the best investor presentations will have the new management team and key reporting relationships in place when the deal is announced to avoid a leadership vacuum that can jeopardize the integration of the two companies. Executives should also address facility closings that require major relocations and headcount reductions before they communicate anything that can easily be misconstrued and spark the rumor mill. Acquirers committed to their employee experience understand that their new experience begins at announcement.

The large technology company that we discussed earlier (under question 1) said that it would achieve $2.5B in cost savings, largely by cutting 15,000 employees over a two-year period. But employees and investors knew that the companies had already planned and announced combined reductions across the two companies of about 11,000 employees prior to the deal. This announcement went over like a ton of bricks with employees since it provided no guidance on where cuts would come from. It also, predictably, created a headhunter's paradise. The uncertainties implied by the announcement of this strategy contributed to the 19 percent drop in the acquirer's shares on announcement. Shares continued to decline as the battle between the target and acquirer heated up in the press.

Consider the clarity of the investor presentation of Avis Budget Group when it announced the all-cash acquisition of Zipcar in January 2013 at a healthy 49 percent premium. The deal would allow Avis Budget to become the leading innovator in the rapidly growing car sharing space and allow Zipcar to accelerate its growth by leveraging Avis Budget's existing vehicle rental infrastructure and technology footprint. The investor presentation stated the deal would generate $50M–$70M in annual synergies from three sources, in relatively equal parts, outlined in detail in the investor presentation: cost (lower fleet acquisition costs; lower vehicle operating, financing, and insurance costs; and lower general and administrative (G&A) expenses and elimination of public company costs), cost and revenue from fleet utilization (meeting Zipcar demand with a smaller fleet by utilizing available Avis Budget cars and expanding Zipcar's weekend opportunities), and pure revenue synergies (from expanding several Zipcar use cases in its customer base, product offerings, and locations).[8]

For employees, equally important was Avis Budget's commitment to the "Zipster" experience, which had focused on the goal of revolutionizing personal mobility. Ron Nelson, Avis Budget's CEO, announced that both the CEO and president/COO of Zipcar would remain in their leadership positions, and also emphasized the deal would enhance personal and professional growth opportunities for employees. Zipcar would also retain its Massachusetts HQ.

The Avis Budget presentation even made clear the difference between yearly P&L benefits versus the run rate they would achieve by the end of each year—a strong signal that senior management had thought this through and had a plan. They also stressed their past acquisition track record in achieving promised synergies. Investors responded with strong positive announcement return of 9 percent (roughly $200M of shareholder value) and exceeded their peers by 64 percent with a 105 percent total shareholder return in the first year.

There is only so much that can be covered in the presentation, so early signals like these matter a lot for employees as well as for investors and customers. The more acquirers can do to shape expectations at announcement, the more employees can begin to sense how they will fit into plans for the future. Early signals like announcing leadership or commitment to shared values or the customer experience—followed shortly thereafter with timelines for knowing the process of talent section and benefits—will calm employees so they initially feel better about the deal, and later spark their interest in how the deal will come together, inspiring them to see their futures with the company (more on this in chapters 7 and 8). Even if uncertainty can't be removed entirely, it can be reduced. And employees who have a clearer view of the future will be better able to engage, or at least be less distracted, with pre-close planning and post-close execution.

3. Does your presentation convincingly link post-merger integration plans to the economics of the transaction?

As we've discussed, acquisitions typically involve the payment of a significant premium to the shareholders of the selling company. That premium is a shock to the system that no one expected—an immediate and direct addition to the growth value of the target and the cost-of-capital clock starts ticking on Day 1. Unfortunately, the message communicated to investors does not always square with the performance required to justify the price being paid.

Even when management offers credible answers to questions 1 and 2, investors will mark down the acquirer's share price to reflect the deal's "true value" if the present value of the synergy numbers does not justify the premium—or if the premium creates a performance improvement problem that is likely not achievable. Think of it like a simple economic balance sheet. If the premium doesn't represent value likely achieved (predictably overpaying for assets), then the economic balance sheet stays balanced by subtracting the predicted overpayment from the acquirer's shareholder value.

To be even blunter: Don't forget that your investors can do math and that they will evaluate the economics of what you are promising.

Nothing is more likely to cause investors to sell their shares than a deal that cannot justify the value being given to another company's shareholders. Failure of the acquirer to provide critical information might cause it to lose even more value than the premium, because of the signals the announcement unwittingly sends to investors that the company might be trying to cover up other internal problems and can't achieve its own stand-alone value.

Consider the case of a large international insurance company that offered an all-stock $5B premium for a US-based insurance company but stated there would only be $130M of annual pre-tax synergies. If we capitalize the $130M at their 10 percent cost of capital—just like investors did—the synergies have a present value of only $1.3B (without accounting for taxes and assuming all synergies would occur in year 1). Investors are smart. The would-be acquirer's market value dropped by more than $3.5B—roughly the gap between the premium and the present value of the announced, trackable synergies—right on the announcement of the bid, drastically lowering the value of the offer and allowing another global insurance company to emerge as the winning bidder.

In contrast, Nexstar offered a 20 percent, or $700M, premium for Tribune. Doing the same calculation, and capitalizing $160M of pre-tax synergies that Nexstar stated would all be realized in the first year, with an effective tax rate of 27 percent and a 7 percent cost of capital, yields $1.7B of value—well above the acquisition premium.

Even long-run, experienced acquirers can run afoul of investors when they announce a transaction that seemingly deviates from their proven business model, predicting benefits for one type of deal based on the success of other, completely different transactions. For example, one large consumer goods company announced its $5.6B acquisition of a branded products company at a 50 percent premium. The acquirer had a successful 30-year track record of making small, single-product acquisitions integrating small "tuck-in" deals that focused on efficiencies. Trouble was, this new deal was 50 times larger on average—10 times larger than their largest deal—and vastly more complex than any of its earlier transactions.

Although both companies sold household products through similar sales channels to the same pool of customers, they competed differently. The acquirer focused on low prices versus premium-priced branded innovative products. They had different production processes and cost-structures. The acquirer would have to defend the revenue trajectory of those premium-priced branded product lines, even without paying a large premium, against increased competitive threats by cheaper knock-off products.

The acquirer's shareholders lost $1B on the news—precisely the amount of the acquisition premium—and its shares plunged by one half in the first year. The CEO later admitted, "We paid too much"—something investors knew right at announcement.[9]

Acquirers, even the best ones, must recognize what they are promising and the challenges that investors will see right from the beginning, and plan their communications accordingly.

These three questions can be summed up in one straightforward question that boards and managers should ask themselves on the eve of the vote on the big deal: How will this deal affect our stock price and why? As a director or leader, you have to believe that the transaction is worthwhile given the price and all the organization disruption that lies ahead, and that it is in the best interests of your shareholders—not just now but through to the completion of the deal and beyond. And your Announcement Day communications process must give stakeholders the same sense of confidence that you feel.

Remember, if you *don't* answer these three questions, investors will assume you *can't* answer them and that you don't have a plan, and they'll penalize you for it.

The Three Questions in Action: PepsiCo Acquires Quaker Oats

Although plenty of companies bungle their M&A communications, those that get it right stand to reap big rewards for their shareholders, both on the day of the announcement and over the longer term. Take, for example, the case of PepsiCo's formal announcement of its $13.4B all-stock acquisition of Quaker Oats Co. in December 2000.

PepsiCo had to overcome significant communications challenges before that deal could be consummated. Reports had been floating in the market for weeks about a not-so-private auction of Quaker, with Coca-Cola and French food giant Dannon Group the other prominent potential suitors. After PepsiCo offered to pay a 22 percent premium for Quaker, it exercised unusual discipline by not raising its bid even in the face of competing higher offers. PepsiCo's announcement was received positively by investors; its shares rose by over 6 percent, or nearly $4B, in the days after the announcement and continued to outperform the shares of its peers over time.

PepsiCo got off to a good start with a detailed press release and investor presentation supported by a lengthy analyst/investor call and webcast. It also sent letters to employees, customers, and bottlers to address their various concerns. In particular, not only did PepsiCo promise that the transaction would be accretive to earnings in the first full year after closing, but it also went so far as to express expected results in terms of return on invested capital (ROIC), which it said would increase by 600 basis points over five years. While sophisticated investors understand this language, it is rarely seen on merger press releases. Detailed materials that outlined the synergies were also available on the company website.

PepsiCo's investor presentation had the three key hallmarks: defendable and trackable synergy targets with clear, understandable "base" cases; clarity of leadership and reporting relationships; and synergies sufficient to justify the premium.

At the outset, PepsiCo reiterated the base case of what it had already led investors to believe. It spelled out to investors what the company had *already* promised concerning revenue, operating profit (EBIT), EPS, and ROIC growth. Thus, the case for improvements—the synergies—could then be clearly expressed as *increases* in profitable growth.

PepsiCo then described in detail where it realistically expected synergies, differentiating these expected gains from those it anticipated but did not include in the investor model. The investor presentation compared the revenue, EBIT, EPS, and ROIC growth rates it expected for the integrated company with PepsiCo and Quaker as stand-alone entities (the new base case). The presentation didn't include any numerical assumptions about the benefits of selling Quaker Oats' Gatorade beverage line through the Pepsi network, which could be substantial. Rather, PepsiCo emphasized the benefits that Gatorade brought to PepsiCo's Tropicana business through better management of the ambient (shelf-stable) beverage aisle in grocery stores. Management articulated clearly how it planned to integrate Quaker Oats and several of its brands into PepsiCo and how capabilities of both companies would be leveraged to achieve additional growth.

The presentation erred on the side of modest cost savings assumptions. A total of $230M of synergies was identified and expressed in terms of their respective contributions to operating profit: $45M from increased Tropicana revenues; $34M from Quaker snacks sold through the Frito-Lay system; $60M from procurement savings; $65M from cost savings derived from SG&A expenses, logistics, and hot fill manufacturing; and $26M saved by eliminating corporate redundancies. Investors and employees felt confident about what they could expect and track as a result of the transaction.

New leadership and reporting relationships were clear. PepsiCo announced that Steve Reinemund would become the new chairman and CEO, Indra Nooyi would become president and retain her CFO responsibilities, and Roger Enrico and Bob Morrison (former chair and CEO of Quaker) would become vice chairmen and report to Reinemund.

Moreover, Roger Enrico, PepsiCo's outgoing chairman, stressed that management used conservative estimates for cost savings and revenue synergies. Despite senior-level management changes at the top of the company, virtually every constituency understood how it would be affected by the transaction.

Thus, all of the stakeholder groups—including investors and employees—were confident about what they could expect and track in every major part of the business. Investors could easily see how the deal would produce improvements in operating profit, more efficient use of capital, and reductions in tax rates that would more than justify the modest 22 percent acquisition premium of about $2.2B for Quaker.

The December conference call announcing the deal generated a positive initial perception of the transaction, and PepsiCo's shares received a strong positive reaction—the nearly $4B increase we mentioned earlier. That perception persisted because of the process that followed the deal closing on August 2, 2002. At that time, PepsiCo released, in Excel format, the restated financial statements for the combination and reviewed all the changes that had occurred since the original presentation. It also hosted a full-day investor conference reviewing the synergies and growth opportunities. Because of the clarity PepsiCo achieved during the closing process, the company actually increased the value of anticipated synergies to $400M from $230M.[10]

Using well-prepared documents, a successful investor conference call, and careful follow-through at closing, PepsiCo was able to paint a rich strategic and financial portrait of the transaction and the effects on the company.

Tactical Preparation for a Successful Announcement Day

The question remains: How do you thoroughly prepare for a rigorous Announcement Day? The "run of show" for a well-prepared Announcement Day runs for many pages of detailed instructions for each participant and each group of stakeholders. To try to address all of those concerns and constituencies, and all of the moving parts, without a carefully prepared guide would be a fool's errand.

There are five elements to consider in Announcement Day preparations:

1. Formally define and document the deal thesis and key messages

2. Define stakeholders

3. Collaborate with external communications

4. Select communications channels

5. Establish timing and presence

Formally define and document the deal thesis and key messages

You should already know how this particular deal fits into your overall strategy. That's what we have been stressing up to this point: creating, articulating, and refining your deal thesis. Now is the time to focus on how to communicate the logic of this particular acquisition to all relevant stakeholders. While you should know the logic cold, articulating it can be another challenge. Announcement Day is the chance to crystalize key messages for how the deal delivers on the future strategy for the company. One concrete tool you can create is a "talk track," or a script that can be used consistently internally and externally for leaders and communications teams to communicate about the deal rationale.

Define stakeholders

What types of employees do you have? Do they work different shifts? What access to technology do they have? Determine what audiences (senior management, managers) would need a preview message and what support, or talking points, should be provided to key messengers. Consider what general outreach you would have across all of your employees and other stakeholders (e.g., email announcement to follow press release), and what specific outreach may be required to address constraints with certain employees (e.g., locations, access to technology).

Collaborate with external communications

The talk track is a central asset in building a set of messages that can be used externally and internally. Assume external communications will be sought out by employees who are looking for any information they can find on the deal, especially in light of how prevalent information is today. Confirm any points that could be perceived negatively on the deal, such as headcount synergies, and have a clear key message that can address concerns head-on.

Demystify any themes or messages in external communication directly in internal messages. We have had clients, for example, who referred to revenue synergies in the press release, and used internal succinct messages to clarify that the opportunity focuses on growth and expanded market opportunities with headcount staying flat. Regardless, absent clarification, employees may become anxious and assume a worst-case scenario.

Consider the local dynamics of the target and consider whether local news could be a risk or opportunity. Consider a non-disclosure agreement (NDA), or an embargoed press release or interviews, with certain influential local media outlets to control the narrative on the deal. Understand the risk of how the deal could be perceived by a hyper-local economy. Consider whether local news will reach certain employee groups, like the night shift, prior to corporate communications.

For internal messages, consider the target employees' main concerns: Do I have a job? To whom will I report? How is my job changing? Address questions directly where possible, or if unknown identify that the discovery process is ongoing and decisions have not been made. Where possible, let employees—yours and the target's—know when you will be able to tell them more.

Consider messages that may be required for other parties like customers and vendors, and provide support to employees who will have to interact with these parties through talking points aligned to the overall messages for the deal.

Select communication channels

When considering communication channels, confirm that all stakeholders have access to multiple communication channels (e.g., internet, computers, mobile access, livestream video, etc.) that enable wide message access. Where good policies and practices already exist, consider how to leverage social media. It's important to monitor how the deal is being perceived across social media so you can tailor your approach as integration planning begins.

Traditional communication methods—email announcements, meetings and town halls, livestream video—can be supplemented with other visual marketing cues (e.g., posters in breakrooms, local signage at entry points to plants) to create excitement. Consider other marketing mechanisms, such as direct mail or recorded telephone messages, for audiences where timing of announcement may not align to employee work schedules.

Establish timing and presence

Determine which members of the leadership team you would want to be present, where, and when. Balance the level of disruption at both the acquirer and target to create prioritization of physical presence. Be conscious of the perception of "bringing the army" if only acquiring executives need to appear on the first day. Determine who from the target leadership team you would or would not want present.

Contemplate the schedule of workers and whether all shifts should hear the news together, or if communications schedule could be shift-based (and whether that creates risk for the night shift if you announce in the morning). In preparation for announcement, consider a leadership pre-session to prepare key leaders and confirm final schedules.

Norwegian Cruise Line Holdings' Announcement Day

To see how these elements come together, we want to tell you about an Announcement Day that can serve as a model of stakeholder communication. One of our favorite experiences was the announcement in September 2014 that Norwegian Cruise Line Holdings (Norwegian) had agreed to acquire Prestige Cruise Holdings, operator of Oceania Cruises and Regent Seven Sea Cruises, for about $3B in cash and stock. The deal would diversify Norwegian's portfolio by joining the upper premium (Oceania) and luxury (Regent) brands with its mass-market Norwegian Cruise Line (NCL) brand known for its "freestyle cruising" (with no set times for meals or formal dress requirement), allowing the operator to compete better with larger rivals Carnival Corporation & plc and Royal Caribbean Group.

This deal was a huge success thanks in part to a well-conceived and well-executed Announcement Day strategy.

Key executives included Kevin Sheehan, CEO of Norwegian; Frank Del Rio, CEO of Prestige; and Andy Stuart, the head of Sales, Marketing, and Passenger Experience for Norwegian.

The deal was announced on September 2, 2014, with a press release that spelled out the logic of the deal, and closed on time on November 19, 2014. The $3B deal, including assumption of debt, included identified synergies of $25M in the first year, with additional opportunities post-integration.

The deal rationale, as outlined by Norwegian, was clear:

- Diversification of cruise market segments through the acquisition of upper premium and luxury brands

- The further enhancement of industry-leading financial metrics

- Opportunities for synergies and the sharing of best practices among brands

- An increase in economies of scale providing greater operational leverage

- The expansion of growth trajectory and global footprint

- The opportunity to complement Norwegian's ship new-build program with an existing order for Regent that provided measured, orderly capacity growth through 2019

The intent leading up to the announcement was to do everything possible to protect and preserve the trust and closeness that exists in the cruising community, and to make sure that in announcing the deal that everyone—from shipboard employees to customers boarding an NCL, Oceania, or Regent cruise—felt touched and connected. Norwegian's objective was to craft an experience that made sure everyone was "touched in a personal way."

First, they looked to understand all of the key leaders in the organization and from whom the employees would want to hear news of the deal (e.g., hearing from the ship captain). Norwegian developed messaging for each leader. While this messaging was similar, the materials catered to each respective audience.

Norwegian developed scripts and calendars for the CEOs and CFOs. They and 10 other key leaders of the organizations had their calendars entirely blocked one day before and two days after the transaction was announced. This gave them blocks of time and also showed just how seriously they had to take the announcement.

News of the transaction was intended to be held close to the vest, so the night before Announcement Day was the first time that news of the transaction was communicated below officers of the company. On this day, the news was shared with the VPs of both organizations.

At the same time, a prep call was held—after business hours—when the "toolkit" for the following day was shared. Norwegian also gave trusted media early notice of the deal, although interviews done the day before were under embargo, which was lifted at 6:00 a.m. on Announcement Day. The official press release went out at 6:00 a.m. as well.

There was some concern about employees learning about the deal on the way in to work (especially in Miami), so when employees arrived, someone at the door greeted them, announcing the deal and handing them a flyer with information for their specific town hall, which their leader held later that morning.

At 9:00 a.m., Andy, the head of Sales, Marketing, and Passenger Experience for Norwegian, stood up to give his town hall based on previously developed talking points, and to field questions from employees. CEOs Frank and Kevin were on the phone with media most of the day. That afternoon, Norwegian reached out to suppliers and customers—including travel agencies and passengers. (Norwegian emphasized agencies, and Prestige their passengers, although both organizations paid attention to each.)

Outreach to suppliers included intentional touchpoints with important passenger-facing groups like unions that represented the talent that performed on board the ships. Echoing the overall culture that Norwegian was trying to promote, they approached suppliers with transparency and honesty, reassuring them that while it was too early in the deal to know how things would evolve, Norwegian wanted to acknowledge their possible concerns and that they would continue to act as good-faith partners. Smaller suppliers received letters—but everybody got contacted.

Frank and Kevin also fielded questions from employees the week after the transaction was announced.

This didn't happen without a hitch. In Miami, the cruising business is a small, tight-knit community. People who were part of the scene knew about the deal ahead of time (even though it was officially embargoed). Originally, the team planned to announce the deal the Wednesday after Labor Day weekend. Instead of wrapping up all of the prep materials the night before, because of the holiday, the team finished all materials before the holiday weekend.

That was a good thing, because the leak happened the Saturday of Labor Day weekend.

Because the materials for the announcement had been prepared ahead of time, all the team had to do was move up the date of the announcement to after the holiday on Monday, and shift the date in the materials from the following Wednesday to Tuesday.

The total preparation time for the materials and timeline was about two weeks. This was not trivial, but you simply can't wait until the last minute to prepare—you've already done so much work just to get to this point. Like other aspects of M&A, a well-orchestrated Announcement Day involves a great deal of work in a short amount of time.

All of Norwegian's work paid dividends. Customer reaction was largely neutral—which in this instance was a positive. There was no loss of customers—a real concern before the deal was announced. While some Prestige customers might have felt that being bought by Norwegian, with its "cruising" style, was a deterioration of their expectations, the high-touch approach to Announcement Day made them feel like Prestige knew them so well that it understood and would address their needs.

On the travel agency side, customers said they appreciated the outreach. Norwegian let the agencies know how this merger would create new opportunities for them to upsell from one line to another and potentially create "customers for life." While they didn't have all the answers, Norwegian made clear that answers were forthcoming. In the short run, nothing would change for customers, and the next deliberate touch point would be when there was something exciting to share about how the merger was moving forward.

Employee reaction was also positive. Those who passed out flyers that Tuesday morning heard directly from employees who had heard about the deal on the way in and were excited in the moment. If someone couldn't answer an employee's specific question, they could note it, pass it on to the executive team, and let the questioner know that that the executives would be able to address it—and they did.

Norwegian's Announcement Day also had legs. Over the next couple of days, the team used "office hours" to reinforce the idea that leadership was available and engaged. Those who were taken aback by the news or who thought of questions later—especially on the Prestige side—could engage with the "other side" and get their questions answered and receive reassurance. This reinforced the goal of being collaborative and open, echoing the world of freestyle cruising. Cutting off this important line of communication would have undermined the trust that they were looking to build.

The preparation and clear, effective storytelling paid dividends in the market as well. Investors reacted positively, with Norwegian's stock price going up by 11 percent on Announcement Day. A year later its stock was up nearly 70 percent.

Conclusion

Communications strategy can make the difference between success and failure. Senior management must anticipate investor demands, and their expectations for answers, long before announcing a deal to the market—just like PepsiCo and Norwegian did. Given the high stakes in M&A, boards and senior executives who understand the real demands of their investors will use those issues as a litmus test in the due diligence process. They will begin constructing a communications program at the earliest stages of a proposed transaction and thus be able to communicate a credible strategic story that enables investors to track management promises through post-merger integration and gives employees some guidance that will set some expectations early on. That said, as evidence from waves of mergers demonstrates, investors eventually will see through a flimsy story if acquirers don't deliver.

Of course, lawyers will caution management teams regarding what should and should not be stated in communications. And some management teams may simply want to be secretive as part of the company's culture. But there may be a big price attached to this secrecy. A new relationship is developing between management, investors, and other stakeholders as they try to tell the "good" guys from the "bad" guys. When investors are in doubt, they tend to assume the latter—so do employees.

In this way, Announcement Day serves as the hinge on which the deal hangs—where the deal thesis, the due diligence, and valuation come together and define the path that the new organization will take immediately after announcement through post-merger integration. The work the acquirer must do to prepare for a great Announcement Day is not trivial, but it will pay dividends. It is, as we noted earlier, the inflection point of the M&A cascade.

Following Announcement Day—and maybe just one glass of champagne—formal integration planning efforts, which are the subject of chapters 6 and 7, will kick off. There is a lot to do.

CHAPTER 6

How Will I Deliver on My Vision and Promises? Part I

From Deal Strategy to Pre-Close Integration Management

If you think you've done a lot of work to this point and have made many decisions, you ain't seen nothing yet. Integration is where the rubber meets the road.

There can be a tendency to race to announcement and treat it like a finish line, but such an attitude can lead to stumbles. Acquirers can be ill prepared for the sheer volume of work that is involved in moving to planning the actual integration. It requires engineering a process that will involve as many as 10,000 non-routine, highly unusual decisions, and senior leaders will have to devote significant time and energy while the rest of the organization swims in fear, uncertainty, and doubt. And remember, investors are smart and vigilant—they will track the results.

In fact, while this chapter comes after chapter 5's focus on Announcement Day, acquirers have to begin thinking about the topics we address here and in chapter 7 well before they go public with the deal. Knowing how much and where synergies will come from, and the resources required to achieve them, should be central to the approval process for the deal.

Non-routine decisions large and small abound in post-merger integration (PMI) planning. They include how to achieve the deal's axis of value (growth vs. cost or some combination of the two) along with a new operating model, how the go-forward leadership structure should be created to meet deal objectives, changing leadership and spans of control, implementing new enterprise management systems, whether to merge sales forces, where to base headquarters and what real estate footprint to retain, and specific synergy targets with owners by function and business.

The list includes seemingly trivial issues like summer Friday schedules and which holiday and vacation policies to adopt. Many of those smaller non-routine decisions won't break the deal, but they will need to be made somewhere. And the longer that decisions go unmade, the more employees will be left wondering and distracted from customer care, product quality, and innovation.

At the same time, acquirers must not run afoul of the anti-trust division of the Department of Justice (DOJ) in the United States or governing bodies in other part of the world (e.g., European Commission in Europe, Ministry of Commerce in China, etc.). The Hart-Scott-Rodino (HSR) regulations in the United States in short require that both parties in a merger act as two separate companies until they are legally one. Although they can do significant PMI planning, they cannot go to market or operate as if they are one company and cannot share competitively sensitive information that could change the way either party did business if the deal did not proceed. (See the sidebar, "Clean Rooms and Clean Teams.")

Clean Rooms and Clean Teams

Clean rooms are a construct of data confidentiality that allows sharing and analysis of competitively or commercially sensitive information. Clean teams have privileged access to that information under specific clean room protocols—rules that govern data access, sharing, analysis, and distribution of outputs. Beyond conforming to HSR regulations, clean rooms can relieve anxiety either side might have in sharing data as well as enable maximal use of the planning time between announcement and Day 1.

Clean rooms are essential for several use cases, including accelerating integration planning, making organizational and operating model decisions (e.g., shared services vs. dedicated in-functional support), and identifying and evaluating potential synergies (e.g., overlapping vendor raw material spend, product pricing and supply chain network optimization, customer rationalization, and evaluating cross-selling opportunities).

Clean rooms and clean teams are used for testing hypotheses developed during the diligence phase and, more important, developing specific plans post-signing that will be implemented after Day 1. For example, making an operating model decision on a direct versus a distributor sales force will require knowing customer revenue and profitability, revenue contributions of various markets, and sales force performance metrics.

Clean room analysis starts with separate data requests sent to both deal parties such that commercially sensitive data can be uploaded in a restricted environment with privileged access only to the clean teams. Clean teams are typically staffed with third parties, including consultants and external legal counsel, to ensure that no one with access to sensitive information would be employed by either side if the deal is abandoned. Leaders nearing retirement might also be involved in the process.

(continued)

Once the analysis is complete, an aggregated output with appropriate masking and anonymization of sensitive information is first reviewed by external legal counsel of both parties and then jointly shared with the relevant integration teams. For example, cross-sell opportunities might be developed using customer-level information, then aggregated at a product or geographical level for sharing with the commercial integration workstream. Detailed data, plans, and initiatives can be declassified and shared with relevant teams for tactical execution after the legal close.

Integration Planning: The Basics

Integration planning provides a short period of time to transfer the deal thesis across parameters of customers, products, technology, go-to-market strategy, and talent into milestones and key performance indicators (KPIs) that are specific and measurable and that will maintain business continuity, deliver on operating commitments, and preserve the momentum of both businesses while providing the blueprints for achieving at least the promised synergies. This is the period when acquirers plan the transition from the current state to the future state where they will deliver new value to customers or operate at a more efficient cost structure than exists at the time of announcement—or both.

Integration planning must accomplish three major goals:

1. Maintain the momentum in both businesses (preserve growth values)

2. Build the new organization (implement new operating model and organization structure)

3. Deliver the promised value (exceed performance implied by the premium)

Without a clear structure, process, and governance to meet these goals, confusion will reign and employees will "vibrate in place." Confusion over roles and pace; lack of clarity in pre-deal strategies and how to translate them to operating plans; and an inability to anticipate and calm customers, suppliers, and employees will likely lead to chaos. Competitors will use this chaos to exploit and poach both talent and customers.

Once this spiral begins, deal value will begin to leak. Lacking functional blueprints that map current-state to future-state processes and the relevant milestones, promised synergies will slip away. Movement toward the new organization will be delayed, eroding employee confidence. Key leadership and talent leave, creating even more confusion. Lack of clarity and planning for synergy tracking can lead to double counting synergies with already planned performance improvements. Failing to understand and orchestrate the interaction and timing of cost and revenue synergies can lead to reducing critical parts of the organization necessary to execute on revenue synergy strategies, possibly even damaging the already expected growth in either company. Cutting too deep can have serious unintended consequences.

On the human side, putting two organizations together can be like a destination wedding where two large families are brought together and meet for the first time at a resort. Will they like each other? The food? What if they don't get along? Emotions will run high on both sides, and whether or not those emotions are uncovered, they won't go away. And those emotions will impact employees' work and how they feel about themselves and the new company.

A successful integration involves seamlessly transitioning the acquired entity into the acquirer's systems, processes, and culture—or creating new ones—while leveraging synergies and executing a defined strategy to create value and enhance the corporate brand.

To achieve a successful integration, those tasked with leading the integration must understand:

- **The Why:** Why did we do the deal? What is the strategic rationale of the deal? What are the deal value drivers? What synergies exist and how will we achieve or exceed them?

- **The What:** What is the new operating model of the combined entity? What pieces will be fully integrated or stand alone? Have the cultural fit, processes, systems, and resources of the target been closely examined and incorporated in the planning?

- **The When:** When will integration planning and implementation begin? What are investor expectations about when value will be delivered by the acquisition? What parts of the integration will take the most time and consideration?

- **The Who:** Who are the key company players on both sides? Who will be the integration leader? What crucial personnel will be involved to create and execute the plan? Who's involved and who gets to make the important decisions regarding the integration? Who are the most important people we absolutely want to retain?

- **The How:** How will processes and systems be integrated? What steps need to be taken to ensure we comply with regulations and relevant laws to reach a legal close? How will we structure a communications plan that will effectively explain the acquisition internally and externally during PMI planning?

Every acquisition is different, and there is no one answer for how to successfully integrate a target into the acquirer's business. But without guiding principles and a formal, clearly defined approach to integration (often referred to as "integration strategy"), this disarray will only be compounded, creating a flawed Day 1 and downstream integration problems—content-light communications, muddy decision rights, employee fatigue from overwork and worry about self-preservation, and less than optimal decisions. The pre-deal planning and assumptions from the diligence phase will get lost, leading to missed functional interdependencies, rework, and erosion of the opportunity to expand or accelerate synergies.

If this sounds like a lot, it is, and the ill-prepared will suffer.

Templates versus vision

This is not a process managed with piles of templates—that's the bad old way. Instead, it's about providing a guiding vision, structure, and governance that will drive decision-making throughout the two organizations as they navigate the integration planning process.

It's also about senior management making important decisions up front—like which ERP system (e.g., SAP vs. Oracle) will be the system of choice—so the teams can work on integration planning instead of distractions from predictable political battles. This chapter and chapter 7 provide principles to avoid potential messes and to capitalize on the deal momentum to rally the troops, energize customers, and lay the foundation for results to report to investors and the board. They also show how to minimize disruptions and preserve momentum.

Here, we focus on the role of the Integration Management Office (IMO), a temporary structure that drives the integration, both top down and bottom up. Working with decisions and high-level plans that were created before the announcement, the IMO produces a finer-grained roadmap for success across the new organization, with targeted workstreams focusing on the axes of value that will guide decisions. The IMO will also keep senior executives closely involved through integration planning, since it is their deal vision and strategy that the IMO is executing.

The more planning and decision-making that gets done pre-close, the more that momentum will propel the new organization into Day 1 and beyond to capture synergies, begin post-close integration execution, and operate as an integrated company. The less planning, the less preparation, the more stand-alone the companies will be on Day 1 without an integrated end state in sight—while the cost-of-capital clock is ticking on all that capital that was paid up front. And "ringfencing," or not integrating the companies, is the start of a death march, leading investors, board members, and employees to ask the question, "Why did we buy this in the first place?" And if they cannot discern a good answer, they will walk away.

Predictable mistakes

In our experience, even seasoned executives make a few predictable mistakes post-announcement that must be avoided.

First, they treat integration as "business as usual"—something to do on top of their day jobs. This approach disregards the sheer amount of work and decisions required and the risks of diverting people who really need to keep the business running against the competition and serving customers. Moreover, they don't grasp that integrations have many functional interdependencies that leaders in functional roles don't normally have or assume someone else is solving.

Second, they declare that "everything is important" and fail to prioritize decisions; nor do they establish a coherent governance structure, leading to collisions, disenchantment, and often mayhem. Third, without a roadmap of major decisions, they kick the can down the road, delaying or postponing decisions that are "hard" in the face of uncertainty, sometimes with the hope it will become some other leader's problem down the line.

Acquirers might also slow decisions in an effort to avoid offending the target company or damaging the culture, or, even worse, will declare to their new employees that "nothing is changing." That is the perfect way to damage trust early in the process because it will be obvious to everyone that *a lot* will change. Remember, there has rarely been a "merger of equals"—a phrase that gets used over and again. The fewer hard decisions made up front, the tougher it will be later to achieve the cost reductions or revenue enhancements required to justify the premium. Kid gloves and happy talk can seem nice, but they ultimately lead to negative unintended consequences. Remember, pay me now or pay me later. But you'll pay either way.

For instance, in one case, during the acquisition of a promising technology company, the acquirer told the target that they wouldn't do anything to compromise their "secret sauce." But to the target, *everything* was part of their secret sauce—from their parking privileges to their free food, generous paid time off (PTO) policies, and office location, right through their killer product (which is what the acquirer thought was the real secret sauce). So once the acquirer started changing policies and systems, the target felt that trust had been broken and talent started walking out the door.

While avoiding the big mistakes is table stakes, the secret to successful integration is in the details. It's often not the one big mistake that will kill integration; it's the collection of ongoing small mistakes. The clock is ticking. Integration must be completed while you have everyone's attention and executive stakeholders agree it is *the* priority. Trust us: The last thing you want is to call in help two or three years later to assist with an integration gone sideways.

Operating Model and Integration Approach: Bringing the Deal Thesis to Reality

Integration planning starts with the strategic intent of the deal but also with an emphasis on keeping the end state in sight. If the team working on integration plans doesn't know that intent, or if the strategic intent was muddy, then having a clear vision for the end state and executing on that become challenging indeed. This is one reason earlier chapters have focused on defining a clear strategy and deal thesis from the very beginning of the M&A process.

The deal thesis drives everything that follows. It answers the question of why the acquirer chose to do *this* deal in the first place, as well as this deal's logic and assumptions for creating value.

Put simply: Why is the combined company more valuable together than apart? The integration approach of a deal built on cost reductions is fundamentally different than one built on growth. Cost-driven deals will typically look toward back office redundancies, while revenue growth–driven deals (aka strategic deals) start and end with the customer offer. In reality, most deals will be a combination of the two, and there will be a tension between those two axes of value that will have to be resolved.

Focusing on the original deal thesis will help align leaders by providing them with the Why. The strategy underlying the deal will also help answer other fundamental questions about short- and long-term objectives, including level of effort, timing, and role of the various parties involved, questions such as:

- What is the value of bringing these companies together?

- How will the new entity go to market differently?

- Just how much do the two companies need to be integrated, and in what way?

- How fast must organization design move to prepare the organization to operate in an integrated way, with a new operating model in light of changing customer expectations and competitor moves?

- How will the new entity exceed the cost and revenue synergies that were already announced?

Operating model

Each organization will already have an operating model: an organization structure that drives how the business is run in different parts of the organization; a service delivery model that guides how parts of the organization interact and the level of centralization of various support functions; and governance processes, behavioral norms, and decision rights that govern who gets to make specific decisions. Taken together, the operating model is a blueprint for translating strategies into how the organization harnesses its capabilities for delighting customers in a way that creates value for the enterprise. Integration planning necessarily changes some or all of that because the new combined entity will likely have a new operating model.

The new operating model is the answer to how the newly merged organization will run its businesses differently, how it will generate value differently than either organization did before. This includes both the enterprise- and business-level operating models (how separate business units interact and use shared services to support going to market differently) and functional operating models (how people, processes, and technologies may change by function to support the needs of the businesses—from expense reimbursements and travel, headcount approvals, and compliance to outsourcing vs. offshoring payroll, and so on).

The new operating model connects a company's deal thesis and business strategies with its capabilities, processes, and organizational structure. It informs the answer to such questions as: Given the markets that are key to our future growth, how do we structure our organization to reach them? How much should we centralize services, decision rights, and governance? How should we redesign incentives to promote the right behaviors on the part of employees?

The operating model is not organization design. Organization design, which we discuss in chapter 7, is concerned with roles and people within the new operating model. The operating model itself is all about the changes to come in how the combined organization does business: who does what, where, and when, and how it will be different than it was before.

Remember, the acquisition took place because of an opportunity that was unavailable to either organization, so change must take place. This will potentially mean breaking a part of the organization that appears to be working well to accommodate the future, but it shouldn't come as a surprise. That might involve, for example, the US DOJ requiring the divestment of a piece of either business. The acquirer shouldn't be surprised and should already have a general idea of what business areas are overlapping and might require a remedy.[1]

One example of a new operating model comes from the changes enacted during the merger of two high-technology component manufacturers, each of which earned approximately $2B in revenue the prior year. Both companies owned and operated manufacturing sites across the globe, and each served as an original equipment manufacturer (OEM) to well-known Fortune 50 high-technology and industrial companies. The acquisition allowed the acquirer to double its capacity. But rather than look at this opportunity through a cost lens to drive additional economies of scale, the acquiring CEO took a bold position. He understood that—as happens with many OEMs—they ran a risk of being commoditized and marginalized by their clients. The act of pleasing your customers by reducing cost based on volume is a one-way street to a cul-de-sac where eventually only a few suppliers can survive. No matter how many acquisitions he would pursue, the CEO understood that using this cost focus, despite the very advanced nature of the technology of the plants, the chance that the company would survive and prosper long term would be slim.

The CEO also understood more than many of his peers that M&A can create a powerful moment for change. He was also aware it is the most natural moment where stakeholders—

executives, employees, customers, suppliers—ask themselves, "What change will this transaction cause?"

The acquiring company had 14 factories with slightly differentiated capabilities, some which had come to the company through past acquisitions under prior leadership. Each was optimized for its own plan. The target was not so different, with 16 factories. The factories for both companies collaborated but were focused on optimizing their own yields, efficiency, customer satisfaction, and capital investment. The acquisition certainly would offer opportunities for the acquirer to lower the combined G&A costs at HQ, increase purchasing power to drive cost savings on direct material spend, and in certain areas enable advanced technologies in growth markets such as electric vehicles.

But rather than pushing his team to optimize for these opportunities, the CEO insisted that the team restructure the operating model to exhibit a higher level of true end-market intricacy, move up in the market to higher margin offerings, and be known for being the best for something—whether it be electric vehicles, smartphones, or medical supplies.

Rather than having 30 plants and trying to win on quality and price, he forced his team to put the customer end market first and to think of the plants together as capabilities to serve four end markets: communications, automotive, medical, and industrial. The CEO honed in on his vision for an end market–focused company, what its key differentiators were relative to the end market (be it certain technologies important for radar or lidar in electric vehicles vs. quick-turn projects in the communications industry, or specific material requirements in medical), and how they could organize themselves around that vision and exceed the demands of their customers.

The acquisition provided the opportunity to change the paradigm and the value drivers of the company by changing the operating model and incentive structure. This in turn kicked off a rapid process of operational and organization design to not only take care of M&A-related issues, but also those related to combining the two organizations from relatively autonomous plants to a company with four end market–focused business units.

A clear operating model is foundational to a sound integration approach: Why and how the integrated organization is going to operate differently forms the foundation for the concrete choices about how the two organizations will be combined.

Integration approach, governance, and guiding principles

Integration approach—what many call "integration strategy"—involves early decisions aimed at translating the deal thesis into the desired end-state operating model—that is, the approach, governance, and principles that will guide the journey from the present to the future. There are many paths and approaches that one could take, but the integration approach defines the parameters within which this particular merger is going to operate.

Clearly defined rules of the road will help the senior integration team confront the harsh reality at the heart of integration planning—prioritization. Prioritization matters because teams must know what is in scope for the integration, and how to set the right pace and determine if it will play out all at once or in phases.

A clear deal strategy and operating model are essential, but they're also somewhat theoretical. Integration approach is anything but: Now you have to start facing practical choices.

The five questions at the heart of the integration approach relate to:

1. **Pace:** How fast must the integration get done?

2. **Degree:** What's in, what's out, and which parts of the businesses will be fully integrated?

3. **Phasing:** Will the integration happen all at once, or in distinct phases over time?

4. **Tone:** Is it acquirer-driven or collaborative or some combination?

5. **Communications:** What, when, how, and to whom will major decisions be communicated?

Different types of deals will require different approaches. Further, even within typical deal classifications there may be vastly different levels of complexity (from geographic reach to anti-trust considerations), whether it's a complete transformation that leads to an entirely new organization; a consolidation, combining two organizations in similar businesses into a larger one; a "tuck-in," where the acquirer absorbs the target; or a "bolt-on," where the target's front office is left intact but its back office is integrated with the acquirer's. While it may be tempting to plot these different deal types into a matrix with rules for each, different deals will often have different characteristics, with some elements of each requiring different integration approaches.

The nature of the deal and its complexity will delimit some of the choices around each element. For a tuck-in with a high premium, for instance, the integration must move fast and happen nearly all at once, with the acquirer setting the tone. In a more complex deal, back office consolidation might need to happen quickly, but rationalizing the supply chain might take longer and require more collaboration in certain areas than in others. Combining two different ERP systems may require an interim-state operating model where both systems run in parallel for at least a year until the cutover to one system can happen.

For example, two large cosmetics companies with operations across multiple geographies and with two distinct operating models in the United States merged in what might be called a consolidation deal. One was strong in the mass self-serve market (e.g., Walmart and Target), while the other focused on large department stores that use beauty advisers. The first phase of the integration was back office consolidation and commercial integration where, although there was some channel overlap, operating models were kept intact. Immediately though, there would be one face to customers (retailers). The next phase focused on supply chain integration that involved warehouse consolidation and the insourcing of the target's fragrance production. The third phase was the "long-pole in the tent" and focused on uniting disparate ERP systems.

Before establishing the IMO, which will oversee the monumental day-to-day tasks of the sprint to Day 1, the new CEO will meet with their direct reports that have been chosen (what we call L1 leadership) and the IMO lead to establish a common understanding—the broad outlines and expectations—of how the integration will proceed, particularly around decision rights. They will agree on what types of decisions will need consultation with the L1 team, which may not be involved with the integration day to day, and those issues that would require escalation to the board. The board in its oversight role should be well informed about the approach and governance for the integration.

Among the decisions will be the composition and role of the executive steering committee (SteerCo)—the ultimate arbiter of major decisions. SteerCo often comprises at least the CEOs of both companies, especially in large material deals. It can also help to have either the COO or CFO who has been involved from the beginning of the acquisition so they can explain potentially confusing financial aspects and synergy expectations of the deal. SteerCo can ratify decisions being recommended by the IMO, clarify strategic questions about the deal, referee big conflicts that the IMO leadership can't resolve, and greenlight and fund synergy programs.

The CEO and their team must also be clear on the guiding principles consistent with the tone of the integration. Is the acquirer in complete control, or will the process be more collaborative? If the merger is going to be guided completely by the acquirer, be clear about this fact up front. It could be a combination of the two, where the sales teams will collaborate and use best practices of both, but the back office processes and systems will move quickly and follow the acquirer's approach.

Other principles might include decisiveness over perfection, speed over elegance, roles before people, guidance like "Don't struggle in silence," using "we" and not "us and them," or not taking actions that would threaten current customer satisfaction. While some of these may be defined by the deal, larger, more complex deals will require explicit principles for different businesses that will help guide the integration over the longer term.

In effect, integration approach and guiding principles help to set expectations for the new organization. The senior team must make sure the approach is logical given the economic rationale of the transaction and that their subsequent actions are consistent with the expectations they set for their organization. In times of tension and doubt, management and employees will need to feel confident the senior team is all on the same page.

The integration approach also makes clear what trade-offs are acceptable. "What will you sacrifice?" is a fundamental question in this process. No synergy, no change, comes for free or without risk. EPS may need to be sacrificed initially to have a smoother integration that will create more value later. Restructuring may require spending precious capital now to replace the IT stack or hire staff or replace the ERP. These may be truly necessary to create an integrated organization, and yet risk EPS in the short term. Is that OK, or is it off the table? What in fact is non-negotiable? Questions like these must be addressed and answered before kicking off an IMO. Many of these decisions will be communicated at kickoff meetings (which we address in the IMO section, below), but they have to be decided earlier in broad outlines by senior leadership.

A useful example of both setting approach and principles, and making trade-offs explicit comes from Deloitte Consulting's acquisition in May 2009 of the federal practice of BearingPoint, KPMG's former consulting arm—a major transaction for Deloitte. BearingPoint was more than twice the size of Deloitte's federal practice in both revenues and people. In the Department of Defense (DOD)/intelligence sector, for example, revenue increased from $14M to over $150M with the deal.

Deloitte's federal practice leadership were emphatic about retaining BearingPoint's talent. Consulting is a relationship business where leaders directly generate revenues. "Startling the herd" could result in a massive exodus of talent. Yet each firm had a radically different operating model when it came to staffing teams. At Deloitte, professional staff came from a general staffing pool that partners had to compete for, whereas at BearingPoint partners "owned" their dedicated staff.

Deloitte leadership made the decision to proceed with the Deloitte operating model but to move slowly to avoid having employees feel like they were being forced into anything: "We need them to stay" was a guiding principle. Leadership met personally with each leader from the seven sectors of the BearingPoint practice—nearly 75 of them—showing a genuine interest in their development and career path at Deloitte as well as their general well-being. Deloitte spent an entire performance cycle crafting new roles and goals where the focus was on keeping staff whole—that is, neither penalized nor marginalized because they didn't come from Deloitte.

Another important guiding principle was avoiding the use of "us versus them." "We" now had a bench of talent that could recruit better candidates, serve larger clients, had better relationships, and could propose on much larger projects. Over three years, the combined platform grew rapidly, with newly recruited professionals making up nearly one-third of the business.

One thing that did have to go fast—very fast—was preparation for Day 1, barely six weeks after announcement. That huge undertaking required arming roughly 4,250 new Deloitte employees with their new badges, laptops, email and network credentials, and compensation and benefits packages on Day 1. Onboarding for Day 1 was so enormous that Deloitte rented the Washington, DC, convention center for the event. Deloitte's federal practice has become well known as one of the major players in federal consulting, and the learnings from that integration have benefited clients as well as the firm's subsequent professional services deals.

Here, you can see how a thoughtful approach and principles can guide the plan to integrate successfully, and quickly where necessary. Those principles and the integration approach go beyond mere planning and affect the employee experience and preparing for Day 1 (topics we address in depth in chapter 7).

The Integration Management Office: Supercharged Conductor for Integration Planning

The IMO is the living and breathing—albeit, temporary—structure that leads integration efforts. It remains separate from the ongoing business by design and facilitates bottom-up and top-down governance. The IMO identifies what must get done by Day 1 and by the end state (what we call the Day 1 and end-state "must-haves"). It identifies the risks of delivering within that scope—and helps reach consensus about what is a non-negotiable priority for Day 1 or what can be deliberately postponed. When conflicts arise or there are competing priorities, the IMO makes the call or escalates the issue to the executive SteerCo. M&A strategy, due diligence, valuation, and announcement are focused on creating value for the acquirer, and the purpose of the IMO is to direct and accelerate the execution to realize that value.[2]

The IMO must be a supercharged prioritization machine for organizing and establishing workstreams, gathering information and ideas from both the acquirer and target, raising issues and problems that need to be solved, setting synergy targets by business and function, developing ideas that will translate to projects for delivering those targets, making decisions, and identifying Day 1 versus end-state must-haves and interdependencies that must be managed across workstreams for Day 1 and beyond.

The job of the IMO is to fulfill the promise of the deal strategy and the new operating model, and to avoid the muddy confusion of jockeying teams operating in their silos. It should propel the new organization through Day 1 toward the end-state operating model.

The pace and amount of work can feel overwhelming, especially given the short amount of time available. And it's true: This is a sprint. Take a deep breath.

Integrating two organizations for reasons that initially might not be well understood or where there are many opinions of how things should be done is a lot like being the conductor of an orchestra. The role of the IMO is—more than anything—that of a conductor, orchestrating the integration teams' attention on the right things to do at the right time, within legal guidance and regulations. No doubt there is a lot of talent on both sides. The target's talent didn't get there by accident, and that may be a big reason you wanted them in the first place. But self-preservation and what's best for their function or business will be their focus. That's true for the talent of the acquirer as well. IMO leadership must prevent that by launching a coordinated effort.

IMO governance prevents people from running around doing their own thing and making their own decisions—which leads to chaos and confusion, and to people vibrating in place, full of anxiety and uncertain of what to do. In this role, the IMO is a sequencing and prioritizing body, aiming to get the bare minimums needed for a flawless Day 1, with no negative customer or employee impact. The IMO also serves a controllership function. It monitors and challenges the estimates of one-time and ongoing costs emerging from the plans of the workstreams for operational integration activities as well as synergies.

The IMO allows for decisions to be recommended deep within the integration workstreams (bottom up) driving to decisions that will be ratified by the SteerCo (top down) regarding organization design and leadership, synergy planning and tracking (both labor and non-labor), and the transition to post-close execution of the end-state vision for the combined company. The IMO must be nimble such that leadership can make decisions quickly and revise them, if necessary, as new information emerges.

While the IMO structure is essential to integration, it can't be overengineered or have too much process because that will result in the opposite of what it is intended to achieve—speed, agility, efficiency. An additional danger exists in focusing too much on process: Teams' focus can shift from defining and tracking results to just publishing their reports. Moreover, the IMO is transient. If it lasts too long, it will leave a legacy of processes that aren't useful to the new organization. Don't forget: The IMO is dispensable once you transition to business as usual.

In fact, part of the IMO's remit is to define when the IMO itself will be fully disbanded. Defining what "done" means—when the integration is complete—is an integral part of planning and will vary across integrations depending on the complexities and interdependencies of the workstreams. The executive team and integration leads will need to know when they've crossed the finish line. In the ideal, the end state is defined as when the two companies are operating in the marketplace as one and the value of the deal thesis is well on its way to being fully realized.

Leadership, workstreams, and staffing

Leading such a complex program—even a temporary one—requires gravitas. The head of the IMO, the integration executive, must know the businesses and the deal strategy, and also must be able to command respect and get business leaders in the acquirer and target to do what they must to support the necessary integration activities. Executives and other leaders may be resistant to change as the shape of their work lives shift and, without clear direction, may do what *they* think is in the best interest of the combined organization—which may be at odds with the integration strategy itself.

There's no other way of saying this: The integration executive will make or break success. The more that must get done, the stronger the IMO must be. Having a weak program head is one big step toward failure. The integration executive must be able to muster dedicated resources both in terms of full-time staff and attention from other leaders in the organization. They should also have access to the CEO.

In one of the most successful mergers that we've been involved with (which we discuss in more detail at the end of this chapter), the CEO chose the head of the most successful and largest business unit to run integration. Such a high-profile appointment served as a signal to the entire organization of the importance being placed on the integration, and it also helped the IMO get the resources and attention it needed to get the job done. This may seem paradoxical—taking a strong leader and using their talents in what seems to be routine project management—but running a major integration effort is anything but routine.

The IMO leader has to be an effective decision-maker. They will refine the master narrative—the compelling vision for the deal—and drive change and communications, set the pace for the timing of operating model–related decisions, oversee the efforts of the clean teams, organization design, and synergy planning, and identify major post-close initiatives that will drive the majority of the deal value.

Choosing the IMO leader must reflect the importance of the integration. That said, choosing the IMO leader also means clearing their plate because they will need to have sufficient time to do the job meaningfully and successfully. The role is going to be intense.[3]

The IMO manages the workstreams that make up the integration planning structure. Beyond typical functional workstreams such as legal, HR, IT, and finance, there may be other workstreams linked to the new enterprise operating model such as insourcing previously outsourced activities or the merging of businesses. For Norwegian Cruise Lines Holdings, which we discussed in chapter 5, that meant workstreams such as vessel operations, call centers, and shore excursions. Each workstream might break into multiple sub-workstreams with their own leadership, charters, and synergy targets. For example, finance will typically have tax, treasury, and FP&A workstreams that report up to the finance functional leaders. (See figure 6-1.)

FIGURE 6-1

Norwegian's integration management structure

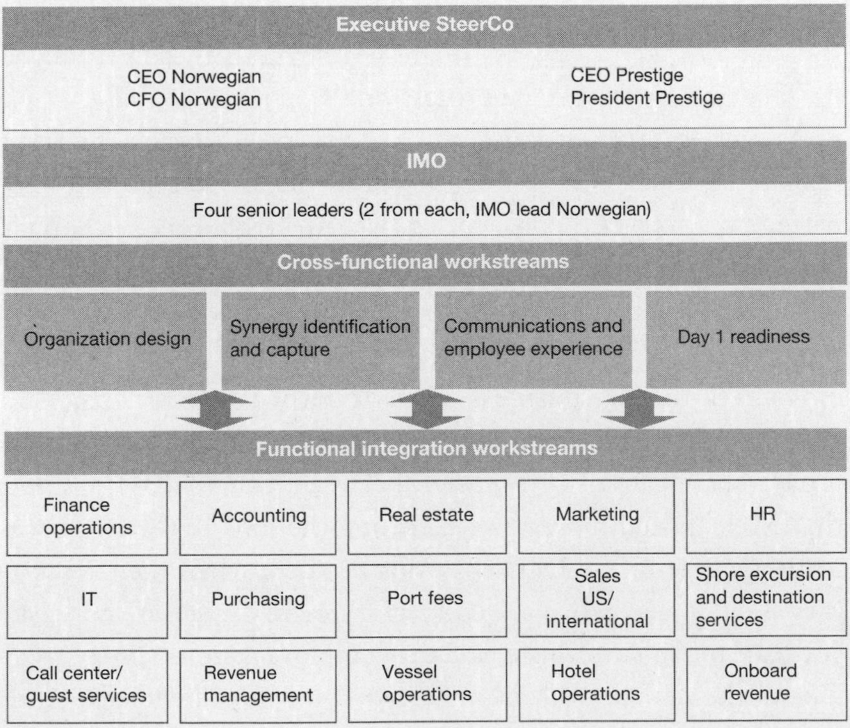

Executive SteerCo				
CEO Norwegian CFO Norwegian			CEO Prestige President Prestige	
IMO				
Four senior leaders (2 from each, IMO lead Norwegian)				
Cross-functional workstreams				
Organization design	Synergy identification and capture	Communications and employee experience	Day 1 readiness	
Functional integration workstreams				
Finance operations	Accounting	Real estate	Marketing	HR
IT	Purchasing	Port fees	Sales US/international	Shore excursion and destination services
Call center/guest services	Revenue management	Vessel operations	Hotel operations	Onboard revenue

There will also be workstreams that cut across all the others. These cross-functional teams (the subject of chapter 7) will typically focus on organization design, synergies, communications and employee experience, and Day 1 readiness. For carve-outs, where you are buying a business from another company, transition services agreements (TSAs) would be a common cross-functional workstream. Cross-functional teams are essential not only because they enable collaboration across functions and crystalize interdependencies, but also because they acknowledge and help lessen the political conflicts that often arise.

Staffing the leadership of the workstreams and sub-workstreams is an important early step in the process of the two organizations learning about each other. Workstreams are typically staffed with the relevant functional or business leaders from both parties—often called "two-in-a-box." This approach allows the full benefit of expertise, knowledge, and idea sharing from both sides—and the opportunity to collaborate to achieve quick wins. It is big mistake to underestimate what you can learn from the business experience of the professionals on the other side.

As one of our colleagues quips, "You need to pick the right people, not the wrong ones." What she means is that you may be tempted to pick people to lead the workstreams who aren't busy, who, if they're seconded to the IMO structure, won't derail business as usual. This is a mistake. The best people are actually the busiest; they will want to get things done so they can fully move back to their business units or corporate positions. This approach isn't without danger. It can endanger business as usual today. There can also be tension between leaders' day jobs and the IMO. Indeed more than tension—the jobs that leaders left to participate in the IMO may not be there when their temporary assignment is disbanded. But if you're aware of that risk, you can make sure those talented employees go back to great jobs in the new organization after planning and execution are complete.

Governance and cadence

The IMO structure ultimately reflects the decisions that have already been made about the new operating model. It engineers kickoff meetings, the cadence of weekly meetings with IMO leadership, external advisers and SteerCo, and interdependency workshops. It sets and assigns synergy targets, leads the development of a prioritized set of initiatives and projects that will deliver synergy targets, facilitates communications, sequences post-close priorities, and facilitates decisions and actions required for a successful Day 1. (See the sidebar, "Enabling Technologies for Post-Merger Integration.")

How big should the IMO and workstream structure be? As with any question like this, the answer is that it varies. IMO dynamics are driven by scope, scale, and degree of integration—by complexity. And remember: Deal size doesn't always equate with complexity (although it often does). Complexity depends on the deal's strategy, the operating model, and degree and kinds of change that will be required during the integration.

A typical weekly cadence starts with a meeting of the integration leader and other members of IMO leadership, which typically includes senior finance leaders from both sides. In that meeting they will talk about the focus areas of the program for the week: major decisions that will need to be made and actions that the integration leader will need to take to push the agenda and mitigate risks. This allows the IMO to act as a forcing mechanism to get teams focused on the right things. At this meeting, leadership reviews activities and reports of the previous week to ensure that the right issues are being raised and prioritized issues are getting resolved, that teams have appropriate resources, and that the synergy program is on track.

Some of this may sound mundane—a workstream may fail to meet its weekly goals and is off track simply because it has insufficient resources—but such a review and setting priorities for

Enabling Technologies in Post-Merger Integration

Several PMI technologies have been developed that enable an acquirer to understand the enormity of the data and information flows that exist, rapidly identify critical decisions, design future-state processes, plan for and track progress of integration plans, measure employee sentiment, and manage complexities inherent in large international deals. They enable the acquirer to keep track and manage an immense amount of data, glean insights, model possibilities, commit to a plan, and track progress against the plan—and connect all the dots so teams are not operating in silos. Such technologies include:

- **Project management tools,** which offer a setting that allows teams to collaborate and share their ideas, data, plans, dependencies, and decisions. That includes serving as a central system of record for new operating model design, blueprints, status reports, synergy planning and tracking, SteerCo and IMO decisions, meeting minutes, plan updates with timelines and upcoming deadlines, and ongoing interdependencies.

- **Organization visualizer tools,** which give teams their first real look at the combined workforce as it exists today, beyond a list of names in an Excel file or paper org charts. This allows leaders the ability to confirm the baseline organization and discover structural inefficiencies (too many managers or too few) inherent in each organization before any design decisions are made and to model and contemplate many possible alternatives for the new organization.

- **Culture diagnostic tools,** which act as a survey that asks questions across several dimensions including differentiating dimensions such as shared beliefs, inclusion, collaboration, sense of pride and ownership, tolerance for risk and ambiguity, and so on. These tools offer an understanding of the current state of each culture, where there are similarities or differences that might create complementarity or conflict, and how to work best together.

· **Change management tools**, which act as a database to enable tracking of all the changes that will happen, to whom, and when. These tools capture change impacts, anticipated reactions to change, planned interventions, status of deployments, participation rates in change interventions—essentially monitoring the efficacy of the change programs so you can course correct if needed. All of this information can integrate into the central project management tool to allow leaders visibility to groups that may be unprepared for the change that is about to come.

· **Contract management tools**, which use NLP to identify, extract, and review contractual data—terms, dates, parties, and so on—at a fraction of the time and cost that any human could. Acquirers can rapidly prioritize opportunities for proactive renegotiation before contracts' auto-renewal, achieve better terms with suppliers and customers, and ultimately accelerate synergy realization.

the week are essential to keep the program on track through Day 1.

Tuesday can involve a one-on-one meeting with the IMO leadership team and each workstream to deliver the weekly status report, a snapshot of the health of a workstream. This is a grueling day and can be unpleasant because some workstreams are falling behind and may be defensive. The meetings stretch all day, one after another, and can be exhausting. But they are vital to make sure each workstream is on track and allow the IMO leadership visibility of emerging interdependencies, Day 1 nonnegotiables, legal and regulatory hurdles, progress on synergies, and anything that might impact the new operating model. Here, it will be clear if the work is on track and if the right resources are in fact in place.

These meetings focus on three topics:

1. Progress to plan

2. Proposed mitigation strategies if not on schedule

3. Decisions

Status reports are especially helpful in spotting when a risk or major issue is on the horizon, but such reports shouldn't require so much detail as to slow teams down. Beyond updates, integration leadership also has the overall view that allows it to surface interdependencies across the workstreams and make required decisions. Making decisions early allows them to be revisited if they don't work out as planned as the path forward becomes clearer. Depending on the number of workstreams, these meetings may take a couple of days—every week.

Thursday or Friday will typically involve an all-hands meeting between all workstream leads and the IMO leadership. That meeting will focus on the outcomes of cross-functional decisions that affect the program as a whole. It will also involve strategy decisions that are going to SteerCo (SteerCo itself could be monthly at first but will meet more frequently as legal close for the transaction approaches).

It's always going to seem like there are too many meetings. People will complain, particularly when the meetings are not well orchestrated or not meaningful or productive. But it is vital for the cadence to drive open communications so that people don't act in silos, ultimately slowing the process while they make misaligned decisions that will inevitably need to be revisited. Making decisions in silos means getting the right parties back together to revisit decisions and discuss alternatives, going back through integration leadership, assessing other decisions that were predicated on those made in the silos, and so on. When leaders struggle to make decisions, IMO leadership must influence those workstream leaders to act.

Workshops and tasks

Kickoff meetings mark the official launch of integration planning. The IMO brings leaders together from both sides—in person or virtually—who will lead the functional and cross-functional workstreams. They provide a platform to gain initial buy-in and to generate excitement on the tenets of the deal strategy, strategic goals, synergy targets, integration approach, and functional implications of the strategy. These meetings are designed to energize the teams and rally the troops who will execute on the new operating model and, at the same time, set the tone for the pace and urgency that will need to be sustained though close. Kickoff meetings should launch as early as possible after announcement to stop chatter and rumors, and to provide facts along with direction of what comes next.

Regardless of whether IMO leadership requires workstream leaders to write charters that set direction and high-level goals for what the workstreams are expected to accomplish or hands out goals to the workstream and functional leaders, everyone must leave these meetings with a clear sense of purpose. They should be able to tell the same story when they get the inevitable questions from colleagues who aren't part of the IMO structure—consistent with the master narrative of the logic and vision of the deal.

Participants leave a great kickoff meeting knowing what they need to accomplish in 30-, 60-, and 90-day sprints, their synergy targets and any initial issues, other workstreams they will need to collaborate with (interdependencies), and a preliminary view of Day 1 non-negotiables and requirements specific for their workstream (e.g., safety, country-specific regulations).

These meetings also establish rules of the road and guiding principles for ways of working, which we discussed earlier in this chapter. Is the acquirer in complete control or is the merger more of a collaboration between the acquirer and the target? The IMO leads will lay out the guiding principles of how the two organizations will work together, including how decisions will be made, transparency, tenets of the customer experience, speed over elegance, decisiveness over perfection, human guidance like "don't struggle in silence," and acceptable trade-offs.

Rules of the road will also include integration planning dos and don'ts related to potential anti-trust issues. Anything that involves the sharing of competitively sensitive information is prohibited, as is making joint business decisions or coordinating marketing or pricing decisions. Clean rooms are required for that. However, sharing and planning office space and facility optimization, IT systems, or financial controls are generally without restriction.

This is a lot of work, and it must move quickly. Many organizations fail to move fast enough and waste substantial time before and immediately after Announcement Day. Don't be one of them. *Time is not on your side.*

Following the kickoff meetings, teams will be focused on functional blueprinting: a map of changes from current state to future end-state processes and technology requirements—the must-haves. Their other focus will be detailed planning for an issue-free Day 1, from financial funding of the deal and any required changes to the legal entity structure to avoiding negative customer and employee impacts, and what employees will want and need to know.

Once workstreams develop their major planning milestones for close, the IMO is ready for an interdependency workshop. Here, each workstream leader walks through their major milestones from now until close, showing each team's path to get to legal close and aligning the critical milestones across workstreams—we call this "walk the walls." This will allow IMO leadership to identify interdependencies between, for example, the tax workstream determining the future legal entity structures and the legal workstream completing the process of getting those legal entity structures in place and filing appropriate regulatory documents for a legal close. Any potential misalignments on upcoming key dates can cause big trouble. The timing and activities of many workstreams such as finance, procurement, and HR will be highly dependent on IT enablement for activities such as paying suppliers and employees across both organizations on Day 1. There will be a long list. Now is the opportunity to make sure interdependent teams are aligned and coordinated.

Ecolab Acquires Nalco

One of our favorite and most successful deals is Ecolab's acquisition of Nalco. Ecolab's approach illustrates the impact of using the deal thesis to guide the integration planning. Ecolab's IMO delivered the initiatives and projects that drove the value of the deal and the future of the combined company.

In 2011, Ecolab, a leader in cleaning, sanitizing, and infection prevention, acquired Nalco, a company specializing in water treatment and processing solutions in a transaction valued at $8.3B. Prior to the transaction, both Ecolab and Nalco were demonstrated growth companies with global reputations for innovation and customer service. Nalco's strong intellectual property portfolio, customer base, and field sales model complemented Ecolab's, particularly in the water business and in emerging markets. You see their products and service trucks everywhere—from the cleaning carts at hotels to oil fields.

Ecolab had completed roughly 50 smaller transactions in recent years, but Nalco was a mega-deal, many times larger than their average deal, and presented the opportunity to create something that could be transformational. The acquisition positioned Ecolab ahead of several mega-trends: rising energy demand, increasing water scarcity, growing public concern about food safety and security, and, finally, accelerating growth in emerging markets. The size of the deal also brought larger risks: that Ecolab would realize neither the cost synergies nor the acceleration of growth that would be required to justify the price. The deal was anything but normal.

To lead the integration, Doug Baker, Ecolab's CEO, chose Christophe Beck, who led one of Ecolab's largest businesses— the institutional business. Christophe was a surprising choice given how important he was to the company, but his appointment was a bright signal to executives and employees of just how important the integration was to the company's future. While many leaders will say they're going to have a great Day 1 and capture or exceed synergies, Christophe made the bold statement: "This is going to be the best integration ever."

Christophe insisted on a full-time team of leaders from both companies with clear reporting lines and responsibilities. He also insisted that the integration team be co-located, which allowed for the immediate resolution of issues and emerging interdependencies. Every meeting started with a reminder of how many days it had been since Announcement Day and how many days remained until Day 1. This "stopwatch" helped provide a sense of urgency and galvanized the teams to keep on track.

Ecolab created a tailored integration approach branded as "Winning as One," and launched the IMO with three overarching priorities, each the focus of a dedicated team: Capturing Hearts, Delivering Synergies, and Accelerating Growth:

- **Capturing Hearts:** This team's planning anticipated the uncertainty and disruption to come inside and outside the

organization. Their planning focused on retaining
100 percent of their most valued customers while maintaining a strong safety record. They also planned for a
smooth employee experience for Day 1 and beyond.

- **Delivering Synergies:** With the goal of making the combined business as streamlined and efficient as possible, this
  team oversaw the planning for cost synergies. Large
  savings were expected from global shared services, facility
  optimization, and immediate savings, post-close, from
  procurement (using a clean room).

- **Accelerating Growth:** The goal for this team was to use
  the combined company's expanded capabilities and complementary market access with major institutions to grow
  existing core businesses, bring innovations to market
  through bold new plays by combining chemistries like
  antimicrobials in energy services, and accelerate presence
  in emerging markets. For example, Ecolab sold drapes and
  hand sanitizers to large hospitals while Nalco serviced
  large hospitals maintaining boilers and chillers. The team
  pursued large opportunities for cross-selling and creating
  bundled offerings for major customer wins. These growth
  synergies were planned and would be tracked as meticu-
  lously as the cost synergies.

With the mantra of delivering the "best integration ever," Ecolab set up a global integration office to drive integration strategy
and planning, as well as regional integration teams in Europe,
Asia, Australia, and Latin America. This structure allowed for
rapid issue escalation and facilitated a consistent worldwide
approach. There were clear governance principles: Functional
teams tackled function-specific issues; business teams addressed
cross-functional priorities such as synergies, employee experience, and operating model design; and regional teams led the
local execution.

The overall financial objective was to deliver an EPS of $3.00. The IMO and workstreams developed their projects and milestones with that goal in mind. In just 61 business days, the IMO and workstreams delivered several layers of initiatives and projects. Twenty mega-initiatives drove the three priorities (capturing hearts, delivering synergies, and accelerating growth). Those initiatives translated into 115 major projects (and 495 subprojects). Each project stated the activity, start and end date, person accountable, and the corresponding benefits and cost to achieve—ultimately approved by the SteerCo and primed to kick off implementation on Day 1.

Ecolab illustrates the intense, interlinked work of the IMO, and how the layers of reporting, workstreams, initiatives, and projects must be designed to support the overall goal rooted in the deal thesis. Without strong leadership, considered structure, and constant orchestration, the sprint to Day 1 will not set up an acquirer for success.

Conclusion

This chapter has focused on the structures necessary to govern and control the integration process, most especially the IMO and its leadership. Integration planning cannot be a process where leaders fill out templates or prepare stacks of forms that are destined for a series of massive three-ring binders—although, years ago, it used to be. Today, integration planning focuses on providing a guiding vision and structure that will drive decision-making throughout the firm and throughout the process. The IMO will take the logic of the deal, the new operating model, and its guiding principles, and translate those into a tightly controlled course of action across many teams and workstreams to achieve the promise of the new end-state vision that will deliver more value to customers and shareholders.

Chapter 7 addresses the major cross-functional work-streams that the IMO will manage. These include designing the new organization, synergy planning, communications and the employee experience, and the sprint to Day 1—and setting up the combined organization for success on Day 1 and beyond. We also discuss the additional planning complexities of divisional carve-outs and associated TSA's with the seller.

CHAPTER 7

How Will I Deliver on My Vision and Promises? Part II

Cross-Functional Workstreams and Day 1 Readiness

Many organizations leap to let investors know of their grand plans for integration but stumble when it comes time to create the combined entity. The sheer volume and pace of work can feel overwhelming.

While chapter 6 focused on how to translate the deal thesis using the Integration Management Office (IMO), here we focus on the cross-functional workstreams typical of the vast majority of pre-Day 1 integration structures, which the IMO oversees: organization design, synergy planning, employee experience, and Day 1 readiness. Don't take your foot off the gas.

After Day 1, each of these cross-functional workstreams will transition, over time, into business as usual, operating as one company. Performing seamlessly during pre-close planning will set up the merged organization for success as it cuts costs and brings its new offerings to market. Acquiring a division presents another layer of complexity for the IMO and workstreams because of transition services agreements (TSAs) with the seller. The fundamental question, then, is how to transition from the theory of the deal to the gritty reality of getting the deal done so the new organization is ready to go to market differently and create sustained value.

Organization Design: Right Structure, Roles, and Leaders for the Future

Organization design addresses the question of whether the right roles are filled with the right people who have the right skill set who will make the right decisions with the right information at the right time—all in support of the new operating model.[1]

Most leadership teams have never engaged in organization design at this scale—and almost certainly not with their own and their colleagues' jobs on the line. As a consequence, organization design can be political, emotional, and disruptive, even in the best of circumstances. If done poorly, it can be paralyzing and demoralizing, ruining the best intentions of the deal. This personal factor ("me"—the first two letters of "merger") can be hard to overcome. Organization design is fundamentally about allocating power and influence in the new organization, so IMO leadership should be prepared for politically charged discussions.

In an effort to avoid these issues (and others, including legal compliance), four things should be in place before design thinking begins: the enterprise operating model, named L1 leaders (direct reports to CEO), synergy targets that have both headcount and associated dollars at the functional or business level, and the functional and business operating model choices (for businesses impacted by the deal). That may sound ambitious, but remember you already have a business case, diligence findings, and a valuation model that have made most of these assumptions.

Some acquirer executives say they don't want to assign targets because they think their teams will come back with more—but they never do. Without specific targets you will almost certainly create frustration and additional remedial work later.

Where the enterprise operating model and L1 leadership are established by the CEO's vision for the new company, it is the L1 leadership—the functional and senior business leaders—who determine their operating model, which sets the parameters for the design of their organizations. For example, the chief human resources officer (CHRO), along with their integration planning leaders, would put in place the new HR model at a functional level. The parameters of the functional operating model must flow through consistent with the philosophy and choices made at the enterprise level, whether those involve shared services or outsourcing, for example, and enable the function to achieve its assigned synergy target. Absent such guidance up front, leaders will create organization structures they *think* make sense but that are unlikely to meet synergy targets or accomplish transformational goals.

It is almost inevitable that several things that "worked" for the old organizations won't be ideal for the new operating model. There's a real tension here, which is why the clarity of the deal strategy and the supporting operating model, and required synergies, are so important. If a centralized rather than business-based accounting and finance function makes the most sense for the combined organization, then make it happen even if the target preferred having business-based support before. But the rationale must be clear and easy to communicate because many will feel "if it's not broke, don't fix it."

The CEO's direct reports—L1 leaders—should be revealed at or shortly after announcement so that those leaders can have meaningful impact on integration planning and decisions. Acquirers may choose to delay some L1 announcements so that it appears that sufficient time and thought have been given to senior talent from the target. Yet such decisions can't take so long that the leaders who will not be involved in organization design decisions might have an impact. Appointments for the next levels of executives, L2 and possibly L3, should be announced just before close (for some companies immediately after) so the rest of the organization understands the senior leadership team.[2] For large mergers with multiple business units that are combining, we find it very helpful to have L3 leaders identified by Day 1, time permitting, to give the employees clearer direction by knowing who their leaders will be.[3]

This necessarily means that a small group of leaders will be involved at this stage. Newly formed leadership teams, who may have previously been competitors, can take time and dedicated effort to find a common true north. Teams may struggle on alignment of business strategy, priorities, and timeline, which only slows organization design efforts. There is a constant push and pull among short- and long-term objectives, balancing the desire to build a transformative organization against the need to "keep the trains running on time." The IMO has to manage that tension and this emphasizes the need to get alignment on the new operating model quickly.

Amid the grand plans for organization design, the heart of your organization—the rest of the workforce—can be full of fear and anxiety. One of the most effective ways to reduce workforce anxiety is through transparency and organizational honesty—not simply communicating company strategy and vision, but the hard truths about job reductions, changing roles, location changes, and other life-altering personal impacts. Until leaders can fully address individuals' personal emotions, and how changes will directly impact people's jobs, employees will likely experience high uncertainty, which can lead to productivity dips and retention risks. (Larger workforce initiatives will take place before and after close, and we'll address them later in this chapter and in chapter 8.)

Leaders should focus on communicating information about the organization design *process* in the absence of final decisions, telling employees about the new operating model, the organization design timeline, how roles are developed and how appointment and selection decisions are being made—and when employees can expect to hear more. A bit of clarity on the topic can produce far better results than a black hole of silence.

Roles not people

Organization design is where feelings get hurt. The senior people involved in and immediately affected by these decisions may have invested their entire careers at the acquirer or the target. The merger may reveal that their particular talents don't fit the needs of the combined organization, and then they are provided transition support for exit. It's hard and emotional work.

Many executives will say let's focus on "roles not people" to take out some of the emotion and diffuse anxiety—but few mean it. We're all human and it's natural that roles have evolved around people and their capabilities as the organization successfully expanded.

Because of these predictably fraught emotions, leaders might think about their people first and then build the roles to fit their people. But designing new organizations around individuals is not only backward, it can also be extremely risky. There is no guarantee those individuals will stay with the company more than a few months down the road. Focusing on people—talent selection—rather than roles first can limit the value potential of the deal.

If you focus on choosing people first, you are liable to design roles around them that are ineffective at bringing the operating model to life. Such a "people-first" approach focuses on the past. Organization design must be forward-thinking in support of the new operating model—both at the enterprise level and within functions. Designing around people fails to recognize the fact that the talent the company needs to move forward, and prosper in the future, may not exist today at either company.

Instead, leaders should first consider the roles necessary to support the new strategy. Focusing on "roles not people" from the outset—rather than treating it with lip service—permits the building of the organization and its constituent roles based on the specific capabilities and experience required to support the new operating model and achieve promised synergies.

For example, a product-centric company is relentlessly focused on creating the best products in a cost-efficient way. But they have just announced a major deal, and the new operating model requires a transformation to a more customer-centric company. The company has a 30-year product designer who has never had to put himself in the shoes of the customer. He has been focused on the coolest products but not one that anticipates customer needs. Everybody loves him and executives may want to put him into a senior product role, but he doesn't have the skills or the required knowledge of the customer who might use the product or how to anticipate their needs.

It should be clear now: The organization design process begins with a clear view of the new enterprise and functional (or business) operating models, synergy targets (from corporate development or the deal team who built the models), and L1 leadership. Organization design is predicated on supporting the new operating models—not the old ones. (See the sidebar, "Elements of Sign-to-Close Organization Design.")

The first organization design workshops with L1 leaders and functional integration team leaders ("two-in-a-box," as we discussed in the IMO section of chapter 6) are to develop a clear picture of the organization charts—the lines and boxes—on both sides. That means not only accounting for all the people that are part of each organization, but also developing clarity about their current roles and understanding what they do and how much they cost. It must be clear who sits in whose run-rate costs. These

Elements of Sign-to-Close Organization Design

- Enterprise operating model

- L1 leaders named

- Functional and business operating models

- Refined synergy targets

- Accurate headcount and cost baselines

- Role development

- L2–L3 talent selection

workshops will immediately yield discussions on which areas are out of scope for reductions or that may need to stay in place for some time to support interim platforms, and areas that may present opportunities for large-scale transformation. This is also the time to document which functional workforces use gig workers and independent contractors that may be easier to impact immediately to achieve synergy targets (of course, the trade-off is that they offer flexibility and are likely more cost-effective in the first place).

Now acquirers have an important choice to make: Design the organization layer by layer, choosing talent for each layer before proceeding to the next, or design it right to the ground and then choose the talent. In either case the organization design team must reach assigned synergy targets, but there are important implications for each option.

Option 1 is a slow-and-steady design process where the L1 leadership, for example, designs the required roles and required talent for their direct reports (L2) and then selects the people for those roles. This layer-by-layer approach allows those newly selected leaders to design the next layer down of their direct reports (roles, talent, and people) and so on. It also allows for arriving at a precise cost for each layer. Design parameters must consider the roles within the bounds of synergy targets for each layer, selection parameters, and timing of transitions (extend an offer and transition the person into the role) so that team can design the next layer. Transitioning also includes remembering the people who were considered but not selected and who may exit if there is not a mutually acceptable role for them.[4] (L4 and below will generally occur post-close.)

The upside of this approach is that leaders get to have their fingerprints on the next layer of roles and talent. This approach can create significant buy-in because leaders have the responsibility to design their roles for their layer, and will hopefully choose wisely when selecting their talent. They will say, "I had the opportunity to design my org and pick my people." At the most senior levels, selection may be based on interviews instead of strict selection criteria (we discuss talent selection in chapter 8). And because it is done layer by layer, the team will have a precise view of the cost of each layer based on the roles.

The downside is that this approach can take a long time as leaders work layer by layer. In a typical organization design process, transformation speed might be less important, but in M&A the cost-of-capital clock will tick on the premium, so there is not the luxury of time. Those who select option 1 also have to be careful they don't subject the workforce to "death by a thousand cuts," as they exit some people and then exit more people, and then some more people, layer by layer, particularly in larger organizations, where it might feel like there are waves of people exiting post-close.

Option 2 is to design the roles and structures without choosing people, all the way down to the ground, with the estimate of the synergies attached and the number of exits and relative costs for each role. Once the organization design team, along with L1 and functional workstream leaders, confirm that the structure meets the synergy targets and addresses the design parameters that deliver on the functional operating models, and that planned roles are geographically where you expect them to be, then talent selection can begin.

The upside of this option is that it gives a good read early on whether you will meet your required cost structure before any names are put into boxes. It's also a lot faster than option 1, so after Day 1 you can get people into those boxes quickly. The organization design team offers a portrait of the end state so that the synergy team can confirm that a path to achieving the business case exists even before close.

The downside, somewhat obviously, is it can feel like it is all being done in a vacuum. Few L1 leaders typically understand what is really done at lower levels of the organization, and they may be missing important information as they design the roles and structure. After close, it can sound like, "Hey Angela, this is the structure I've designed for you, now pick your people." Those new leaders may want to challenge your recommendations. You won't have their buy-in because you didn't have their input. It will be important to design the end-state structure with a plus or minus factor if you use this option, so there's some latitude to make adjustments in compensation or people.

With option 2, acquirers will have a picture by close of the shape and roles of the new organization. The roles will be designed at the necessary compensation level, with a description of the talent required—for instance, years of experience, skills, geography, and other criteria that matter most. This process also documents the strict selection criteria that talent selection must follow later. In the world of M&A, where speed to value creation is paramount, option 2 is a popular approach with many acquirer executive teams. They also avoid the death by a thousand cuts so they can quickly exit people without creating unnecessary stress on the organization, allowing those who remain to refocus on delivering the future (more on this in chapter 8).

Option 2 has two other benefits. First, it helps illuminate potential areas of risk early on—especially single points of failure throughout the organization—where there might not be sufficient redundancy. That might be a major enterprise account rep role for an important customer that should have backup support, or, say, a payroll accounting clerk who recognizes that their job will be eliminated when payroll gets consolidated. Individuals like that will be looking for a new job, so you need to have a backup plan for someone who has the necessary skills, especially in satellite locations, where an exit will be an immediate problem.

Second, because the acquirer is designing the organization to the ground, option 2 offers an early line of sight on whether there is any chance of reaching headcount synergies from organization design. Admittedly, headcount synergies will be approximate because option 2 doesn't place names in boxes. That said, it gets more quickly than option 1 to the probability that synergy targets will be missed before any names are even attached or expectations about future roles are cemented.

In either approach, most labor-saving synergies are found in levels 1–4 of the organization, at the senior manager and leadership levels; if synergies aren't found there, you will have to dig deeper in the organization and potentially cut away organizational muscle. The truth is, deferring these kinds of hard decisions will make it that much harder later on, and can destroy trust and legitimacy—before you even have a chance to earn it.

In either case, the more you determine at the top, the less cost-saving burden will trickle down through the rest of the organization. Beyond that, often the most productive or skilled employees are the most at risk of attrition during a deal. They likely have the best exit options and may be the most impacted by changes in their networks and lost political capital within the organization. They often hold themselves in high regard and are in fact well regarded in industry. They're going to be unsure if they will want to deal with the potential mess and stress created by the merger. If these people are key to the future of the new organization, these organization design exercises will help identify them so that you can incentivize them to stay.

A final point: The rest of the workforce is watching what is going on, making assumptions about how the new organization will run based on the people chosen. Clarity of process, even if you don't have the answers, will help the rest of the workforce face the inevitable uncertainty.

Synergy Planning: The Devil Is in the Details

Synergies were central to the deal thesis and the justification of the premium paid to the target's shareholders. They were also presented to the board, investors, and employees. Integration planning and execution is the time to make them real: defendable, achievable, aggressive. The work acquirers did during the due diligence phase should be in the forefront, and a strong connection must exist between the diligence team and the synergy team. Without the specific assumptions developed during diligence, the synergy team will be flying blind, or worse, reinventing the wheel.

The synergy leadership team should comprise an executive finance sponsor with sufficient gravitas for setting targets, financial planning and analysis (FP&A) people from both sides who understand the cost structure and accounting systems, and someone from corporate development who can serve as the link between the synergy team and the original diligence team—a person who can make clear what was assumed in the deal.

Synergies are easy to talk about, but let's not forget what they really are: operating gains over stand-alone expectations. Acquirers must generate performance improvements that exceed the growth value embedded in the shares of both companies. And remember, synergies don't come for free; nearly every synergy has a cost to achieve. Think of this as the "synergy-matching principle," where we consider the cost to achieve each benefit.

Synergies take the form of cost savings—labor and non-labor—or revenue enhancements, and there is often a tension between the two. Revenue synergies typically involve more risk than cost synergies because they depend on introducing new offers into an uncertain environment. Will customers appreciate it, want it, and be willing to pay for it? Will competitors react with a comparable offer with similar value at a lower cost? Can the sales force really cross-sell products they don't know? Any new offer is introduced into a world of "ifs." Further, those growth synergies will often arise from new offerings and "co-specialization"—that is, the result of combining distinct capabilities from both companies. Leakage here will come from a failure of the companies to effectively collaborate in the marketplace post-Day 1.

Cost savings on the other hand are largely under the acquirer's control and as a consequence are much easier to estimate and develop. Although some potential cost synergies, like procurement or real estate synergies, may require negotiation and executive alignment, acquirers will still have a clear view of the data required to zone in on potential savings. This is where clean rooms and clean teams can yield synergy plans that can be effected immediately after closing, particularly on procurement savings or immediate cross-sell opportunities.

All acquirers will face a "fact of life" regarding synergies: leakage. What is leakage? It's when you thought you were going to get "X dollars" of synergy but there's a perfectly good reason why you can't. For instance, in one deal, the acquirer planned to sell some real estate in Germany (and had counted on both the revenue and savings from the real estate deals) only to discover unexploded ordinance from World War II in the basement of the building, squelching the real estate plan. While you might not find British bombs in your basement, some of the synergies you were counting on will be difficult or impossible to realize.

Everyone will have reasons they can't achieve synergies, so the synergy process should stress test whether the reasons are real or not. More important, synergy targets will need to significantly exceed those built into the deal model. Beyond allowing for leakage, aggressive targets will force the workstream owners to think about a *portfolio* of projects with a range of risks that will collectively allow them to achieve aggressive targets. They'll have to get creative to find both low-risk, low-hanging fruit and high-risk, high-reward projects, which they might have chosen to avoid with lower targets.

Setting a baseline

The first step in synergy planning is establishing a combined baseline for costs, revenue, and people. Looking ahead to tracking benefits post-close, the baseline will ultimately be used as a benchmark to validate whether synergies have been realized. It is an often difficult but always a necessary exercise.

While the organization design team is focused on labor synergies, the synergy team should build a baseline by mapping the target's and acquirer's costs, revenues, and full-time equivalents (FTEs) to a common taxonomy of functions (e.g., finance) and sub-functions (e.g., tax, treasury, FP&A, accounting). For instance, in the target, payroll costs might roll up under finance, while in the acquirer payroll could appear under HR. The combined baseline is important because not all companies roll up functions and sub-functions the same way. It takes planning and coordination to ensure that the right costs are bundled together. No matter what you do, the synergy targets must be coming out of that baseline. In practice, we often say "costs follow the target" because the baseline defines the "bucket" a synergy target will be attributed to.

The synergy team should stay closely aligned with the organization design team, using the same taxonomy across both labor and non-labor initiatives. Even though these two teams may have been working in parallel, it is their *combined* cost reductions that allow acquirers to meet the synergy targets. That's why it is important the same taxonomy is used to roll up revenues, costs, and FTEs to the same functions and sub-functions. Although those taxonomies may not be fully consolidated before close, they certainly must be shortly after Day 1.

Baselines also serve as the basis for sanity checks when developing top-down synergy targets.[5] For example, if legal has a synergy target of $2M, the baseline can serve as a useful comparison to make sure that the total legal cost structure seems reasonable for this cost-saving objective. Functional benchmarks from high-performing peer companies can also be used to test whether targets are too aggressive or not aggressive enough—offering an opportunity for the acquirer to transform the combined organization into a superior performer while it transacts the deal.

Top-down synergy targets

The deal model and prior due diligence from corporate development or the deal team that drove the offer price is the starting point for setting synergy targets.

Top-down targets should be delivered to the functional teams without the details of how to achieve them—that's *their* job. Functional teams and impacted business will ultimately pull the levers that deliver synergies, so they need to be responsible for brainstorming initiatives that will evolve into projects and workplans. The synergy program lead might include sample initiatives for their specific function or line of business, but it's the job of the functional or business leads to figure out how to achieve those synergies. Requiring the teams to develop a plan will purposely challenge them to build their own perspective on opportunities within their line of business or function.

Top-down targets should give functional or business teams significant stretch goals. In our experience, top-down targets will typically be at least 40 to 50 percent greater than the total synergies needed to meet, and hopefully exceed, externally communicated synergy objectives—to allow for leakage, overlaps of initiatives, and just plain bad forecasts. Stretch targets of 75 to 100 percent greater than announced synergies are not unusual. Teams will inevitably experience overlap of initiatives with other functions as they are developed, another source of leakage. As synergy leadership develops a range of targets, they will share the high end with the teams. Sharing the high end of the range provides a buffer to still hit publicly stated synergy objectives.

Bottom-up synergy targets

Developing bottom-up synergies is even more work—and the devil is in the details. The initiatives and projects that will drive specific synergies evolve over time because for every day that goes by teams learn more about one another and have better line of sight to synergy initiatives and opportunities for improvement. Brainstorming non-labor initiatives begins at the kickoff of the IMO. Functional and business heads identify initiatives and give a rough range of what those initiatives might be worth. Is this a large initiative or small one? If it's large, just how large is it? Is it between $1M–$2M, $10M–$20M? More? Less? It's useful to require some rough range that can be refined later on. Clean rooms and clean teams will be extremely valuable where identifying and planning for synergies rest on detailed information that HSR regulations would not allow to be shared.

Typically, this process will have initial, second, and final submissions (with many iterations in between) that could contain well over 100 distinct initiatives each across multiple functions, businesses, and individual owners. Because so many potential opportunities exist, a standard format is necessary to capture initiatives. Remember, garbage in, garbage out: The lack of a standard structure, format, or software will lead to poor quality of submissions and waste a lot of time—and likely delay the overall program. Each bottom-up synergy initiative should have a name, start and end date, specific amount, cost to achieve, and owner. Without those five minimum requirements, you have no bottom-up synergy plan.

Another important detail is the early prioritization of what information for each initiative is needed and by when. Teams just won't know enough to have all the details from the get-go, so the first submission should include items like the name of the initiative, description, owner, team impacted, rough range of value, and complexity (high, medium, low). The follow-up submissions will provide updates to previously submitted fields and more detailed value estimates by period, with detailed costs to achieve the estimates by period—so the initial ranges become narrower and can be submitted for approval from the IMO, and later SteerCo, and ultimately built into executive plans.

Leadership must stay involved in the initiative development process to both provide strategic direction on initiatives and approve funding when required, since some initiatives will be costly. (Remember, synergies aren't free.)

Finally, the synergy lead should work with finance to understand any nuances that may exist around what counts as a synergy for external reporting. For examples, at one prior client, only roles that were open for a certain number of months and then closed could be counted when reporting externally. But all teams must agree to basic synergy rules of the road. (See the sidebar, "Synergy Rules of the Road: An Example.")

Workplans

An IMO requires workplans by Day 1 so that execution can begin right away at close on both short-term operational integration milestones and accomplishment of quick-win synergy initiatives. Workplans can prioritize the value capture portfolio of

Synergy Rules of the Road: An Example

Acquirers will find it valuable to give general guidance to all the workstreams as they discuss and build their synergy workplans— so they are all following the same rules.

What Counts as a Synergy?

- **Headcount:** Any role eliminations or reductions in compensation after deal close, including voluntary terminations that are not backfilled. Reductions in budgeted open roles will be tracked and counted as a synergy.[a]

- **Non-headcount:** Any positive, non-labor financial impact that directly increases revenue above plan or reduces costs and/or capital expenditures versus the baseline run-rate costs and that is a direct result of the acquisition.

What Counts as a Dis-Synergy?

- **Headcount:** Any non-budgeted, non-approved additional roles or increases in compensation after deal close.

- **Non-headcount:** Any recurring, non-labor cost increase due to adoption of new operating policies, technologies, processes, or procedures.

What Counts as a One-Time Cost?

A one-time cost will include the costs necessary to implement and realize synergies.

- **Headcount:** Some examples would include severance, relocation, retention bonus, and recruitment.

- **Non-headcount:** Some examples would include hardware or software purchase costs, lease breakage or vendor sunsetting fees, travel and consulting fees.

(continued)

What Are Cost Synergies?

Cost synergies are cost savings achieved through the consolidation of the two companies' processes and systems through initiatives that leverage economies of scale, eliminate duplicative costs and departments, and improve efficiencies in the combined baseline. This includes cost savings associated with the elimination of previously budgeted capital projects or one-time project costs.

What Are Revenue Synergies?

Revenue synergies are revenue increases over the forward-looking revenue plan as a result of specific revenue initiatives (e.g., new, bundled value propositions for customers), achieved through increased customer penetration, better geographic presence, cross-selling, and accelerating product time to market.

How Should I Think about "Business as Usual" Improvements When Defining Synergies?

Synergies from the integration should not include any "business as usual" improvements (e.g., a planned or ongoing upgrade of an ERP system unrelated to the integration). The impact on the budget of existing cost-saving initiatives should be included as part of the baseline. Exceeding planned cost savings from an ongoing transformation can be counted as a synergy.

Who Gets Credit for a Recognized Synergy?

- **Headcount:** When corporate functions or the businesses identify synergies, credit will go to the corresponding function or business, with close attention paid to not double counting synergies.

> • **Non-headcount:** Synergies for corporate costs, such as finance or legal costs, that sit in a business would be owned by the business.
>
> **Do Transfers between Functions Count as a Synergy?**
>
> No, movements between functions have no synergy impact.
>
> a. These need to be *genuine* budgeted open roles. On either side, though, leadership must be vigilant for budgeted open roles that magically appear. This also applies to budgeted costs in general.

synergy initiatives and label "quick hit" initiatives that can be accelerated to rapidly realize synergies on or shortly after Day 1, so they can, as we say, "ring the bell."

Initiatives will require projects with associated milestones—and owners—in final submissions to make each initiative real. A $100M insourcing initiative involving multiple product lines and facilities will be far more complex than a $300,000 initiative consolidating booths at global trade shows. But they will all need to add up to your promised synergies. A few synergy initiatives—say five to 10—will often drive more than two-thirds of the total synergy value. These major initiatives should have entire workplans built out to support them.

The synergy team will share these workplans with IMO leadership, along with a timeline for when synergies will be realized. This will allow leadership to provide strategic direction, drive iterations, and weigh in on priority, timing, and sequencing. Once the synergies are prioritized, they must be funded. For instance, moving from five ERPs to one would involve significant one-time costs. Ultimately, SteerCo will approve the short list and funding of initiatives that will drive the majority of the value.

Delivering workplans will also help teams and leadership maintain vital momentum, so they are ready to launch priority initiatives quickly after close—when they *must* begin. Remember, there's lots of work and little time.

Labor and non-labor synergy perspectives will come together in tracking and reporting (which we discuss in chapter 8). Until this point, labor synergies (headcount reductions) and non-labor synergy initiatives will often be developed in parallel. However, in internal tracking and reporting, both labor and non-labor synergies will have to be formally rolled up for financial reporting. That will also help build the fact base for external communications.

In summary, the major elements of a synergy program are:

- Appoint the right executive sponsor for synergies

- Establish the baseline

- Assign aggressive synergy targets

- Formulate initial ideas for savings and growth

- Develop actual initiatives and projects and document how you have met your commitment

- Refine and prioritize projects and fund them

- Gain approval from IMO and SteerCo

- Create accountable targets for executives

Ecolab's synergies

For their part, Ecolab emphasized growth synergies beyond the $150M that would come from cost reductions, which meant focusing on capturing the hearts and minds of customers, and on internal sales and marketing teams. From sign to close, this meant confirming the growth synergy estimates from diligence in a clean room.

The synergy team analyzed growth synergies from cross-selling opportunities and bundled solutions for customers, leveraging new shared infrastructure and the joint development of new products and services. The majority of the synergies came from the top 50 overlapping accounts.

The clean room was crucial to confirming, expanding, and accelerating the growth synergy targets. It allowed the team to appropriately use more data from both companies and to draw on the expertise of each of the relevant leaders from both organizations for the growth synergy workstream. It also helped planning for synergy realization by cascading targets to accounts, businesses, and regions. Recognizing the importance of the clean room, leaders on both sides engaged in thoughtful and focused clean room–friendly dialogue.

The other critical reason for Ecolab's success was the strong support from the C-suite for the growth synergy estimates and execution program. This C-suite attention created buy-in throughout both organizations. For example, sales and marketing teams planned "Top to Top" meetings at key accounts, which helped facilitate the execution and realization of growth synergies.

By Day 1, the Ecolab growth synergy team had produced synergy estimates by type, by business, by region, and by account. They had created communication plans for the top 50 accounts. And they had produced an agenda and plan for a sales conference shortly after close to ensure all sales and service professionals were well versed in the newly combined go-to-market capabilities and offerings.

Communications and Employee Experience: Reducing Uncertainty, Preparing for Change

Stakeholder communications and employee experience are most emphatically not about having more cake. You already had a chance to celebrate on Announcement Day and will again on Day 1. What stakeholders really want is reduced uncertainty and clear expectations—and engagement. As one of our colleagues says, "You are borrowing trust you have not yet earned," so start earning it now—and happy talk about a "merger of equals" won't do it.

Communications for all stakeholders—employees, unions, retirees, customers, vendors, contractors, and of course investors—must be intentionally crafted. Create the messaging for each group of stakeholders aiming for transparency and frankness. If answers for their questions don't exist, let the group know when they will. Think of the communication plan around Day 1 preparations as akin to those of Announcement Day: coordinated, calendarized, diligently rehearsed, and informative. Remember: Everyone sees through fluffy emails.

While clarity is essential in all communications about plans pertaining to the integration, employee experience focuses solely on the needs of the employees and includes everything from the nitty-gritty of defining new roles to the change management planning and leadership required to reach the new organizational structure. It's much more than just communications: It encompasses all of the enterprise-wide changes across all departments in both companies, which will have large-scale, cross-functional impacts. It should live as a workstream managed by the IMO rather than with functional leaders. It's a vital part of the integration: It stabilizes the organization, helps employees understand the new strategy and fosters excitement about their roles within it, and creates a strong and consistent feedback and communication loop. (See the sidebar, "Employee Experience Vision.")

There is also the potential for real conflict arising from profound choices on culture and employee experience—and employees know it. If the acquirer talks about "family," "trust," "teamwork," and "togetherness," while the target says they "get shit done by being nimble, agile, and breaking stuff" while privately telling

Employee Experience Vision

The employee experience vision should serve as the guiding principles for all change management activities throughout the integration and needs to encompass:

- Building confidence in employees by helping them understand the intention behind the deal

- Establishing trusted leadership to inspire confidence in the future of the combined organization

- Reducing employee uncertainty and anxiety on the future of their roles through targeted communications

- Leveraging the collective strength of each of the companies and maintaining cultures that enable success

- Allowing two-way feedback mechanisms to understand strengths and weaknesses through the integration process

its employees, "If you want warm and fuzzy, you'd better get yourself a dog"—well, you've probably got some work to do. You won't be able to establish a new culture—how work gets done, shared values and norms, and what gets rewarded—until you know what already exists. Before Day 1, leaders need to begin to grasp how the cultures of the organizations are similar and different, and establish how to work together so the organizations can operate successfully post-close (we discuss more on change and culture in chapter 8).

Even without a profound culture clash, the changes that inevitably accompany a merger can trigger an emotional response. Mergers turn employees' worlds upside down, bumping them down to the bottom of their hierarchy of needs. They've gone from being concerned about self-actualization in their work and their life to worrying about their physiological and safety needs:

if they have a job, if they are secure, where their next paycheck is coming from. It can be terrifying. The merger will also make new demands on employees' time, and potentially disrupt their day-to-day experience. The job of the employee experience team is to "get ahead of the pain," not to downplay or eliminate it, so that employees feel that your plan is thoughtful and authentic.

As a result, the charge of the employee experience team during sign to close comes down to three things:

1. Identifying what changes are forthcoming

2. Planning for what the new organization will do to support the changes

3. Confirming that employees are ready for the changes throughout the life cycle of the deal

The employee experience team will define the changes for every stakeholder group on a timeline, and plan accordingly. Once they've identified the changes that are coming, they should start developing a thoughtfully orchestrated set of words and actions by leaders, and a curated set of experiences that may include learning or rotational programs. Employees should also be offered options to participate in learning experiences, in the normal course of their day, that will help prepare them for Day 1 and beyond.

For instance, a customer service rep may have 15 major changes over the next 12–18 months, with a cadence of changes associated with sunsetting old systems and implementing new ones, learning new products and new scripts, and finding out where to get answers to frequently asked questions. Some teams will also have interim operating models as they transition from the old way to the new way (e.g., navigating ERP systems that will be consolidated over the course of a year).

On Day 1, both systems will be running, but the teams should know how the transition will take place. If Sergio managed the old ERP system and knows he will be transitioned out, he must know why he should continue to help and how he will be rewarded for staying and putting in effort when he knows that he will be obsolete within the year. There will be other transitional functions as well across the organization. Successful employee experience management is predicated on identifying all of the "Sergios" in the organization and managing each.

Remember, not all functions or businesses will be impacted in the same way, so it's necessary to understand how different employee groups with different needs will have unique experiences—and to craft the appropriate experience for each. For example, finance may be cut substantially while sales will get to hire aggressively. Such seeming disparities will require serious conversations with each function so that employees understand what is changing, what isn't, and why.

Managers from both sides with new cross-reporting relationships will need to be equipped with procedures to follow when they have to manage these new employees. You don't want someone to walk in one morning bemoaning, "I've got another 45 people reporting to me in different locations. What do I do? I don't even have job descriptions!" Give them tools to deal with the fast-moving situation.

With a complete picture for the whole of the organization, the employee experience team will determine how to help each group through each of the changes. How are we going to support them? When will we need leaders to talk with them? When will we send messages that make them feel supported? How do we get their feedback? How will we reward them? This is the essence of getting ahead of the pain—knowing and anticipating those often minute, sometimes large, but always meaningful changes to employees' lives.

Clearly, employee experience cannot just be another email— or series of emails. Knowing what will change (and what won't) means the employee experience team can plot the change experiences over time based on anticipating the employees' needs. The team must understand not only the integration plans but how this transformational effort will impact employees over the lifecycle of the integration. This includes knowing the workforce and broad personas (including their exits, new roles, cross-selling assignments, and other changes over each functional area's life cycle) and working to craft their experience and smooth the impact. Day 1 should reveal a clear line of sight to the end state, which means that a big part of the pre-close work is developing that vision.

First is anticipating all of the processes that are a predictable part of everyday work life that will change because of the merger. These include basics such as providing training in new processes and procedures where work will be done differently (e.g., travel planning and per diems). Basics like this affect an employee's day-to-day work.

But this evaluation goes deeper than basic processes. It also means evaluating which functional areas and teams require leadership site visits, and assessing how employees will feel about major events and who should have the conversations to help guide them. But more generally, once the changes are known, the next step is to plan what the new organization will do to support each group of employees through the changes.

In one particularly successful merger, the acquirer actually visited the target's product R&D team—and turned the visit into an event. The target set up tents on the corporate campus, had a barbecue, and had their R&D team show off what they were most proud of. The team put their top 5 products in the spotlight during a "gallery walk" and talked about their "babies" with an air of celebration—and why they were proud.

While this event made everyone feel good, it also demonstrated to the target's team the commitment of the acquirer in getting to know them and respecting their accomplishments. Both groups could share their history, talk about what motivated them, and exchange knowledge of the products and their future collaboration. It allowed them to develop a sense of camaraderie. But this isn't just about making people feel good—such exchanges also enhance the ability to better cross-sell and achieve revenue synergy targets.

Not every merger will have a carnival-like celebration on the home campus, but crafting employee experience with the same level of care is an absolute necessity. If employees don't feel taken care of, they're not going to be taking care of customers. As with the other integration workstreams that are sprinting toward Day 1, planning the overall employee experience is imperative. That planning should reflect core principles of the integration approach, and include a calendar for coordinated timing of training and resources for those who are doing the messaging, including, for example, customized decks for executives, and prep sessions for all-hands meetings on Day 1.

No matter how well you plan and execute, you will need to confirm that employees have the tools they need for their new jobs and that they have acquired the necessary knowledge or know where to find it when they need it, and that employees feel ready for the change. During sign to close, a readiness assessment is typically done through a survey. The employee experience team uses the results to identify pockets of risk and coordinates with the IMO to address each prior to Day 1. Often, this takes the form of a readiness team being deployed to teams that are least prepared in the days leading up to Day 1.

Engagement

Remember, acquirers are not onboarding the target's employees. They are not new recruits. The target's employees did not decide to join your organization. In fact, in some mergers, they may very well have had the opportunity to work for you and chose the target instead. The point is, they chose to work for the target, which means that the effort must focus on engaging them, not onboarding them. Create excitement and a sense of belonging and identity for employees.

What employees want—need, really—is a clear narrative and a reason to belong. Employees hate ambiguity and uncertainty. If given the chance, they will assume the worst. Those at the most senior level will worry about achieving the promised synergies, but employees are worried if their badge will work, if their internet will be on, if their laptop is changing, about the quality of coffee and their business cards, when they'll get paid, and if their benefits are changing. Don't forget, the word "synergies" may terrify employees—because synergies mean layoffs, change, and hard work.

At the same time, people can take bad news. Instead of telling them, "You're all important to us, we'll let you know about changes later," tell them, "We'll be transparent and give you six months' notice with enhanced severance and outplacement services." Even if detailing everything that's going to happen is out of scope, setting expectations about when employees will have all the answers is both possible and necessary. The "must-have" is letting them know *when* they'll know, providing them with some surety about their future. Further, make sure outreach to employees is coordinated so they don't get distracted, sidetracked, and overwhelmed by multiple and possibly conflicting messages from IT, HR, and finance, but rather get a holistic picture of new procedures through orchestrated communications.

This approach to employee experience isn't just to be nice to employees for humanitarian reasons. It will help prevent false narratives from leaking out to competitors, suppliers, and customers. Further, having the new employees on your side means that in the future they won't stick a knife in your neck when they have the chance.

This all underscores the need to announce the new CEO and top management as soon as possible, providing some signal of the direction the company will be moving in and how it will be managed. Executives' reputations may have preceded them, so employees will want to know what they're getting—again, reducing uncertainty. Use those announcements to showcase the leadership to build excitement about the future.

Leaders alone cannot do it all. The employee experience team will identify and enlist influential employees—people whom others trust—to connect people and information. These integrators can be extremely valuable in supporting a clear message about the transformation and help define the combined organization's shared values, beliefs, and behavioral drivers—fundamental dimensions of culture. Achieving these goals will require knowing how different functional areas will be affected and who the "change agents" are within the organization.

Between Announcement Day and Day 1, Ecolab, for instance, planned their change management initiative that they would launch post-close. They identified roughly 500 "culture partners" throughout both organizations and created the environment for voluntary dialogue with groups of 8–10 employees. These groups were designed to discuss the merger, determine how to best leverage strengths of both legacy companies, and internalize messages across networks. The culture partners not only cascaded and reinforced communications throughout the organizations but also provided an invaluable feedback loop to the integration planning team and executive leadership team on what was working, as well as on specific organization concerns. The change readiness team used standard tools like pulse surveys as well as more novel ones like change councils and cross-functional team forums that were tasked with creating an environment of change and discussing integration-related change tactics.

The overarching purpose of the communications was to cascade clear and transparent information throughout each organization and to align on key messages that focused on the business case, business as usual, and what's on the hearts and minds of employees. To do so required knowing and having the key messages for every area, and, for the entire organization, an internal communications plan and timeline, and a feedback mechanism. The resources needed included enterprise-wide leadership alignment on the master narrative and meta-messages, as well as the support of corporate communications teams on content creation and delivery. At Ecolab, internal communications focused on the meta-message of what were the three overarching priorities of the deal: Capturing Hearts, Delivering Synergies, and Accelerating Growth (see chapter 6).

Being clear and transparent, and working actively to engage employees, will go a long way toward telling employees just what their lives are likely be like. On Day 1 each employee should know where they sit; what, if anything has changed for their role; who their boss is; and what their compensation and benefits are. A structured employee engagement process should take each employee through the first day, month, and year, and the critical junctures associated with each time frame. And remember, if you can't give them specifics, then give them the date when you will.

As we said in chapter 5, "Culture starts at announcement." You started by prioritizing clear, consistent, and transparent communications on Announcement Day—and you want to continue the philosophy of that experience through integration and beyond. By positioning the value of the two companies together and stating clearly how employees will fit in, you will provide employees with certainty that will pay dividends.

Day 1 Readiness: From Planning to Execution

Day 1 may seem like a daunting milestone, and readiness for that milestone can seem like a never-ending list of complex decisions and integration activities. But getting to and successfully executing Day 1 is less about boiling the ocean and more about placing laser focus on a small number of bare-minimum and non-negotiable tasks. Some companies do much more on Day 1, announcing new initiatives or bold new programs. It could be good to go big—especially if you have extra time. But meeting the bare necessities is a must.

Here's the short version: You want to close as fast you can. Avoid regulatory scrutiny and be prepared to achieve synergies fast. The goals of Day 1 are to minimize what can go wrong—especially something that could land someone in jail—and to preserve business continuity. A great Day 1 also includes ensuring that everyone is excited about such a big milestone—the first day of the new organization. Keep the lights on, prepare for a new mode of operating, and have the plans in place to launch the combined company (to "rock 'n' roll," as one of our colleagues puts it).

While Day 1 readiness may only amount to a handful of activities, it is by no means simple. The consequences of achieving anything short of perfection can be deadly. Failure to achieve Day 1 readiness can destroy a deal overnight as operations at the target and acquirer are disrupted and market cap is destroyed. Anything short of a flawless Day 1 can also complicate post-close execution as internal (employees and the board) and external (customers and suppliers) perceptions of the deal sour while disruptions are highlighted in the media and the narrative around management's ability to execute on integration sours. Moreover, lack of Day 1 readiness delays post-close execution, leading to leakage of synergy value and jeopardizing customer relationships.

One of our colleagues likes to say, "Day 1 is like a baby. It's going to come, you know the due date, but you don't know exactly when it will happen." Have a plan for what you must accomplish if it comes sooner than expected and what more you can get done if Day 1 pushes out later. One way to add "nice to haves" is to ask if a goal is core to the deal strategy. If the answer is yes, you can further ask if it is practical to complete and if it is scoped appropriately to achieve by Day 1. If you can answer yes to both, it can stay on the list.

What does "minimal" mean? Tasks for Day 1 focus on enabling acquirer and target to transact business after close without any interruption. Achieving these necessary goals means ensuring legal and regulatory approvals across all geographies, receiving the required authorizations for employees and vendors to continue operations and receive payment, and confirming safety-related operations remain in place. Missing the mark in these three areas not only disrupts operations but, in the extreme, could lead to legal consequences. As such, Day 1 perfection must be viewed as a table stake for any successful deal. Day 1, like a baby, *could* come early, in which case the bare minimums become even more important.

As a result, Day 1 is a prioritization exercise—and what you want to prioritize are those goals that are core to closing the deal and creating the most value. You can create a closing conditions checklist to close on time, including mitigation plans for what happens if you miss a certain goal. If there are items on your list that aren't for Day 1, then they're for the end state. That's not to say that they're unimportant; it's just that they're not necessary for Day 1. This may include decisions that require more data (e.g., those related to customer behavior). And that's why Day 1 requires a laser-like focus on what you need to close the deal without negative legal consequences.

Ecolab prepared carefully for its Day 1, creating blueprints and dashboards to ensure that the new Ecolab would run smoothly, that regulators would be satisfied, that customers would be delighted, and that employees would be ready and able to take care of customers and excited to get on with the business of the day. Remember, Christophe Beck aimed to make this "the best integration ever" and wanted to deliver on that promise.

Central to this effort was the creation of four command centers around the globe that were central points of contact across Ecolab and Nalco, empowering regions to resolve issues at the local level. The command centers were designed to respond rapidly to resolve any outstanding issues. They identified common risks and shared mitigation strategies, and provided real-time executive leadership visibility. Rather than create something new, they used existing business processes (e.g., HR help desk, IT service desk) to surface issues and share progress.

The IMO created timelines to prepare both leaders and employees. Leaders named in the L2 and L3 leadership communications received the announcement, organization chart, and talking points prior to the all-employee announcement on November 21, eight days before Day 1. A week later, the Ecolab and Nalco executive teams were invited to attend a webcast to prepare them to deliver key messages and understand their role on Day 1. After the webcast, Ecolab E-level leaders and Nalco directors and above received the "Leader and Employee Day 1 Guides." After the all-hands webcast on Day 1, those same leaders received customizable slides to use with their teams. Employee preparations followed a similar path.

Ecolab also identified six essentials for Day 1: Day 1 certification for systems (HR, ERP, IT, and so on), synergies, organization design, communication plans, 2012 priorities, and implementation governance. These were presented to the IMO for approval and sign-off.

Ecolab's Day 1 was a major success. At headquarters, they rented out the St. Paul Convention Center, complete with a massive balloon arch in Ecolab's colors, for an all-employee celebration where the go-forward strategy and the new purpose, mission, and values were shared. Similar events where held around the world. Further, part of Ecolab's and Nalco's culture—valued by employees—was giving pins to celebrate milestones at 5, 10, and 15 years, and so on. On Day 1, everyone received a newly designed Ecolab pin representing their respective tenure.

Ecolab also rolled out its new safety program and its go-to-market plan for cross-selling and approaching customers as a combined company in the first week post-close. Day 1 built massive momentum for post-close success through being laser-focused on taking care of customers and employees.

Carve-Outs and Transition Services Agreements

Coming out of due diligence, buyers will have estimated the one-time and run-rate costs for standing up the divested business. Now buyers must also develop a complete view of the true operating expenses to run the business on Day 1 with transition services that will be provided by the seller.

This interim state will create additional costs because the buyer is relying on TSAs from the seller before they can begin to realize the synergies. Deal teams and lawyers from both sides typically have agreed to a high-level legal framework (e.g., a non-binding term sheet) for what services the seller will provide for business continuity. The term sheet provides a mechanism for both sides to continue their negotiations on TSAs even after signing the deal regarding exactly what services will be provided, for how long, and at what cost. At signing, the term sheet mechanism is useful because the buyer will be worried about being over-charged without understanding all of the service details from the seller. As a result, there will often be a negotiated cost ceiling included: "Thou shall not charge me more than the current cost allocation for the divested business from the parent."

During the due diligence phase, the seller will be the buyer's best friend. But once the deal is signed, interests diverge immediately. The seller doesn't want the business anymore; it wasn't a core business, so they don't want to spend any more time or money. There is no incentive for the seller to provide the TSAs other than to get the deal done. The seller now has stranded costs from shared infrastructure, services, and procurement deals with the divested business. Their focus will be on removing those costs as soon as possible versus supporting the buyer. So, they may not give the buyer their best people, and they will likely play hard-ball on the duration and scope of the TSAs. This dynamic is important to recognize because the buyer will want more time to open the hood and understand what people, processes, and systems they are actually getting, and may need to demand more time and flexibility so they can make an educated decision on TSA scope, pricing, and duration.

During sign to close, TSAs must be defined, costed, and negotiated in a coordinated, cross-functional manner. Typically, the integration leader, who has that cross-functional view and operational knowledge and expertise, can serve as the central point of contact to negotiate with the seller. Timing of TSA exits presents a unique functional interdependency beyond buying a company outright. For example, exiting HR TSAs for payroll, benefits, and performance management systems (HRIS) may be highly dependent on the IT integration timeline and related HR systems. Until the buyer can exit the IT TSAs they will have to continue paying for those HR TSAs, meaning those TSAs may turn out to be much more costly than first imagined.

Day 1 implications for carve-outs are also unique. TSAs will provide business continuity where the seller has not disentangled the business by Day 1. That said, there will be areas where separation will happen, and those must be thoroughly pressure tested by the buyer. For example, the seller will need to transfer the business as a legal operating entity, and this will require separation of things such as bank accounts, legal employee transitions, federal and state tax IDs, and third-party contracts. Developing a comprehensive separation plan with the seller is the first step for an issue-free Day 1. Actively participating in Day 1 readiness activities, including dress rehearsals (dry runs) leading up to legal entity cutovers, will help pressure test that the seller is ready to flip the switch and hand over a fully functional business.

Conclusion

Integrations used to look different. They were about templates and bureaucracy. A CEO would have a binder from a consulting firm with the two companies' logos on the front. In it was a playbook—and a pretty static one. The binder would have pages that laid out the IMO team, guiding principles, charters, Day 1 readiness, synergy communications, post-close vision, the names of the workstreams, and so on. The consultants would gather everyone for a kickoff and give them the templates that they would inevitably struggle with. Worse, they would make the leads feel juvenile, forced to comply with status reports and roadmaps that they had no control over or investment in. And this was followed by months of positioning and posturing.

The approach we've laid out in chapters 6 and 7 gets investment and buy-in up front, where leaders can make many of the major decisions together. Instead of getting the IT teams together to fight it out over the major choices over six months, those leaders can make facilitated decisions right up front. That provides the right structure and frame for the teams to proceed with their planning and provide clear guidelines to employees and those reporting to the head of the IMO.

This level of integration planning prepares the new organization to immediately deliver on pre-close planning operational decisions, achieve early wins on synergies, and complete the post-close planning for the end-state vision.

In chapter 8, we'll discuss how this massive amount of planning moves from the transitional state of planning to becoming post-Day 1 business as usual, fulfilling the promise of the deal thesis.

CHAPTER 8

Will My Dreams Become Reality?

Post-Close Execution

Day 1 is an exciting milestone, but, operationally, it should be relatively quiet, involving communication with employees and customers, ensuring regulatory hurdles have been met, and that bank accounts are ready to go. But once the deal has closed and Day 1 celebrations have come and gone, the road to integration and the future state of the new firm begins. Buckle up, because all of this will be under public scrutiny as you begin to report results.[1]

Post-close execution must receive the same level of management attention that Announcement Day and pre-close planning did. The key to post-close success is maintaining momentum. Thousands of decisions have already been made before Day 1, but they have not been tested and implemented by the new organization. This chapter focuses on how to improve the odds of successful execution of the deal thesis and the fulfillment of all of the pre-close planning without stumbling—and how to do it quickly and efficiently. But first, a word on the risks.

New significant risks begin to enter into the deal after Day 1. Issues such as overlooked interdependencies or change programs without adequate leadership authority can build with a slow drip until they reach the point where senior management takes notice. Critical employees can leave, taking their legacy knowledge with them and causing damage to the underlying businesses—even if some synergies are realized. The result can lead to not only loss of confidence from investors but also loss of vital relationships with customers, employees, and suppliers.

Post-close is also the period when many acquirers also begin to transition the attention of executives who saw a deal through from inception back to their operating roles. Executives will begin the handoff to managers who will be focused on the integration program. This shift in focus can present real challenges to pre-serving the teams' attention on execution.

The biggest mistake that we've seen is that acquiring leaders move their attention away from the deal, sometimes even put-ting some of the integration back into the hands of the manag-ers from the target—asking them, for instance, to change their processes, or to achieve synergies that they aren't invested in, or to deal alone with change management issues. We can assure you that it is unlikely the target has the same goals as the acquirer, and its managers will prefer to keep operating the way they did pre-acquisition.

Another pressing issue is having no clear definition of the end state—that is, not knowing when the transition is complete, when the two organizations are truly operating in the marketplace as one combined entity.

Other roadblocks exist as well. Among them are a failure to have a clear understanding of the synergy projects in play, lead-ing to a subsequent failure to properly track synergies. Frankly, everyone is tired from the sprint to Day 1, and that fatigue can lead to bad decisions, including disbanding the IMO too soon. The discipline of the IMO will be necessary post-close, when the IMO shifts to a different structure.

What are the signs and symptoms of "the wheels coming off a deal"? It can be a long list, but telltale signs include when integral managers, feeling disaffected and uninvolved, start to leave; when employee satisfaction and morale suffer because employees don't feel like they belong and are not being appropriately integrated; when dissatisfied customers leave for competitors because their needs haven't been met or promises have been unfulfilled; and when deal goals lose priority, as those who are responsible for execution feel removed from the planning and find the goals too challenging to meet. All of this adds up to a failure of financial performance, when the deal falls well short, 12–18 months in, of the synergies that were announced.

The fact is, the longer post-close execution takes, the less likely management will be able to deliver on the value detailed in the original deal thesis and promised to shareholders and customers. In an unforgiving market this can lead not only to adjustments in earnings expectations but also to management losing the ability to achieve the financial results expected for both companies before the deal. Moreover, as post-close integration activities continue, time and money the business could have otherwise used for growth continue to get consumed, taking attention from other opportunities and limiting follow-on acquisitions and growth.

The majority of post-close execution activities should occur within a year of close—certainly no longer than 18 months. Much longer than that, and interest will surely wain. Inability to execute major integration tasks within the first year not only reduces deal value as the present value of forecasted synergies decreases but also means that tracking operational gains becomes more complex. Slow execution also complicates change management as manager and employee behaviors calcify and they start treating the transition way of doing business as "the new normal."

The first step in successful post-close integration, then, is to ensure there is a dedicated transition team—typically the IMO—that focuses on integration activities with a clear group of leaders and trusted functional and business leads who are solely focused on integration and transitions and empowered with decision authority.

The core post-close task is to drive the new company toward fulfilling the initial deal thesis and implementing the plans and decisions made before Day 1. Post-close execution should therefore center on getting the integrated business and its new operating model to business as usual as quickly as possible. Together, there are five major transitions to manage:

1. From the IMO to business as usual

2. From organization design to talent selection and workforce transition

3. From synergy planning to synergy tracking and reporting

4. From the clean room to the customer experience and growth

5. From the employee experience to change management and culture

These are addressed individually in the sections below, which focus on the details—the substance—of how to track the necessary transitions that lead to superb post-close execution.

Transition 1: From the Integration Management Office to Business as Usual

The IMO and the structure it governs don't end on Day 1, but they do go through a definite shift. Sprinting to Day 1, the IMO managed and oversaw the workstreams, paying particular attention to interdependencies and priorities that were bigger than any one functional area. After Day 1, the IMO begins to graduate functions into business as usual. While the pre-close IMO focused on defining the end state and creating plans and synergy projects, the post-close IMO becomes all about execution, transition, and orienting structures to achieve the promised goals.

Because Day 1 can bring a lull in efforts—caused by fatigue from the sprint combined with the feeling that Day 1 constitutes a finish line of sorts—the IMO must preserve momentum so the integration doesn't fall off the rails as people get distracted. Remember, this is just the beginning of executing on all of the pre-close planning. Short-term solutions or workarounds that got you through an issue-free Day 1 now must be confronted as you transition from the IMO structure to business as usual.

Post-close, integration planning will confront the realities of execution. While the idea of "realizing the value of the deal thesis" is an elegant rule of thumb, one of the major aspects of the post-Day 1 IMO, practically speaking, is managing ongoing interdependencies across the workplans and the day-to-day overlap among workstreams, making sure plans and milestones are on track and that the integration machine is running smoothly. It's only when the integration work no longer requires this extra level of coordination that it is time for a workstream to graduate and move to business as usual.

What does "business as usual" actually mean? For our purposes, it refers to the typical ways that functions work together and will continue to work together into the future without the additional coordination across workstreams provided by a body like the IMO.

The objectives of graduation to business as usual are threefold:

1. Allow teams to transition execution to business units and exit from participation in regular IMO meeting cadence

2. Ensure that a clear path exists for workstreams to complete all integration objectives and achieve synergy targets

3. Signify to executive sponsors and SteerCo that a work-stream no longer requires active coordination and efforts of the IMO

A common mistake is to tie achieving business as usual status for a workstream to achieving a certain amount of synergy realization. For example, IT or finance may have realized 100 percent of their synergies but may still be held back from graduating because other workstreams are still dependent on their other integration activities. IT and finance may remain on the critical path for other workstreams to realize their synergies or operational integration requirements. Graduation to business as usual must truly be about not needing to coordinate integration activities any longer.

Once a workstream does graduate, the IMO will no longer oversee program management for the workstream. This means attendance at IMO meetings is no longer required—the purpose of these meetings, remember, was input into coordination efforts and status reporting on milestones and overall workplans. After their transition to business as usual, integration workstreams will no longer exist as their projects and activities are added to the existing portfolio of projects and initiatives of the ongoing businesses or functions. Budgets are integrated into the normal annual operating planning and budgeting process. And project managers become responsible for supporting documentation and workstream deliverables.

As a consequence of graduation, workstream leaders will assume responsibility for remaining integration-related commitments, including staffing of resources necessary to execute on plans.

Workstreams will still need to update integration readiness projects in a central planning tool for tracking and reporting, while tracking of synergy capture and integration spend will be ongoing, led by the IMO and FP&A.

Migration rates from IMO to business as usual will differ by function. Often back office operations like HR, IT, and finance require the most attention from the IMO since they are the "long poles in the tent"—the initiatives that take the longest to realize and that other functions depend on. Integration of the acquirer and target may begin with heterogenous systems in those areas (IT, HR, and finance) that must be normalized as the new organization moves to business as usual, a process that can typically take more than a year. In a carve-out, transition to business as usual happens when the TSAs are fulfilled and exited. HSR-mandated divestments also must be resolved before business as usual is reached.

As a useful example, consider the synergy cross-functional workstream. It will formally transition to business as usual when the individual workstreams have approved targets and bottom-up plans have been incorporated into the functional or business financial budget (which will now have a lower spend or higher revenue expectations). Tracking the results ultimately becomes the job of FP&A—as would normally be the case for tracking business performance. For some companies, the synergy team will dissolve when the company has met or exceeded the run-rate commitments made at the deal announcement. Other companies have used markers such as when synergy realization is well under-way and trending at or above expectations before transitioning to FP&A.

Until that formal transition to FP&A, the IMO must make sure synergies are being documented and tracked, otherwise a business or functional unit can game the system for their first year so the IMO will stop bothering them. Without established synergy targets and a mechanism for validating achievement, the business unit might sandbag and give the IMO synergy numbers it can easily beat, counting it as synergy when it really isn't.

Knowing when the IMO itself will be fully disbanded is part of the integration end-state vision up front. Defining what "done" means is an integral part of planning and will vary from integration to integration and the complexities of the workstreams. But the executive team needs to know when they've arrived for each function and business. In the ideal, the end state is defined as when the two companies are operating in the market as one and the value of the deal thesis is fully realized.

Because workstreams will roll off over time, the IMO structure will flex, shrinking in size and diminishing in importance— either by reducing the number of members, reducing the number and frequency of meetings, or by allowing workstreams to leave the governance structure. The cadence of meetings and executive report-outs will become solely related to synergy capture rather than to procedural integration. The IMO's end is typically indicated by the IMO leader taking another role, and many team members resuming pre-IMO business roles or finding new positions. There is often a less senior person from the IMO team who assumes controls to address the final close-out duties.

But remember that until the integration is done, the IMO in some form is still intact. (See the sidebar, "Illustrative Business as Usual Graduation Process.")

Transition 2: From Organization Design to Talent Selection and Workforce Transition

Following organization design and role decisions, it's time to choose the talent that will help lead and execute the new company's plans and transition the rest of the workforce.

Talent selection

Talent selection—led by the organization design team—is more than just about picking the right talent. It's fundamentally about who remains and who departs from either company, and who

Illustrative Business as Usual Graduation Process

1. Core IMO identifies workstreams that are candidates for graduation. Workstreams can reach out to IMO if they feel they are ready.

2. IMO works with eligible workstreams to complete the documents required for graduation.

3. IMO and eligible workstreams participate in a combined review of required documents and seek approval from the respective workstream executive sponsor.

4. Upon approval, workstream leadership acknowledges full responsibility for the integration and workplan as it pertains to their organization.

gets which role. Further, it's also about the faithful application of agreed and prioritized selection criteria—relevant experience; skills; compensation (cost); performance ratings; geographic location; diversity, equity, and inclusion (DEI) targets; and so on. By Day 1, L0 through L2 (or possibly L3) leaders have been chosen at the top of the house and announced—important signals for the future direction of the combined company. The job now is to select, notify, and transition L3 or L4 leaders and below—a much larger workforce.

Now is the time to execute on whichever option you chose during the pre-close planning process described in chapter 7: option 1 (where each selected leader designs their organization and roles and then selects their people, layer by layer) or option 2 (typically L3 leaders design their structure and roles from the top all the way down to the ground, and talent selection follows). Either approach will be guided by the synergy targets for each impacted function or business, where it is much easier to achieve synergy targets at the more expensive top of the house (L1–L4) than digging for savings deeper in the organization.

Whichever option you chose, though, the task now is to match the open positions to be filled to the pool of candidates—the candidate slate. The organization design and HR teams must ensure that the business leaders who are selecting talent are familiar with agreed criteria and that they apply those criteria consistently (and that the right people are considered). There will almost always be tension between fit, criteria, and cost in either option.

Option 1 can offer leaders on both sides the opportunity to give input on talent, which can be priceless given their historical knowledge. That said, this option can be influenced by the relationships that leaders have with candidates. Option 1 is prone to "hallway campaigning" because it is done layer by layer. This can lead to biased outcomes because it becomes harder, perhaps unintentionally, to apply the agreed talent criteria clearly and fairly. We all have coworkers we regard highly enough to imagine they can do virtually any job even if they don't have the "right" background.

But option 1 has advantages too. Namely, the cost of each layer can be sanity checked to ensure that it is tracking to synergy targets before proceeding to the next layer. Problems arise because there can be the temptation to keep higher-priced talent (often the most productive) that leaders believe they just can't live without, but then cuts must be found in subsequent layers—and that can lead to another case of "death by a thousand cuts."

Let's play this out: Mark is chosen as an L2 leader, a divisional executive vice president, and one of the direct reports he chooses is Ami. Mark notifies Ami and installs her, then Ami designs roles and picks her people and notifies and installs them. They subsequently choose their own teams, and so on. If leaders at the top are not aligned with their synergy targets, they will push the savings burden down to the next layer and the next to the bottom of the house. As it gets harder to find savings deeper in the organization, they may have to go back and go through the process again—sometimes several times. When that happens, leaders can either go back and make difficult choices they didn't make the first time or give up on the synergy goal, which is not uncommon (this is an example of leakage we discussed in chapter 7). And since the talent has already been informed, it can be painful and difficult to undo.

Option 2 allows a more data-driven approach for talent selection that's overseen typically by L3 leaders along with their HR business partners all the way to the bottom-most layer of the organization. An advantage here is that it can facilitate the fair, and strict, application of the agreed-upon criteria to arrive at selection decisions across the enterprise, not just department by department. The design phase already considered the average cost of a role, but the selection phase now involves the specific cost of individual talent. It's possible that such a straightforward application could result in sub-optimal choices or one that's too costly because, for example, the highest producers are often the most expensive. This means that in the end the most expensive people might be chosen because cost was prioritized last. On the other hand, the new organization risks being *without* its best talent because it prioritized cost over something else—resulting not in a cost issue but a talent issue (which may be fine if the pool consists of younger high-potential talent who can grow with the role).

More tension arises when leaders don't want to readily accept the results of the strict application of criteria. Leaders may feel that not only did they not design their organization, but they also couldn't pick their best people. Although option 2 has less risk of unfairness or inconsistencies overall, people might feel resentful or unhappy with what they feel stuck with. The synergy target has been met, but they didn't get the team they would have chosen. If upper-level management is unhappy with the results, or if lower-level managers revolt, adjustments may be necessary.

The criteria can be revisited in the event of not meeting the synergy target. If lower-level managers are unhappy, the organization can help them be successful with the team they have—which might mean longer transition times, training programs, or more leadership time.

Regardless of which approach is used, it must include legal and synergy team reviews. Legal is looking for consistent application of the criteria with no unfairness or bias. The synergy team is looking to confirm that leaders didn't deviate—intentionally or otherwise—from the approved synergy estimates and goals. Legal and synergy teams are often in the unenviable position of being the enforcer of the rules.

A review of the entire workforce can provide a chance to understand where processes may have created inequities (e.g., through unconscious bias) and to resolve or to reinvent those processes to foster long-term DEI goals. Day 1 can offer a time for the new organization to be transparent about where and how each company has had challenges, and to proactively address those inequities in the selection decisions. At the very minimum, redesigning the workforce should not unravel any progress either company made and should—looking forward—create career paths consistent with larger DEI goals.

Workforce transition

There are two major themes in workforce transition. First is the notification of all employees, as well as regulatory bodies, works councils, unions, and so forth, on the nature of how they will be impacted. Most countries will have their own employee notification requirements for plant closings and layoffs that have to be followed, such as the Worker Adjustment and Retraining Notification (WARN) Act in the United States. Notification includes presenting employees who are staying (in new roles) with offers, presenting those who are needed short term with retention agreements, and presenting employees who are leaving with an exit plan and outplacement services. It is also important that employees who are not impacted understand the major organizational changes that are going on around them.

Second is the knowledge transfer that must happen for the smooth operation of the business as employees move into their new roles. Some employees will possess such valuable knowledge that they might need financial incentives beyond recognition and praise of their value, even to be simply "on call" during transitions. But the total number of employees who receive such retention bonuses should be minimal.

Other major considerations for orchestrating an orderly workforce transition include questions of timing, logistics, and sequencing—again, on 30-, 60-, and 90-day horizons. One important decision is which functions should transition at the same time and which should not. The organization design team can assess the relationships, documents, major account changes, and shifting technology changes that are coming and how they will affect different populations. For example, the sales force might be learning a whole new CRM on top of a new customer base and new metrics for accounts, as well as forming new relationships internally with support people who are *also* learning new things. Questions of sequencing revolve around the right amount of time and support to minimize disruption to the customer and stress for the employee.

As a consequence, workforce transition looks different function by function based on the level of risk attached to a poor transition. The most common approach is to quickly notify the enabling functions and realign employees as soon as possible before transitioning customer-facing people. On Day 1 it can be unclear who owns the major customer relationships, because that knowledge resided in the clean room planning. Companies typically view their customer relationships as competitively sensitive as well as their top talent, so leaders need to fully absorb the

customer portfolio and sales relationships before making important decisions.

It is common to know how the back office–enabling functions
will be impacted because pre-Day 1 planning included decisions
on outsourcing, shared services centers, and IT system choices.
That said, these changes may need 12–18 months to fully implement, which would mean retaining a substantial portion of those
supporting people (e.g., systems administrators for payroll) for
the duration of time that systems are being retired.

Timing, logistics, and sequencing are also important factors
in knowledge transfer. With rapid notification and quick exits,
vital knowledge that comes through years of experience can walk
out the door. If an exiting employee wants to help, retaining them
may require a short stay bonus of 30 days or more. Bonuses can
be predicated on the successful transfer of knowledge, introduc-
tions to key relationships, or transmitting important documents
as enumerated in the transition contract or retention agreement.

For instance, if Ellen gets picked to stay and Michael doesn't,
knowledge transfer planning should ensure that normal operations are not negatively impacted when Michael steps back and
Ellen steps forward. Conversations that prompt self-reflection
should account for the knowledge, relationships, documentation—
the history of Michael's engagement with the job and the information Ellen needs to continue to seamlessly serve the client,
internally or externally (what we called the service delivery model
in chapter 6). The aim is to create consistent if not elevated service delivery.

This process can be burdensome to the workforce, so it's necessary to also account for the extra time and effort that the transition creates. This time might be tumultuous for an employee's
customers, while at the same time the employee is losing their
finance or HR business partner and engaging with someone who
is effectively a stranger and also unfamiliar with the new processes (with no bond of trust or shared history)—and that can

be overwhelming for some talent. The workforce transition team must manage the sequence and timing of those changes.

The organization design team will also need to assess which functions can go faster than others. Ensuring that transitions happen in a way that's least disruptive for employees and customers is vital. Of course, there are times when a culture is so broken and so toxic that disruption may be welcomed as an immediate fix, but this is rare. A more normal window for exits might be two weeks for many back office employees; customer-facing functions that are being redeployed but not exited could span a couple of months. But, again, the main message here is that both the workforce transition and knowledge transfer must be as thoughtfully sequenced as the rest of the acquisition has been.

Transition 3: From Synergy Planning to Synergy Tracking and Reporting

Pre-Day 1, the synergy team pushed the workstreams to develop initiatives and workplans, with a roadmap of milestones for each initiative. These plans should aim to achieve at least the cost or revenue synergy targets they were assigned. SteerCo has approved the plans, and they have been built into executive plans and goals with actual project codes attached to them. That was the easy part. There is a long way to go.

Now, the clean rooms are open, data is readily available, and the two companies can operate as one. The new company must begin to cultivate investor confidence in the deal because the acquirer has just formally purchased the target's shares at a premium. The synergy plans, both labor and non-labor, must be revisited and confirmed in the light of day by the synergy team and the workstreams and immediately assessed for additional initiatives in each function that might be possible now that the new management team is in place.

More important, the IMO along with the synergy team will kick off an aggressive financial reporting and tracking process, designed and approved prior to Day 1, that will ensure that claimed synergies are auditable and directly attributable to the initiatives and workplans that will generate those synergies. Real synergies are discrete line items that will ultimately impact the P&L. They must be distinct from the operating plans already in place for both companies ("if but for the deal"), and the claim that they have been achieved must be able to withstand challenges that they are indeed real.

In our experience, acquirers will benefit from a tracking cadence—preferably weekly—that keeps a hot spotlight on progress and celebrates achievements by "ringing the bell." At Ecolab, they were able to ring the bell in the first week after Day 1 as they recognized more than \$21M from procurement synergies. Although the cadence can flex over time, the functions have to prepare for the long haul until at least the announced run rate for their net synergies (gross financial improvements less incremental ongoing costs to achieve) has been reached.

Synergy plans and results that are not managed and tracked aggressively will likely go off plan. Business leaders will want to do the minimum to achieve targets that weren't their idea in the first place—and that they may secretly believe are unrealistic even though they have delivered initiatives and plans to achieve them. They may be tempted to game the synergy targets by exceeding their operating plan (e.g., by not spending their budget in the short term and counting it as a synergy). People don't fail to honor plans because they don't understand. They fail to honor plans because doing so is hard. They may attempt workarounds so they can go back to the old ways of doing things. That's why establishing a process to monitor plans and recognize achieved synergies is so important, as is communicating and emphasizing significant financial incentives for both meeting and exceeding synergy targets immediately following Day 1.

For example, when two large environmental services companies merged, the new company announced up to $70M in synergy achievement bonuses to top executives and nearly 700 employees if they could meet a synergy target EBIT run rate of $150M. They would also be well rewarded if they met the lower target announced to the street that would yield a range of 25 percent to 100 percent of the maximum award, as long as the one-time costs and ongoing costs to achieve the synergies did not rise above an agreed amount. Incentives like this matter inordinately.

As we discussed in chapter 7, the synergy program is made up of a portfolio of prioritized initiatives. Each of those initiatives has an owner and requires a workplan—a series of milestones based on the number of projects that will be required to accomplish the initiative and achieve associated net synergies. After Day 1, the IMO will need to integrate the synergy workplans and milestones with the end-state functional operational integration plans to highlight what synergies are dependent on general integration activities.

That may sound like a large, complex endeavor. It is.

Only the IMO, however, has the full line of sight of all workplans, and realizing synergies must be coordinated with the operational integration on which synergy plans are dependent. These include such milestones as the first combined quarterly close or consolidating real estate or facilities. Reaching these milestones leads to direct cost savings for the newly combined organization.

Ultimately, this is a critical prioritization exercise for the IMO because some synergies may have fewer dependencies yet offer higher value relative to those that are more complex and less valuable (and that will also take longer to realize). Further, sequencing synergy workplans and operational integration activities must be aligned with the new operating model and leadership priorities beyond those of the deal (e.g., ongoing priorities of the businesses), so changes in priorities will require SteerCo approval.

A successful synergy reporting and tracking program will have three reinforcing components:

1. **Financial reporting,** which establishes the mechanism of tracking benefits and associated costs from each synergy initiative that is tagged to an internal cost center, department, or project code.

2. **Milestone tracking,** which is driven by the IMO and tracks the project milestones for each initiative to ensure dates and dependencies are being met as planned and are on track.

3. **Leading indicators,** which are KPIs developed based on the primary synergy drivers to proactively monitor their dependencies and provide a forward-looking (vs. reactive) approach to course correction. Leading indicators are an ongoing "health check" that raise an early warning signal that synergy initiatives are likely off track and will likely not reach their milestones. Large initiatives with big payoffs and several major milestones are the prime candidates for using leading indicators. Those initiatives typically take longer, are more complex, and may need ongoing monitoring to keep them on track.

Remember our favorite CEO, Chas Ferguson of Homeland Technologies? Well, Homeland went ahead with its acquisition of Affurr Industries. They had an issue-free Day 1 and are now implementing their synergy reporting and tracking program. Consolidating attendance and sponsorships at tradeshows and other events is an initiative where Homeland believes it can realize millions in run-rate cost savings with Affurr because both companies go to many of the same ones. Milestones for such an initiative would include determining which tradeshows they had in common and the allocated spend; agreeing on a strategy for combined tradeshow footprint and which shows or conferences offered the best opportunities to consolidate; negotiating new terms; and the sequence of consolidation. A leading indicator might be how many tradeshows out of the total to be consolidated have been negotiated successfully.

Or consider the merger of the cosmetics companies we highlighted in chapter 6. The target had outsourced its production of fragrances to four contract manufacturers. A major source of synergy was insourcing fragrance production using the acquirer's facilities. Major milestones included reconfiguring the acquirer's manufacturing facility, buying new equipment that mixes chemicals and fills containers, conducting pilot production runs, ramping up production and hiring additional labor, and rolling off the contract manufacturers. Leading indicators included getting the technical specifications for the new machines ready and placing the orders for the new machines (that would take at least six months to deliver), monitoring the progress of hiring and training new employees, and progress of rolling off the existing outsourcing arrangements.

This leaves us with financial reporting and tracking, which involves six major concepts: the baseline, the assigned synergy targets, the functional or business financial plans, the periodic forecast, the actuals, and analysis of variances to spotlight problems and reforecast in either direction.

Figure 8-1 illustrates how these six items combine to form the financial reporting and tracking process. The starting point is the combined baseline of the forward plan without synergies. The assigned stretch targets are the minimum targets for the functions or businesses to achieve at the run rate. The plan is the bottom-up financial plan developed by the functions or businesses on Day 1; the plan must at least meet the targets but often will exceed the targets, especially with incentives. The forecast will equal the plan on Day 1 and will be re-forecasted every month or quarter based on the actuals—the recorded cost or revenue synergies that have been verified by FP&A. The variance between

FIGURE 8-1

Synergy financial reporting and tracking illustration

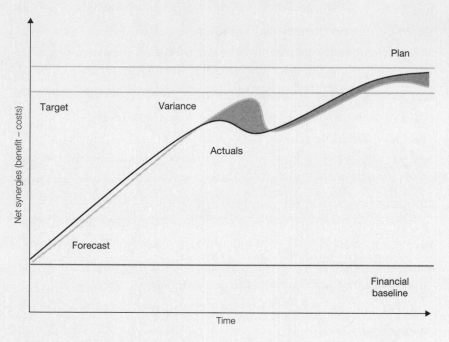

Note: For simplicity, we've held the baseline, target, and plan flat to focus on forecast, actuals, and variance on the way to achieving the plan.

plan and forecast will need to be understood as the new forecast for both labor and non-labor synergies is refined for the next period.

It is this financial reporting and tracking process along with milestone tracking and leading indicators that the synergy team, the IMO, and senior management will use to manage the revenue and cost synergy programs and deliver the performance promises the acquirer has made.

In practice, the synergy team and the IMO have to instill a cadence of monthly actuals tracking; a quarterly evaluation and reforecast; a variance analysis against forecast and plan to understand why the company is exceeding or missing expectations; and executive reporting for the IMO, SteerCo, and the board. Initiative achievement will be aggregated across both labor and non-labor synergies. That means the IMO and synergy team work together to develop a standard approach and timeline that all will adhere to, on a regular cadence, to consolidate data on headcount and operational (cost and revenue) synergies.

Not having an agreed combined baseline in place prior to Day 1 is another invitation for mischief. Remember, the combined functional baseline presents the forward plan for costs and revenues that would have been in place without the merger. It is the starting point for the synergy tracking program because synergies will become part of the new budgets in business as usual for the combined company. Not pushing for that baseline before Day 1 will allow significant gaming as either side might pad their budget, from which synergies will be measured and rewarded.

Note a couple of important distinctions: one-time cost versus ongoing costs to achieve synergies, and the difference between run-rate synergies and P&L impact. One-time costs will typically be external advisers, lease breakage or vendor sunset fees, new equipment, or startup costs for new IT systems. Ongoing incremental cost would come from a growing sales force, for example, to drive growth synergies. Remember, net synergies are the gross improvements minus the ongoing costs to achieve them and result in increases in EBIT and NOPAT.

In chapter 4 we discussed the ramp up of synergies and assumed the full P&L impact for a given year. The "run rate of synergies" is a term often used and is the go-forward projected annualized savings, where the P&L impact is the actual total for the year (we equated run rate with P&L impact in chapter 4). Consider the following example of a $200,000 engineer who leaves in the middle of the year. The quarterly savings impact is illustrated as follows:

2020	Q1	Q2	Q3	Q4
Expected synergy savings	$0	$0	$50,000	$50,000

In this example, we have an expected run rate at the end of the year of $200,000 ($4 \times 50$), but the P&L impact for the year is only $100,000 (the sum of the year's improvements). The P&L impact will equal the run rate when synergy increases have leveled off and are in effect for a full year.

The synergy team will need to stay in place until there is sufficient confidence that the functions or businesses are well on track to meet or exceed the commitments that were communicated on Announcement Day and can be moved into the FP&A office as part of ongoing executive plans and budgets.

Transition 4: From the Clean Room to the Customer Experience and Growth

Although cost synergies represent the axis of value for lots of mergers, many deals also focus on growth. Valuable M&A revenue growth depends on preserving current revenue, achieving future growth expectations already in the stand-alone businesses' financial goals, and then realizing additional revenue as a result of the strategic benefits of the deal—the revenue synergies. Revenue synergies will typically take longer to realize than cost synergies because they are subject to competitor and customer reactions and often depend on new sales systems, customer offers, and realignment of the sales forces.

These improvements are often facilitated by operating model changes that will make the combined company more customer focused—meaning that new growth depends on customers who believe they are being served better with higher-value offers by the combined company than they were before the deal.

An effective customer experience, in and out of M&A, can increase customer retention, spur higher and more frequent spend per customer, or lessen price sensitivity. It is predicated on delivering the right messages and products or services through the right channels at the right time at a price that customers are willing to pay. Any growth plans must be built around enhancing the customer experience.

The customer experience strategy and revenue growth planning began during the due diligence stage and were carried through the sign-to-close period in the clean room. Up-front considerations should have included drivers of customer purchasing behavior; improving current offers; how changes in offerings will impact customers and how they will likely respond; which customers are at the greatest risk of switching to a competitor and why; and what will be communicated to customers at announcement, during sign to close, on Day 1, and beyond.

Customer churn is a real danger during the merger. Customers leave for many reasons: disruption of services, lack of information, competitive behaviors between sales forces (often due to misaligned incentives), and predictable competitor reactions with aggressive customer communications of how bad the deal will be. Much of this churn is avoidable by evaluating the current customer experience by segment and channel, listening to what customers tell you, and then prioritizing customer experience improvement opportunities along the roadmap of touchpoints.

Engaging directly with your customers even before Day 1 is also a real option. For instance, when a semiconductor equipment manufacturer acquired a complementary cleaning business, the acquirer's top customers previously had poor customer relations with the target's sales force and leadership. Work to mitigate these issues prior to Day 1 included extensive meetings with customers to explain the acquisition, the new leadership team, and how their account teams would be impacted. Opening such a dialog before the deal closed (provided you're not going to market as one combined company before it's legal) allowed customers to air their concerns and the acquirer worked to mitigate revenue leakage and enable growth related to combining sales efforts immediately after close by explaining the enhanced benefits of the combination.

Even without such direct conversations, an enormous amount of data on customers and their behavior should be readily available. The combined sales force and data from all sales channels are extremely valuable assets in fully understanding customer needs. With enough of the right data, analytics and AI will allow the development of algorithms that have proved very valuable in offering more value to customers.

The sales force, specifically, is the connection point with customers. Their relationships and knowledge are the bedrock of revenue growth. Great salespeople understand why customers buy or don't, when they buy, and how much they buy, as well as their satisfactions and dissatisfactions or unmet needs, what price they are willing to pay, and why they would switch—and even what they complain about over lunch or in the field. As such, members of the sales force must be ready to answer questions and be comfortable representing the voice of the customer to leadership as planning in the clean room transitions to executing on new growth opportunities.

From the clean room to growth opportunities

During sign to close, the clean room offered a sterile environment to assess the product and service portfolio across both companies, including overlapping customers, overlapping products and services, pricing, direct versus distributor approaches, and customer profitability and sales trajectories by customer and geographies—all to size and prioritize potential opportunities for driving revenue growth and profitability.

But let's get back to basics. Revenue synergies are in fact just a special case of the general issues all companies confront when they evaluate and consider changes in their go-to-market strategy to improve their growth trajectory. Broadly speaking, improving go-to-market strategy boils down to either expanding how much of the addressable market can be served (beyond what we called "serviceable market" in chapter 3) or making better offers based on improving the customer experience, creating new offers, or a combination of those two that customers value.

Expanding the serviceable market starts with a focus on capture points or the moments that allow a business to get in front of the customer—the "at bats," as it were. In financial services, for instance, the bank branch is a traditional capture point, a concrete place to attract depositors and offer new, relevant, valuable products or services. It's where customers—even millennials—still prefer to show up and engage.[2]

Go-to-market strategy changes will often focus on "win themes" that focus on strengthening or expanding customer capture points (customer segments, geographies, channels) or addressing customer preferences you aren't doing today (service, responsiveness, product quality) or offering bundles of existing products they really want and may create less price sensitivity because of the new benefits. Internally, that might mean redesigning sales incentives and sales teams, streamlining the sales process by offering faster pricing approvals, using better CRM, or using better sales systems from order and billing to delivery.

In M&A, the issues are no different, but they can certainly be more complex. Acquisitions bring with them an entire portfolio of new possibilities and opportunities—myriad new capture points and potential offerings that presumably were not available as separate companies. Company A might have stronger relationships at large accounts or better digital channels than Company B. Company B may have better geographic or international presence than Company A. Collectively, they have a portfolio of products or services that can be sold together, enabling a cross-sell of existing products, attractive new bundles, increased geographic presence, or brand-new products or services.

Let's start with an organic growth example that would-be acquirers should appreciate: the successful transformation at IDEXX, a veterinary diagnostics and information management company. It's a great illustration of a dramatic change in go-to-market strategy that involved a combination of cross-selling and new and better offers.

In 2013, Jay Mazelsky, leader of the North American Companion Animal Group at IDEXX, undertook a commercial model transformation to engage customers in a more compelling way. The transformation involved moving away from an emphasis on individual products to a market model built on solutions for companion animal veterinary clinics. That thesis kicked-off a multi-year, two-step go-to-market strategy transition to redefine how IDEXX touched customers.

The original commercial model had included a specialized sales force organized by product or service, and three large national distributors that touched the same veterinary customer base. That meant that diagnostic analyzers, laboratory services, and a rapid "SNAP" blood test for early diagnosis were separate product groups often sold by different salespeople. This segmented approach to customer engagement impeded cross-selling opportunities that could take advantage of multiple offerings to the same buyer, and salespeople had siloed career paths with little movement across product segments. It also meant there were insufficient IDEXX commercial resources who had the time or account coverage to build trusted adviser relationships with their customers. Any cross-selling that did occur required complex coordination.

IDEXX first restructured the commercial model into an account manager model with sales professionals owning accounts within an assigned territory instead of only selling individual products or services. That empowered customers to choose what was best—single products or an integrated solution—for their practice. It allowed, for example, diagnostics equipment sales to include discussions on laboratory support, SNAP tests, and a new offering that facilitated an integrated IDEXX software solution, including software that served as a data warehouse of all the historical test results for an individual animal patient.

Immediate impacts included an increased level of cross-product sales at points of sale; increased access to the veterinary clinic as the solution model allowed salespeople to serve as "strategic advisers" with a broader view of the business challenges facing clinics (which are essentially small businesses); and a more coordinated commercial operations framework that supported pricing, contracting, and service visits. This go-to-market strategy change—which effectively paired cross-selling with new and improved offers—was so successful in the first year that, for the second major step, IDEXX announced a distributor exit strategy at the end of 2014, replacing their distributor contacts with their own sales force. A larger commercial footprint with subject-matter experts in diagnostics resulted in dramatically faster topline growth, higher customer satisfaction scores, and ultimately a successful global rollout following the success of the new North American operating model.

Acquirers should have the same, or greater, opportunity than IDEXX to rethink their go-to-market strategies. In M&A deals, any analysis of growth synergies should reveal a long list of opportunities that will vary in degree of anticipated value, time to realize, complexity, and required investment. Prioritizing those opportunities must allow both quick wins to achieve early momentum and investment in longer-term projects like new innovative products to fully achieve the promise of the deal thesis.

Cross-selling—selling more of Company A's products through Company B's channels or relationships and vice versa—can provide quick wins by immediately expanding your serviceable market. It also supports the building of the new company's brand. Leadership must clearly define these opportunities so the sales forces know who sells what to whom (so both companies aren't calling on the same customer) and how to reach them—and be ready to announce a sales compensation plan that incentivizes cross-selling on Day 1.

Sales forces are typically excited about the opportunity to cross-sell, but many questions must be answered. Can Company

A really sell Company B's products? Are the procurement professionals the same for the individual products where they sell? Where there are overlapping sales forces at an account, will procurement be looking for discounts, just like you are trying to do with your suppliers for cost synergies post-Day 1? Can the companies reconcile different contracting and pricing terms? Can sales teams be sufficiently incentivized and trained to sell the other company's products?

Whether it is pure cross-selling of existing products or considerations of new bundles or new products, inevitably the term that will emerge in revenue synergy discussions is "complementary": "We have complementary sales forces" or "We have complementary products," or "Customers will just love our bundled offers," and so on. The bottom line is that capture points, or products or services, are not complementary just because leaders say they are. The new company must be able to better penetrate existing customers, reach more customers, and make offers that will delight them in new ways.

Examples of successful bundled offerings cleverly stitching together existing products and services abound. A simple but powerful bundled offer that many young families loved was when Amazon bought Quidsi (parent of Diapers.com) and offered a discount on diapers paired with a three-month free subscription for Amazon Prime—resulting in greater sales on both sides.

A more involved bundle was a deal that brought together transmissions and engines for heavy trucks. With some modification, the combination brought a powertrain with greater fuel efficiency than if customers purchased them separately or from other providers (any other transmission with a particular engine). Another example is when a chemical company acquired a data services firm, which allowed it to automate ordering so that customers no longer had to pay close attention to inventory, reducing the risk they would run out of key chemical components. Bundled offerings might unlock a customer segment that is less price sensitive and more focused on other benefits, such as when two airlines consolidated routes and offered better non-stop access to more destinations with more choices, which attracted the more lucrative business traveler.

Brand-new products will often have the longest lead time to value realization and will emerge from joint innovation where companies reimagine what the products or services can be beyond the bundling of offers. The two companies will already have their own innovation roadmaps at various stages of progress. Joint innovation should be led by examining a joint product development roadmap, combining intellectual property and technological capabilities, and exploring the "art of the possible" that would not have been available if not for the deal. That exercise will also aid leaders on a go-forward vision and decisions on which developing products to advance, which R&D efforts need to be rationalized, and what the future pipeline will be. Joint innovation can be as simple as creating a new application for a normal business process through new chemistries or technologies.

Valuable M&A revenue growth is challenging and complicated—but far from impossible.

New growth depends on customers who believe they are being served better with higher-value offers by the combined company than they were before the deal. Building on the work of the clean room team, relentlessly focusing on customer needs, and leveraging knowledge about customer behavior will form the solid foundation to create opportunities for growth that otherwise wouldn't have existed. Cross-selling, new bundles, and new products can each provide pathways to real, sustained growth.

Growth at Ecolab

Ecolab and Nalco complementary products and services were the foundation of the combined company's growth strategy, presenting opportunities for cross-selling, bundled offerings, and new products and services. Ecolab defined success as building and growing market momentum and increasing penetration in key accounts by leveraging existing channels and relationships.

With these and other growth objectives in mind, Ecolab held a three-day global sales conference in the first 10 days after close. The conference included the top 50 account leaders (from both companies) as well as key business leaders. The agenda included product demonstrations, cross-training, account leader meetings, and the development of action plans for each account, including jointly integrated value propositions.

Attendees discussed synergy and growth opportunities against the backdrop of the sales force reorganization, revised coverage models, and the drawing of new territories and responsibilities. These discussions revealed new opportunities to expand the pie for the combined company, and owners were assigned. Product experts from both sides offered training sessions to explain the joint product roadmap and identify innovation opportunities.

Ecolab and Nalco also focused on their top accounts and customer needs, making sure to use their sales forces to determine the long-term objectives of their top accounts and to understand how the combined company could best respond to customer needs. According to *Harvard Business Review*, "The company's model was to provide on-site evaluations and training for customers and build them customized portfolios of products and services based on those visits."[3] Many of their customers had worked with both companies for years, and it was essential to maintain those strong relationships.

Cross-selling was a key opportunity for Ecolab post-close. One of the largest hotel chains in the world was a key account of Ecolab. They used Ecolab cleaning products throughout their operations from washing towels to cleaning corporate offices. Nalco, however, had not been able to penetrate that account and provide their extensive water solution services. The combined sales teams worked to articulate how the combination of Ecolab with Nalco services could enhance its existing water services and create a more complete end-to-end solution. Together the "new" Ecolab enhanced capabilities also provided specific customer-focused field services. For example, the water used for washing hotel towels could now be used to water on-site landscaping—a bundled solution as a result of the merger.

Ecolab also focused on new products and services. For instance, one of Nalco's existing services included sensor monitoring in heating and cooling towers. These sensors collected data to help monitor operations and identify pre-emptive maintenance needs. As a long-term product development goal, Ecolab explored creating a new monitoring service that used Nalco's sensors to track in situ product effectiveness. For example, Ecolab offered descaling chemicals used to clean and sanitize pipes that have become blocked due to buildup. Using Nalco sensor technology, Ecolab derived a method for monitoring the progression of buildup, subsequently tracking the effectiveness of their products when used by their customers to descale their pipes, allowing for predictive maintenance and reduced downtime.

Transition 5: From the Employee Experience to Change Management and Culture

In chapter 7, we wrote about how part of planning the employee experience focuses on "getting ahead of the pain"—that is, anticipating important changes for employees, function by function, across employee groups and addressing their needs so they are ready for the changes and transitions to come. Indeed, this chapter has detailed many post-Day 1 changes. They might appear straightforward to plan, but change management is hard. As Todd Jick, a Columbia Business School professor, writes in his classic piece "On the Recipients of Change":

> For most people, the negative reaction to change is related to *control*—over their influence, their surroundings,

their source of pride, how they have grown accustomed
to living and working. When these factors appear
threatened, security is in jeopardy. And considerable
energy is needed to understand, absorb, and process
one's reactions. Not only do I have to deal with the
change per se, I have to deal with my reactions to it!
Even if the change is embraced intellectually ("things
were really going bad here"), or it represents advancement ("I finally got the promotion"), immediate accep-
tance is not usually forthcoming. Instead, most feel
fatigued; we need time to adapt.[4]

The nature of M&A change management is even more involved
because there are so many moving parts—workforce planning
and transition, executing on the employee experience plan, implementing the new operating model and organization design, and
managing the merger of not just two businesses but two cultures
and accepted ways of working.[5]

Executive teams are expected to quickly create inspiring points
of view about the possibilities for the future that investors and
customers find believable while simultaneously needing to calm
anxieties of the workforce and then inspire employees. These two
goals require two carefully crafted—but different—messages,
which creates a natural tension and necessitates the prioritization of parallel paths of work for executives. In the first, they
manage external enterprise-level requirements. In the second,
they methodically address the workforce by elevating them
through their hierarchy of needs: job security, rewards, affiliation, and growth.

At the enterprise level, executives must "inspire, spark, and
calm." Inspiration and spark begin on Announcement Day and
carry through to Day 1. The external market wants to know the
strategy and vision: how value will be created, where the synergies lie, and the new operating model to achieve those goals. Mes-

saging sparks their belief through sharing more detail of how the deal will improve the customer experience and create growth and value. Executives later calm the market and the board by demonstrating how the merged company is navigating the future post-Day 1, as it starts realizing the anticipated benefits.

Employees have a different set of expectations. For them, executives must "calm, spark, and inspire"—seemingly the opposite of the needs of the market. Employees care less about vision at the outset. They want to be calmed by knowing they have a job and benefits—a process that starts pre-close. Spark happens after close. Once they know they have a job, employees want to be sparked by exploring the vision for the company and the brand, building on their curiosity about the future. And then they want inspiration that will help them both affiliate with their new company and envision themselves remaining and growing at the company for the rest of their career with a sense of belonging and purpose.

Tensions can arise because the two groups—the market and employees—are looking for competing information at the same moment. A small group of executives are operating at 30,000 feet, but thousands or tens of thousands or more employees see the organization from one foot off the ground. The employee experience team often transitions to focus on change management and as the change management team they are charged with continuing to help resolve this tension. They must approach their task by refining and executing on the change management initiatives that were considered and developed pre-close.

During pre-Day 1 planning, the employee experience team worked to address employee anxieties about their future—explaining the talent selection process, communicating timelines, announcing new leaders, clarifying benefits, and preparing employees for change—the essentials of reducing uncertainty for employees as they confronted the reality of the merger so they could better focus on their role. Post-Day 1, questions like

"Do I have a job?," "To whom do I report?," "Do I have to move?," and "Did my benefits change?" should be answered swiftly. No one should be wondering if their ID card will work, who their insurance provider is, to whom they report, and where they sit come Day 1. This is the calm.

Once employees are assured, the issues begin to shift. It's time to spark. The change management team will focus on creating a sense of affiliation, addressing questions like "Does this company's values, community commitment, and brand align with my beliefs?" As employees develop a sense of connection and belonging to the organization, the moments for inspiration arrive. The change team must illuminate possibilities for employees' future. Will they offer employees the possibility of growth, addressing questions like "What are the opportunities for advancement, mobility, and leadership?" so they will feel fulfilled for years to come.

The approach, though, requires a similar level of detail: By understanding major milestones and communicating them in a "day in the life" way, the change management team will help employees (now levels 3 or 4 and below, a much larger employee population) build a sense of affiliation and empower them to see a desired career path in the new organization.

Organizations that don't engage in robust change management—those that rely on the mere communication of who the new leaders are or that just move employees into new roles—see attrition rates and dissatisfaction levels that are sky high. Why? Because employees simply didn't know where they belonged—and subsequently left or became unhappy and frustrated and stayed. Other mistakes include reducing employee autonomy or making other major changes without clear explanation. If employees feel like their rights are being taken away, they'll become unhappy and be confused about their role and their future. For example, if someone loses their direct reports, they may still opt to boss those people around if that's what they prefer. People will selectively remember what they want and act accordingly. Remember, people don't fail to transition because they don't understand—so part of the change management effort is taking the time to help them feel that change makes sense and is in their best interest for the future.

The tactics of change management can include training sessions, two-way communications, and rotational opportunities. It can also include a heavier leadership engagement, with personal attention from leaders and managers to recognize and motivate employees. Each touchpoint is a chance to demonstrate core values and make them tangible. The experience must be fair for everyone but personal for each employee—including not just monetary rewards but also gestures of gratitude that show their work is valued. If you haven't anticipated how some employee communities will experience change, then they will reject you. So post-close change management must be as carefully crafted as the pre-close employee experience: with milestones set at 30, 60, and 90 days that recognize the changes that employees are facing—especially those tied to integration milestones.

The entire process must be fair for everyone—including those who are leaving—to help those who remain work through any possible survivor guilt. As Joel Brockner, a social psychologist at Columbia University, has shown, a high-quality process ("procedural fairness") that includes input, consistency, and accountability can help everyone feel better about the outcome.[6]

Culture

Any discussion of change management in M&A will converge on culture. Discussions of culture can come off as "fluffy bunnies." But in reality, issues associated with merging cultures are complex and meaningful problems, deeply connected to integration efforts. Shared beliefs on "how work gets done around here" involve decisions rights, access to information, and rewards and incentives that can be dramatically different across companies. Those shared values and expectations didn't happen overnight. They took years to evolve and were passed down through the generations of managers and employees.[7]

Company cultures are so taken for granted that someone from a different culture may view the practices and beliefs of the other as absurd—creating the seeds of a so-called culture clash. At its core, culture allows behaviors to become reasonably predictable. As a consequence, it's imperative to pay attention to developing a shared culture early—beginning on Announcement Day. We've seen clients fall down when they say, "We'll deal with culture after the work from the integration has slowed down and we have more time." By then, it's too late.

Organizations can differ across many dimensions that need to be assessed on what matters for the new operating model and the vision for crafting the culture of the new organization. Culture assessments will reveal differences in a sense of pride and ownership in the organization, attitudes toward inclusion, risk and governance processes, the appetite for change and innovation, a focus on customers versus products, how employees collaborate and team, the importance of informal networks, and even daily routines and rituals that impact how work gets done and what are acceptable behaviors.

Culture is also a supporting rod that can hold together the organization and drive performance. Take the extreme example of one CEO who focused relentlessly on maximizing profit. In meetings, when making decisions, it was what she and her leadership team asked about first. When they approved new products, they did so only if they met a clearly defined operating margin threshold. Employees internalized this and went to outrageous lengths to conserve costs, even foraging in dumpsters for copper wiring to use in their new product designs. Their profit-maximizing, cost-conscious culture was reinforced by a profit-sharing mechanism that paid out more than 35 percent of their base pay every year. Consider how tightly integrated that aspect of culture is: strategy to execution, supported by reinforcing incentives with a vision set by leadership.

Or consider the care that Disney took to preserve culture when it acquired Pixar in 2006 to breathe new life, technology, and innovation into its animation division. Not only was Pixar's creative head, John Lasseter, appointed to lead Walt Disney Animation, reporting directly to Robert Iger, then CEO of the Walt Disney Company, but both parties negotiated a "social compact" of culturally significant issues. Disney promised to preserve everything such that employees felt that they were still Pixar—email addresses and signs on the building would still say Pixar and rituals like monthly beer blasts and the welcoming new employees would be retained. As Iger writes in his book, *The Ride of a Lifetime*, "If we don't protect the culture you've created, we'll be destroying the thing that makes you valuable."[8]

Culture signals and symbols that began at Announcement Day and that were reinforced pre-close are now becoming embedded post-close, whether you want them to or not. Which leaders are chosen and their styles and values send important signals about the new culture. Employees will also observe and have feelings about the new priorities, who has influence and how will decisions be made, what gets rewarded, who has a say and gets to participate in decisions, and even what systems will be used to run the business. Each of these is a signal to employees about the shared culture that is developing through the merger. The post-close period also presents the opportunity to publicly celebrate early wins—like new accounts or successful cross-selling—to show employees what is important for future success.

And yet, each of these is under your control and should be addressed deliberately with an appreciation of the effect they will have on employees: not just on culture but on employees' sense of affiliation and growth, keys to keeping them satisfied and productive and seeing themselves as part of the company for a long time to come. If culture is the shared norms around how work gets done, and how work gets done is going to change, then the opportunity is to take an active role in shaping new shared norms, rather than coming to them too late when employees have already decided and their new behaviors have calcified.[9]

Culture at Ecolab

In the April 2016 issue of *Harvard Business Review*, Jay Lorsch, of Harvard Business School, and his associate, Emily McTague, interviewed Ecolab CEO Doug Baker on how he shaped the company's culture. Baker had taken over at Ecolab in 2004 when revenue was $4B and grew it to $14B in 2014 by completing more than 50 acquisitions, including Nalco as the largest. The workforce had more than doubled during his tenure.[10]

As Ecolab absorbed new acquisitions, complexity and organizational layers grew and divisions and managers became siloed. As Lorsch and McTague write, "The expanding bureaucracy was eating into Ecolab's customer-centric culture, and that was hurting the business."

Baker aimed to restore customer focus and customized offerings as a core strength—and that meant a major change effort. He focused on pushing decision-making to the front lines, to the employees who were closest to customers. Ecolab also engaged with those frontline employees by training them on all Ecolab's products and services so they would be better equipped to figure out on their own which solutions best fit customers' needs.

Although it seemed risky to push decisions down, Baker "found that the bad calls were caught and fixed faster that way. Eventually, managers began to let go and trust their employees—which was a huge cultural shift." Ultimately, that fostered frontline responsibility and allowed Ecolab to stay connected with its customers as their needs evolved.

Baker championed an important tool in change management and culture shaping: public acknowledgment through promotions and recognition. Lorsch and McTague write:

> Baker also emphasized the importance of meritocracy in motivating employees to carry out business goals. 'People watch who gets promoted,' he says. Advancement and other rewards were used to signal the kind of behavior that was valued at the company. Baker found that public acknowledgment mattered even more than financial incentives over time. 'What do you call people out for, what do you celebrate, how do people get recognized by their peers? The bonus check is not unimportant, but it is silent and it's not public," he points out. Kudos went to managers who delegated decisions to customer-facing employees and encouraged them to take the lead when they showed initiative.

This collaborative approach across divisions had long-lasting positive effects on the new Ecolab:

> As frontline employees were rewarded for owning customer relationships and coordinating with one another, a culture of autonomy emerged. (This also freed up senior management time, allowing executives to focus on broader issues.) Once people throughout the ranks felt trusted, they in turn trusted the company more and began to view their work and their mission— to make the world cleaner, safer, and healthier—as real contributions to society. And in their enhanced roles, they could see firsthand how they were making customers' lives better. This shift took time, though, because the process had to happen again and again with each acquisition.

"When we buy businesses, they're not going to love the new company right away," Baker says. "Love takes a while."

Conclusion

Leading up to Day 1 is a sprint. Post-close is marathon. While Day 1 is an exciting—and important—milestone and should rightly be celebrated, there is still much work to do after Day 1—but it's finite. The goal, remember, is to create a fully integrated and aligned organization—strategically and operationally—that can achieve the promise of the deal thesis. With thorough planning and disciplined execution, that goal is attainable—helping the organization to achieve greater returns and create even greater value than employees, investors, customers, and the board expect.

CHAPTER 9

Can the Board Avoid the Synergy Trap?

Tools for the Board

Directors have the primary fiduciary duties of loyalty and care in fulfilling their responsibilities. The duty of care asks whether they have acted as "ordinary and prudent people would act under similar circumstances." Boards are routinely given a board book that reviews the strategy and valuation of the deal that management is promoting, and directors will certainly ask several questions based on the information they are given. But are they asking the right questions or having the right discussions, given that so many bad deals make it out of the boardroom?[1]

Although acquiring boards are protected by the broad protections of the business judgment rule, what if directors asked the questions that ordinary prudent people might ask regarding these major capital investment decisions? For example, how much shareholder value are we putting at risk if synergies don't materialize? Does it make a difference for our investors if we pay with cash versus stock? What percentage reduction in cost or percentage increase in revenues are we promising our investors (and telling the market), and are those beliefs at all sensible or plausible? Do we know how much the integration will cost, and how many people will be involved? Do we have a clear structure in place that will guide the process for integration planning before closing with a real business plan? And what if there were tools that could quickly raise major red flags that would drive specific questions to management about the viability of the proposed deal and help spot the high-probability losers?

Directors need more and better information about proposed deals before they cast their votes. Remember that negative market reactions are often driven by a gap between what management believes and what investors perceive, so presumably boards will want useful lenses to stress test deal economics, the messages CEOs are about to give the market, and the level of preparation required to immediately begin delivering on their promises. Indeed, no longer would any board worth its salt rely merely on an investment banker's fairness opinion to justify the payment of a significant acquisition premium.

This chapter offers several simple analytical tools and straightforward questions that can help boards spot those deals that are likely to result in negative market reactions and drive more informed discussions about potential material deals. The tools include:

- *Shareholder Value at Risk (SVAR)*, which is a measure of the materiality of a deal.

- The *PMI Board Pack*, which sits alongside the valuation and strategic rationale in M&A board packages.

- The *Meet the Premium (MTP) Line* and *Plausibility Box*, which plot the point of cost and revenue synergies, as will be reflected in the investor presentation, to see if the proposed deal lies above or below the line and if the combination is plausible based on company and industrial history of synergy realization.

- The *Capabilities/Market Access Matrix* and the *Synergy Mix*, which are another sanity check of whether or not the proposed combination of cost versus revenue synergies makes sense given the nature of the assets coming together.

These tools will help close the gap between what management believes and what investors are likely to perceive *before* the market does. Senior management—it should go without saying— should know the answer to all these questions before the board gets involved. With these tools, boards will be better able to answer the fundamental question: *How will this transaction affect our share price and why?*

Shareholder Value at Risk

In chapter 4 we made the case that the purchase price of an acquisition is typically driven by the pricing of other comparable acquisitions ("compaqs," or precedent transactions)—often without a rigorous assessment of where, when, and how management can drive real performance gains. At the minimum, boards should be able to articulate how much shareholder value is immediately put at risk by their decision to approve a deal. Further, other choices that management recommends—particularly using cash versus stock to pay for the deal—impact the risks that boards should be able to understand.[2]

Before committing to a major deal, both parties will need to assess the effect on each company's shareholder value should the synergy expectations embedded in the premium fail to materialize. In other words, boards must ask "What percentage of our company's market value are we betting on the success or failure of the acquisition?"

A useful tool for acquirers assessing the relative magnitude of synergy risk is a straightforward calculation we call Shareholder Value at Risk (SVAR). SVAR is simply the dollar premium paid for the acquisition divided by the market value of the acquiring company's shares before the announcement is made.

This index also can be calculated as the percentage premium multiplied by the market value of the target relative to the acquirer. We think of it as a "bet your company" index, or a measure of the materiality of a deal, which shows how much of your company's shareholder value is at risk if no post-acquisition synergies are realized. The greater the percentage premium paid to sellers and the greater their market value relative to the acquiring company, the higher the SVAR. As we've discussed, it's possible for acquirers to lose even more than their premium (if there is damage done to stand-alone growth value of either company). In these cases, SVAR *underestimates* risk.

The use of cash versus stock as the method of payment has profound ramifications for the shareholders of both acquiring and target companies, and a substantial impact on SVAR. In a cash deal, the roles of the two parties are clear-cut, and the exchange of money for shares completes a simple transfer of ownership. But an exchange of shares presents a far less clear picture of who is the buyer and who is the seller. In some cases, the shareholders of the target company can end up owning most of the acquirer that bought their shares.[3]

Companies that pay for their acquisitions with stock share both the value and the risks of the transaction with the shareholders of the company they acquire. The decision to use stock instead of cash can also affect shareholder returns. Past research on M&A has consistently found that, at the time of announcement and beyond, shareholders of acquiring companies fare worse in stock transactions than they do in cash transactions. What's more, the findings from our M&A study confirm this and show that early performance differences between cash and stock transactions get greater—much greater—over time.[4]

Despite their obvious importance, these issues are often given short shrift. Boards, executives, and journalists tend to focus mostly on the prices paid for acquisitions. It's not that it's wrong to focus on price; price is certainly an important issue confronting both sets of shareholders. But when companies are considering making—or accepting—an offer for an exchange of shares, the valuation of the company in play becomes just one of several factors that managers and investors need to consider. Let's look at the basic differences between stock and cash deals.

Back to basics: cash versus stock trade-offs

The main distinction between cash and stock transactions is this: In cash transactions, acquiring shareholders take on the entire risk that the present value of synergies embedded in the acquisition premium will not materialize. In stock transactions, that risk is shared with target's shareholders. More precisely, in stock transactions, the synergy risk is shared in proportion to the percentage of the combined company the acquiring and target shareholders each will own.

To see how that works, let's look at a hypothetical example. Homeland Technologies wants to acquire Affurr Industries. Homeland has a market capitalization of $5B, made up of 50 million shares priced at $100 per share. Affurr's market capitalization now stands at $2.8B—40 million shares each worth $70. The executives of Homeland estimate that by merging the two companies, they can create an additional synergy value of $1.7B. They announce an offer to buy all the shares of Affurr at a price of $100 per share. The value placed on Affurr is therefore $4B, representing a premium of $1.2B over the company's preannouncement market value of $2.8B.

The expected net gain to the acquirer from an acquisition, the net present value (NPV), is the difference between the estimated present value of the synergies obtained through the acquisition and the acquisition premium (as we defined in chapter 1). If Homeland chooses to pay cash for the deal, then the NPV for its shareholders is simply the expected present value of synergy of $1.7B less the $1.2B premium, or an expected gain of $500M.

But if Homeland decides to finance the acquisition by issuing new shares, the NPV for its existing shareholders will be reduced. Let's suppose that Homeland offers one of its shares for each of Affurr's shares. The new offer places the same value on Affurr as did the cash offer. But on the deal's completion, the acquiring shareholders will find that their ownership in Homeland has been reduced. They will own only 55.5 percent of a new total of 90 million shares outstanding (50 million original plus 40 million new) after the acquisition. Their share of the acquisition's expected NPV is only 55.5 percent of $500M, or $277.5M. The rest goes to Affurr's shareholders, in addition to the premium, who are now shareholders in an enlarged Homeland.

The only way that Homeland's original shareholders can obtain the same NPV from a stock deal as from a cash deal will be by offering Affurr fewer new shares. They could try to justify this approach by pointing out that each share would be worth more with the expected synergies included. In other words, the new shares would reflect the value that Homeland's executives believe the combined company to be worth rather than the $100-per-share pre-announcement market value.

But while that kind of deal sounds fair in principle, in practice Affurr's shareholders are unlikely to accept fewer shares unless they are convinced that the valuation of the merged company will turn out to be even greater than Homeland's estimate. In light of the disappointing track record of acquirers, particularly in stock deals, this is a difficult sell.

On the face of it, then, stock deals offer the shareholders of the target company the chance to profit from the potential synergy gains that the acquirer expects to make above and beyond the premium. That's certainly what the acquirers will tell them. The problem is that the shareholders of the target company will also have to share the risks.

Let's suppose that Homeland's purchase of Affurr is completed with an exchange of shares, but none of the expected synergies materialize. In an all-cash deal, Homeland's shareholders would shoulder the entire loss of the $1.2B premium paid for Affurr. But in an all-stock deal, their loss is only 55.5 percent of the premium. The remaining 44.5 percent of the loss—$534M—is borne by Affurr's shareholders.

In many takeover situations, the acquirer will be so much larger than the target that the target's shareholders will end up owning only a negligible proportion of the combined company. In that case, the target's board must decide whether they would recommend a decision to own the acquirer's shares in the first place (and worry less about the plan).

So let's see what the SVAR numbers are for our hypothetical deal. Homeland was proposing to pay a premium of $1.2B, and its own market value was $5B. In a cash deal, its SVAR would therefore be 1.2 divided by 5, or 24 percent (or relative size of 56% ($2.8B/$5B) times the percentage premium of 43%). But if Affurr's shareholders are offered stock, Homeland's SVAR decreases because some of the risk is transferred to the target's shareholders. To calculate Homeland's SVAR for a stock deal, you must multiply the all-cash SVAR of 24 percent by the percentage that Homeland will own in the combined company, or 55.5 percent. Homeland's SVAR for an all-stock deal is therefore just 13.3 percent (see table 9-1).

The SVAR for a mix of cash and stock is the weighted average of the percentage of the deal value from cash times the all-cash SVAR plus the percentage of the deal value from stock times the all-stock SVAR, so SVAR for a combination deal will be somewhere in between the SVAR for an all-cash or all-stock deal based on the mix of cash and stock. Using the data above for Homeland, with a mix of 50 percent cash and 50 percent stock, would yield an SVAR of 18.7 percent $((0.5 \times 24\%) + (0.5 \times 13.3\%))$.

A variation of SVAR, what we call "Premium at Risk," can help shareholders and the board of a selling company assess their risks if the synergies don't materialize. The question for sellers is, What percentage of the premium is at risk in a stock offer? The answer is simply the percentage of ownership the seller will

TABLE 9-1

Acquirer SVAR% in all-cash versus all-stock deals

Ratio of stand-alone value of target to stand-alone value of acquirer

		.25	.50	.75	1.00
ALL-CASH DEAL					
	30	7.5	15	22.5	30
	40	10	20	30	40
Premium (%)					
	50	12.5	25	37.5	50
	60	15	30	45	60
ALL-STOCK DEAL[a]					
	30	3.75	7.5	11.25	15
	40	5	10	15	20
Premium (%)					
	50	6.25	12.5	18.75	25
	60	7.5	15	22.5	30

[a] Acquirer owns 50% of the combined company

have in the combined company. In our hypothetical deal, the Premium at Risk for Affurr's shareholders is 44.5 percent (40 million new shares divided by 90 million total shares outstanding). Once again, the Premium at Risk calculation is actually a conservative measure of risk, as it assumes that the value of the independent businesses is safe and only the premium is at risk. But as many acquirers have demonstrated, unsuccessful deals can cost both parties more than just the premium.

How Can Companies Choose?

Given the dramatic effects on value that the method of payment can have, boards of both companies have a fiduciary responsibility to incorporate those effects into their decision-making processes. Acquirers must be able to explain to their shareholders why they will have to share the synergy gains of the transaction with the shareholders of the target. For their part, the target's shareholders, who are being offered stock in the combined company, must be made to understand the risks of what is, in reality, a new investment. All this makes the board members' job more complex.

Questions for the acquirer

The management and the board of an acquiring company should address two economic questions before deciding on a method of payment. First, are the acquiring company's shares undervalued, fairly valued, or overvalued? Second, what is the risk that the expected synergies needed to pay for the acquisition premium will not materialize? The answers to these questions will help guide companies in making the decision between a cash and a stock offer. Let's look at each question in turn.

Valuation of acquirer's shares. If the acquirer believes that the market is undervaluing its shares, then it should not issue new shares to finance a transaction, because to do so would penalize current shareholders. Research consistently shows that the market takes the issuance of stock by a company as a sign that management— who is in a better position to know about its long-term prospects— believes the stock to be *overvalued*. Thus, when management chooses to use stock to finance an acquisition, there's plenty of reason to expect that company's stock to fall.

What's more, management teams that offer what they believe to be undervalued stock to pay for an acquisition often base the price of the new shares on the current "undervalued" market price rather than on the higher value they believe their shares are worth. This can cause a company to pay more than it intends, and in some cases to pay more than the acquisition is worth. Suppose that Homeland believed that its shares are worth $125 per share rather than $100. Its managers should value the 40 million shares it plans to issue to Affurr's shareholders at $5B, not $4B. Then if Homeland thinks Affurr is only worth $4B, it ought to offer Affurr's shareholders no more than 32 million shares.

In the real world, though, it's not easy to convince a disbelieving seller to accept fewer but "more valuable" shares. If an acquiring company's executives believe that the market significantly undervalues their shares, their logical course is to proceed with a cash offer. Yet the same CEOs who publicly declare their company's share price to be too low will cheerfully issue large amounts of stock at that "too low" price to pay for their acquisitions. Which signal is the market more likely to follow?

Synergy risks. The decision to use stock or cash also sends signals about the acquirer's estimation of the risks of failing to achieve the expected synergies from the deal. A really confident acquirer would be expected to pay for the acquisition with cash so that its shareholders would not have to give any of the anticipated synergy gains to the target's shareholders beyond the premium.

But if management believes the risk of not achieving the required level of synergy is substantial, it can be expected to try to hedge its bets by offering stock. By diluting its company's ownership interest, it will also limit participation in any losses incurred either before or after the deal goes through. Once again, though, the market is well able to draw its own conclusions. Indeed, empirical research, including ours, consistently finds that the market reacts significantly more favorably to announcements of cash deals than stock deals.

Stock offers, then, send two powerful signals to the market: that the acquirer's shares are overvalued and that its management lacks confidence in the acquisition. In principle, therefore, an acquirer that is confident about integrating an acquisition successfully, and believes its own shares to be undervalued, should always proceed with a cash offer. A cash offer neatly resolves the valuation problem for acquirers that believe they are under-valued as well as for sellers uncertain of the acquiring company's true value.[5]

But it's not always so straightforward. Quite often, for exam-ple, an acquirer does not have sufficient cash resources—or debt capacity—to finance a cash offer. In that case, the decision is much less clear-cut, and the board must judge whether the addi-tional costs associated with issuing undervalued shares still jus-tify the acquisition.

Questions for the seller

In the case of a cash offer, the selling company's board faces a straightforward task. It has only to compare the value of the com-pany as an independent business against the price offered. The only risk is that it could hold out for a higher price or that man-agement could create more value if the company remains inde-pendent. The latter case certainly can be hard to justify.

Let's suppose that Affurr's shareholders are offered $100 per share, representing a 43 percent premium on the current $70 price. Let's also suppose, without considering taxes, that they can get a 10 percent return by putting this cash in invest-ments with a similar level of risk. After five years, the $100 would compound to $161. If the bid were rejected, Affurr would have to earn an annual return of more than 18 percent on its cur-rently valued $70 shares to do as well. So uncertain a return must compete against a bird in the hand.

More than likely, though, the target company's board will be offered stock or some combination of cash and stock and so will also have to value the shares of the combined company being offered to its shareholders. In essence, shareholders of the target will be partners in the post-merger enterprise and will therefore have as much interest in realizing the synergies as the sharehold-ers of the acquirer. If the expected synergies do not materialize or if other disappointing information develops after closing, the target's shareholders may well lose a significant portion of the premium received on their shares.

If a target company's board accepts an exchange-of-shares offer, it is endorsing not only the offer as a fair price for the company's shares, but also the idea that the combined company is an attractive investment—so it needs to evaluate the deal logic and integration plan (see the PMI Board Pack below). Essentially, then, the board must act in the role of a buyer as well as a seller, and must go through the same decision process that the acquiring company follows before it recommends an investment decision on behalf of their shareholders.

No matter how a stock offer is made, the target's shareholders should never assume that the announced value is the value they will realize before or after closing. Selling early may limit exposure, but that strategy carries costs because the shares of target companies typically trade below the offer price during the pre-closing period. Of course, shareholders who wait until after the closing date to sell their shares of the merged company have no way of knowing what those shares will be worth at that time.

The questions we have discussed here—How much is the acquirer worth? How likely is it that the expected synergies will be realized?—address the economic issues associated with the decisions to offer or accept a particular method of payment for a merger or acquisition. There are other issues of tax treatment and accounting that the advisers of both boards will seek to bring to their attention. But those concerns should not play a key role in the evaluating SVAR.

The PMI Board Pack

As we discussed at length in chapters 6, 7, and 8, post-merger integration (PMI) is a highly complex process. The pace, importance, and sheer number of decisions that will need to be made for a merger far outstrip the normal rate of decision-making.

Combining two organizations with distinct cultures while trying to manage business as usual and protect the day-to-day cash flow is daunting. In most organizations, PMI is not a core skill.[6]

Directors must feel confident that the claims of management are supported by at least the foundations of an integration plan before approving a deal—and senior executives, knowing this, should be prepared by all of the work they have done to assess the deal. Ultimately, investors will want to feel confident that management has a plan.

Boards are regularly presented with a review of the strategy and valuation of the deal, often supported by a fairness opinion, but there is usually little about how the companies will be integrated. The PMI Board Pack is designed to help the board ensure that senior management is ready to avoid the common pitfalls of PMI. As a summary for board members, there are four major reasons that PMI efforts fail to deliver what has been promised:

1. **Loss of focus:** There is little structure to the PMI so executives and employees are distracted from running the businesses and worrying about customers and competitors. Employees spend a lot of time looking for other opportunities.

2. **Wasted time:** The organization does not appear able to begin generating synergies at closing so the present value of any synergies eventually obtained is greatly reduced. As delays continue, employees lose confidence in the deal's strategic rationale and competitors have time to respond. Management fails to prioritize and make tough decisions, either not addressing the big, tough decisions early, or getting mired in slow decision-making processes.

3. **Competitor reactions and changing business environment:** The PMI is carefully planned but lacks a structure that will allow the organization to quickly revisit and modify plans as needed. In short, the PMI becomes so internally

focused that the organization is not prepared to respond to changing business conditions.

4. **Failure to follow through on plans:** The PMI focuses on designing the new organization and delivering early synergies but not on resolving the thousands of bottom-up issues to transition the organization through the end-state vision. The result is a failure to deliver the new organization needed to support the businesses and achieve the synergy targets.

During its review of the deal, the board is in a unique position to ensure not only that a proposed transaction makes sense strategically and financially but also that the groundwork has been laid to deliver the promised results. Without such plans, deal value may begin to leak. By making specific demands of senior management, directors can have a tremendous influence on the outcome. Before a deal is approved by the board and announced publicly, senior management should present the following five essential elements:

1. A *PMI process calendar* showing phasing of activities and decisions

2. The *key top-level shaping decisions* to be made up front

3. A *tailored integration approach* that is clearly articulated

4. The *structure, teams, and resourcing* to deliver the PMI

5. The *business plan* that delivers the performance promises for the deal

PMI process calendar

A successful PMI is a structured series of events that begins long before and continues long after the deal closes. A proposed calendar of activities, along with a timetable of what is to follow, should give the board a good view of the phasing of PMI activities. In many disastrous transactions, the CEOs have stated for the record that there was little in the way of PMI planning. By reviewing a calendar and timetable, the board could have easily seen the problems that were to come. In fact, by the time directors even consider an M&A proposal, the PMI process planning should already be well underway. At this stage, there are hundreds, if not thousands of key decisions yet to be made. Yet, senior management should be able to discuss the basic elements of a PMI plan.

Senior management will not be able to go into the detail that we lay out earlier in the book, but they can walk the board through an overview of the phases of a typical PMI, how they will be addressed, and on what timeline. Those phases are:

- Up-front planning and direction setting

- Data gathering

- Design and decision-making

- Implementation

Up-front planning and direction setting coincide with due diligence and valuation work. In hostile transactions, it will have to be completed only with publicly available information on the target. At this point, senior management determines the integration approach and the broad outline of the new operating model (which connects a company's deal thesis and business objectives with its processes, capabilities, and organizational structure), and makes key decisions on timing, team structures and roles, resource allocation, and performance targets. These elements, which form the rest of the PMI Board Pack, must be in place before the deal is announced.[7]

Data gathering and analysis, which began during diligence and can now be readily facilitated, should begin immediately following Announcement Day. Integration workstreams will collect information on the current operations of the two organizations, then share and compare them to identify key differences and similarities—particularly with an eye toward major integration activities and synergies. Clear guidelines must be established, with the help of legal counsel, for what data can and cannot be shared between the two companies prior to closing and what competitively sensitive data will have to be put into a clean room. Analysis will examine such issues as establishing the financial baseline for the combined organization, and how to stabilize the businesses during PMI.

Design and decision-making will include issues like integration opportunities consistent with the new operating model, organization design, synergy targets, and integration workplans that will deliver results. This will start as data is shared and, depending on the speed of regulatory approval, will likely continue after closing once the clean rooms are open. In this critical phase, which will begin to shape the new company, teams gain a deeper understanding of each company's history, culture, strategies, and decision-making styles. This understanding should emerge as integration options for the new company are developed, evaluated, and debated. The recommendations developed in this phase need to deliver the promised synergies.

Implementation starts at deal closing and continues until all key integration steps are taken—which may take as much as a year to 18 months after closing. At this point, a management priority is leading the transition from an integration team structure to business as usual in the new organization. This must include rigorous integration and synergy tracking that maintains high visibility of synergy commitments and accountability for the actions needed to deliver them, in addition to preserving the momentum of the underlying businesses.

The point here is, again, that the management team will not have all of the answers. But they should be able to present a calendar and timeline outlining all of these steps, as well as early principles that will guide the merger.

Key top-level shaping decisions

At the outset, several key decisions need to be made—or deliberately postponed—by the senior team for the PMI to move forward. These shaping decisions focus on integration scope and high-level organizational issues. They include what parts of the two companies are being fully integrated, for instance, and other top-level decisions like who will be the CEO (L0), their direct reports (L1), and initial details of changes to the operating model and the structure of the new organization.

The extent and nature of these up-front decisions will depend on the situation, but in general these decisions are not easily delegated to an integration decision-making structure. Some of these decisions might have been a critical part of the deal negotiation.

Some important decisions may have to be deliberately postponed. In a recent financial services merger, for example, the issue of how to merge the two branch networks was postponed for some time because of significant strategic branding issues that needed time to resolve, and because of data-protection laws that would constrain the sharing of customer data. Again, not all details will be available, but these shaping decisions, which help to set the direction for the new organization and have significant impact, should be made clear to the board.

Tailored integration approach

Few issues pervade organizational life during PMI more than uncertainty. If this uncertainty is not managed well, it will become destructive and almost surely undermine the process. Because all M&A deals are different, the senior team must agree on a clear, tailored approach to the PMI and be prepared to clearly communicate this to the board. This approach will include the scope of the integration, as well as its pace, tone, early integration priorities, and how key decisions will be communicated and when (see chapter 6 for more details).

If expectations are being set for the new organization—and they are—then the board should be privy to what those expectations are. The senior team must make sure the approach is logical given the deal thesis that is guiding the acquisition and forms the heart of the deal, and that their subsequent actions are consistent with the expectations they set for their organization.

In times of tension, management and employees will need to feel confident the senior team is "on the same page." Mistakes in approach can lead to PMI failures that will later likely be blamed on culture clash. By exercising careful oversight, the board can pressure test the approach and help management avoid this pitfall.

Structure, teams, and resourcing

After key decisions are made and the approach to the integration is clear, a discrete integration structure, separate from running the individual businesses, is needed to manage the PMI. Senior management cannot be fully involved in the thousands of decisions, large and small, that must be made during PMI. Therefore, empowered PMI teams must be created with clear roles, responsibilities, and reporting relationships to make clear recommendations for top management (the SteerCo) to ratify.

Central to this is the Integration Management Office (IMO) and the workstreams that it oversees. The IMO and its workstream teams facilitate the structured collection of information on the companies and create early working relationships between the companies that will make possible some early successes. Teams within the IMO structure also drive the bottom-up approach that, combined with a tight calendar, forces senior management to make or ratify tough decisions and maintain momentum in the process. The board should have a view of the IMO and major workstreams, and who will be taken off day-to-day business to focus the integration, how many other staff will assist and for how long, and how much any external support will cost.

Senior management should also consider how to resource the PMI teams, especially the IMO. It is not unusual for 10 percent or more of senior and middle management to be heavily involved in the PMI process. Because these managers should be the most talented people from either organization, who and how much time will be required must be clear so that focus is not lost in keeping the ongoing businesses competitive during the PMI.

In short, the board should understand this structure, the key executives within the structure, and the likely timing and level of HR needed to drive the integration process—consistent with the chosen integration approach.

The business plan

Senior management must devise and present to the board a credible business plan for the new entity that spells out the synergy targets, major initiatives and goals, and one-time costs of the integration effort. Of course, all of that might be presented in the valuation, so the board should understand these broad targets and how management expects to achieve them—including the new operating model and any potential go-to-market strategy changes that will drive growth synergies or cost savings and justify the premium. It should be clear to the board that these synergy targets exceed a "baseline" of what the two firms were expected to achieve if the merger had never taken place. The detail of the business plan will evolve as the PMI moves forward from initial top-down synergy targets through to final synergy commitments built into internal budgets and plans.

Synergies are often not developed with sufficient rigor and may be buried in financial plans, or even the valuation, with little clarity or visibility. This can make it virtually impossible to know 6–12 months later whether any synergies have actually been achieved. To give performance targets more visibility, the board should see some additional integration measures and milestones, such as the timing of projected labor and non-labor synergies, facility closings, or new product offerings, so that the board can later assess the progress of the integration effort at future meetings.

The business plan is an operationalization of the business case and deal thesis: why the merged organizations will beat the performance trajectories already built into both companies' share prices, and how it will offer more of what customers want and can get nowhere else, in ways not easily replicated by competitors. The integration process involves refining and gaining commitment to the business plan. The board must see not only a broad plan, but a process for testing, adjusting, and then keeping score against the plan during the implementation phase.

The PMI Board Pack offers the board an opportunity with every deal to assess these five elements—the calendar and phases of activities; top-level shaping decisions; the integration approach; structure, teams, and resourcing; and the business plan that delivers the performance promises for the deal.

To the last point—the business plan—we offer a suite of tools to help the board stress test that the financial goals of the deal are sound and plausible before they are presented to investors on Announcement Day.

The Meet the Premium Line and Plausibility Box

While much has been written about the shortcomings of relying on earnings accretion and market multiples to reach acquisition decisions, short-term earnings accretion to the acquirer remains one of the most popular thresholds in judging whether or not to do a deal. It's also typically the first order of business in investor presentations. So rather than present one more argument against the popular use of earnings in evaluating M&A transactions, we show here how to use earnings-based financial information in a way that would be much more useful to senior executives and boards before they agree to pay a significant premium for another company.[8]

For any transaction with a significant SVAR (with significance to be set by the board), we present a simple "earnings" model for the target that yields combinations of cost reductions and revenue enhancements that would justify a given premium. This way, any talk of a deal being accretive to earnings—along with the logic of the deal—can then be readily scrutinized in operating terms that are familiar to most corporate managers and investors. While this is no substitute for a properly executed DCF valuation, it is another way of enabling boards to avoid obvious mistakes—especially when deals appear to be "accretive." Our approach also yields some simple metrics that allow a sanity check of the PMI business plan.[9]

The equity market value of a public target (MV_T) prior to the acquisition announcement can be expressed as a multiple (P/E_T) of its after-tax earnings (E_T) as follows:

(1) $MV_T = E_T \times P/E_T$

When an acquirer offers a premium (%P) for the target company, the dollar value of the premium offered is simply the product of the premium (%P) and the pre-announcement target equity market value (MV_T).

That offer premium can also be stated in terms of the after-tax earnings of the target (E_T) and its price-earnings multiple (P/E_T):

(2a) $\%P \times MV_T = \%P \times (E_T \times P/E_T) = (\%P \times E_T) \times P/E_T$

Equation (2a) implies that, in order to earn the dollar premium offered for the target, the target's after-tax earnings (E_T) must increase by %P and then be maintained *in perpetuity*. But this assumes that the earnings multiple (P/E_T) of the target remains unchanged.[10] Assigning the same P/E also assumes that any earnings improvement from synergies will be assigned the same P/E as the pre-deal P/E.[11]

To illustrate: If an acquirer offers a 20 percent premium over the target's pre-announcement market value (and provided we assume a constant P/E), the target must generate a 20 percent increase in after-tax earnings. Substituting pre-tax profit margin (Π), revenue (R), and the effective tax rate (T) for E_T, we have an expression of the incremental after-tax earnings required:

(2b) $\%P \times E_T = \%P \times (R \times \Pi) \times (1 - T)$

Because this increase in after-tax earnings must be delivered through the generation of *pre*-tax synergies, these pre-tax synergies—$\%P \times (R \times \Pi)$—are our focus.

Some acquirers focus exclusively on cost reduction or revenue improvement, but the more common approach is to seek a combination of the two.

In the case where an acquirer intends to earn the acquisition premium entirely through cost reductions, we define *%SynC* as equal to the pre-tax earnings improvement required as a percentage of the pre-acquisition addressable operating cost base of the target. We find *%SynC* to be a useful measure of how challenging it will be for an acquirer to justify the acquisition premium from an operational perspective. By putting the cost reduction in percentage terms, a CEO or business leader would need to defend the feasibility of the reduction.

(3a) $\%SynC = \dfrac{\text{Pre-tax synergies required}}{\text{Operating cost base}}$

Alternatively, using both pre-tax operating profit margin (Π) and revenues (R) to reflect the operating cost base in the denominator, we arrive at the following expression:

(3b) $\%SynC = \dfrac{\%P \times (\Pi \times R)}{(1 - \Pi) \times R} = \%P \times \dfrac{\Pi}{1 - \Pi}$

Equation (3b) shows that, by considering just the percentage takeover premium and the pre-tax operating profit margin (which we set as EBIT), the proposed pre-tax earnings improvement from a deal can be quickly evaluated from percentage cost reductions alone. So, for example, a proposed deal at a 35 percent premium on a target with an 18 percent pre-tax margin will require a 7.7 percent $[0.35 \times (0.18/(1 - 0.18))]$ decrease in operating costs to achieve enough pre-tax profit improvement to justify the premium and just break even. And remember, for those cost reductions to represent synergistic gains from the merger, the cost savings would have to come on top of any reductions already expected in the stand-alone plans of the two companies.

Although this may be intuitively obvious, the model suggests a more aggressive $\%SynC$ for higher-margin businesses for a given acquisition premium. This reflects the simple fact that a higher-margin business has a smaller percentage cost base. An aggressive $\%SynC$ in such a business requires going deeper to make a difference to the bottom line, and going deeper may mean cutting away fat and muscle—which makes meeting the premium through cost reduction more challenging.[12]

In cases with potential revenue as well as cost synergies, a simple adjustment to equation (3b) can be made to estimate the cost reductions that would be required after taking account of the benefits of the expected percentage increase in revenue, or revenue synergies (%*SynR*). In other words, the more synergy from revenue gains, the less the burden on cost reduction.

(4a) $\%SynC = \dfrac{\%P(\Pi \times R) - (R \times \%SynR \times \Pi)}{R(1 - \Pi)}$ or,

(4b) $\%SynC = \dfrac{\%P\,\Pi - \%SynR \times \Pi}{1 - \Pi} = \dfrac{\Pi}{1 - \Pi} \times (\%P - \%SynR)$

Using equation (4b), we can compute the cost synergies required to earn the offer premium for any deal, given three variables: the premium offered, the pre-tax operating margin (EBIT), and the expected percentage revenue synergies.[13] If %*SynR* equals the premium percentage, then no cost synergies would be required in this model for a given acquisition premium.

The equation yields what we call the Meet the Premium (MTP) Line. Figure 9-1 shows the MTP Line that depicts those combinations of %*SynC* and %*SynR* that generate enough pre-tax synergies to equal—but not exceed—the hurdle posed by a 35 percent premium and a pre-tax operating profit margin of

FIGURE 9-1

The MTP Line

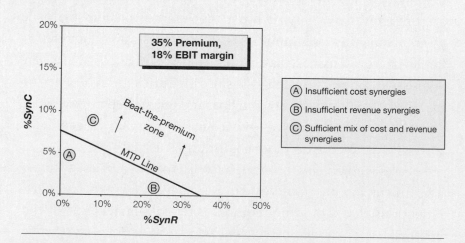

18 percent. If the expected percentage revenue increases equal the premium percentage (35% in this example), then no cost reductions would be required to justify the premium. And, as we have already shown, in the absence of any expected revenue increases, the cost reductions necessary to meet the premium are 7.7 percent. (Those endpoints effectively represent the *%SynC* or *%SynR* required to meet the premium in the absence of the other.)

The importance of the MTP Line for senior management teams and boards is straightforward: Deals whose benefits put them below the line should be avoided—or at least put under more scrutiny. Points A and B are deals an acquirer should seek to avoid, whereas the expectations for the deal represented by point C would more than justify the premium using this approach. And the higher the premium paid for the target, the larger the combination of *%SynC* and *%SynR* necessary to earn the premium. (In terms of figure 9-1, any proposed increase in the premium above 35% would call for a parallel upward shift in the MTP Line.)

This simple picture can be used to inform and guide detailed discussions about the combination of revenue and cost synergies that management believes it can achieve in a potential deal— which should become the focus of management's communication to investors. The upshot: *If you can't plot a point, what will you tell investors?*

Besides testing the competitive assumptions that would drive projected revenue synergies, several other questions need to be answered. For example, what is the addressable cost base—that is, how much of the cost base can actually be reduced (does it include overheads, indirect expenses, etc.)? Deals with a seemingly high cost base may in fact have few components that can be managed, unless the acquirer has specific capabilities to do so. It also begs the big question of what the experience has been for the acquirer, and other acquirers in the industry, in realizing synergies in similar deals.

In our experience, companies are generally more successful in reducing costs than in increasing revenue. It is easier to take out costs by, say, closing facilities and reducing headcount; these are internal issues that are controllable, visible, and tangible. Cost considerations also generally come first. They tend to be approached by fresh troops with all their energy focused on getting something done and achieving quick cost-reduction wins.

Revenues, on the other hand, are affected by competitor and customer reactions. For this reason, they are harder to anticipate and control, particularly in cases where the benefits are expected to come from cross-selling initiatives. Moreover, the analysis and commitments required for growing the revenue line are often deferred until after the businesses are stabilized and the cost issues are under control. (See chapter 8 for a more detailed discussion on revenue growth.)

That delay, however, often has unwanted consequences. Competitors are given time to react in the marketplace by protecting their customers and approaching those of the new combined firm. They will anticipate the acquirer's moves and court the best customers of the acquirer and target by playing up the disarray of the new firm and the lack of customer service that is likely to follow. Delaying the focus on revenue synergies also allows plenty of time for headhunters and competitors to poach the best salespeople. And it also often means that the organization is fatigued from the demands of PMI by the time it worries about its new go-to-market strategy and how it will serve customers in ways it couldn't before. Moreover, when cost reductions take priority over revenue growth—or are just viewed independently of it—the infrastructure required to support potential revenue growth can end up being cut.

When evaluating projected synergies, setting reasonable thresholds above which successful cost reduction and revenue improvement become implausible is critical in assessing the extent of the operating challenges associated with any deal being contemplated. In figure 9-2, we show how these thresholds form a

FIGURE 9-2

The Plausibility Box

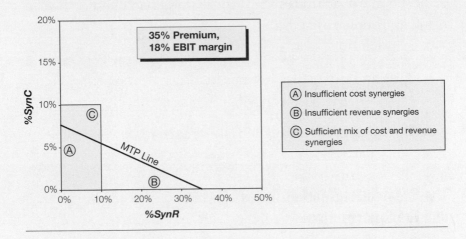

"Plausibility Box" that can be used to assess whether the envisioned combination of required synergies for a given target is reasonable, even when that point lies on or above the MTP Line.

Figure 9-2 illustrates a hypothetical box with an upper range of 10 percent operating cost reduction and 10 percent revenue synergies.[14] (Only point C is both plausible and sufficient to meet the premium.) In practice, an acquirer can set the parameters of this box any way it wishes *provided it has the supporting evidence.* The evidence can be drawn from an acquirer's experience or industry synergy benchmarks. This is also a useful sanity check tool for assessing a sensible price range, given various combinations cost and revenue synergies.

Our assumption is that synergies will begin immediately, so any expected differences in the timing of revenue versus cost synergies must be made explicit and addressed. Any projected delay in realizing the synergies required to justify any significant premium will cause investors to mark down the price of the acquirer's shares to reflect those delays right at announcement. As our M&A study clearly shows, that price reduction puts the acquirer into a hole and sets a negative tone that can affect organizational morale, especially those employees whose pension assets are invested in the acquirer's stock.

In summary, boards must consider these two questions when evaluating a proposed deal:

1. Does the proposed combination of percentage cost reductions and percentage revenue increases, the synergies, fall above the MTP Line?

2. Does that point also fall inside a range that is plausible?

The Capabilities/Market Access Matrix and the Synergy Mix

Having set the stage for those two questions, the next step in the analysis is to consider whether the proposed combination of cost and revenue synergies—even if that point falls within the Plausibility Box—makes operating sense, given the strategic intent of the deal and the assets the transaction brings together. In this section, we present a framework for having that discussion. Then we use four major deals to illustrate how it might be applied.

There is a vast literature on the effects of diversification and relatedness on the value added by M&A.[15] The objective of that literature has been to classify deals into a single category— typically "related," "unrelated," or some intermediate category— and then compare the average performance of the categories to judge which is better or worse. This literature also reflects a long history of academic debate, with a stream of conflicting findings.[16] But while the debate has provided grist for the academic mill, it has given practitioners little help in assessing specific deals. And, unfortunately, the practitioner literature on the subject has also resorted to such "categorizing." In this body of work, deals are typically referred to as "core," occupying an "adjacent" space, or constituting a "diversifying" move.[17]

The problem with putting deals into such categories is the failure to consider the very real possibility that any given deal will span a range of categories, depending on the capabilities and market access that are brought together in the combination.

Figure 9-3a presents a three-by-three matrix that we have found far more helpful in both operating and board-level discussions than assigning deals to a single category based on a vague idea of relatedness. Using our framework, deals can fall into different combinations of categories, depending on the strategy for creating value and the assets that are being combined.[18]

With the help of figure 9-3a, any deal can be characterized in terms of 1) the parts of both businesses that offer the *same* capabilities (e.g., R&D, product design, product portfolio, operations, cost structure, supply chain, systems) and market access (e.g., channels such as sales force and third-party relationships, geographic presence, brand, channel power); 2) the parts of the businesses where one company has a clear advantage over the other and is simply *better*; and 3) the parts of the businesses that bring together *new*, or non-overlapping, capabilities or market access.

The shaded zones in the Synergy Mix chart in figure 9-3b illustrate how different spaces in the Capabilities/Market Access Matrix

FIGURES 9-3A AND 9-3B

Capabilities/Market Access Matrix and Synergy Mix

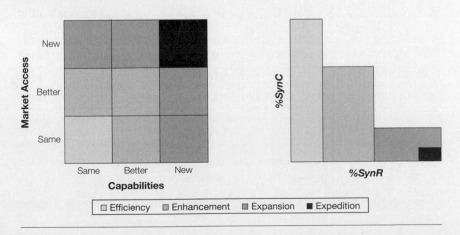

translate into different types of potential synergies, and thus map to a range of different cost and revenue synergy combinations on the %SynR/%SynC graph (on which we showed the MTP Line in figure 9-1). The result will form the basis for the mix of synergy expectations that management will hold up for investors.

Different spaces in the capabilities/market access matrix suggest the potential to yield mainly cost or mainly revenue synergies, or a combination of both. Deals that bring together the same capabilities and market access will yield mainly cost benefits ("efficiency") because of the potential for scale and redundancies. Deals that have overlap but bring better capabilities or market access can yield both revenue synergies and cost synergies ("enhancement"). And deals that bring together new capabilities or market access, with little overlap, will be expected to add value mainly through increases in revenue (referred to as "expansions" in cases where there is some overlap and as "expeditions" where there is none). Most significant deals will involve some combination of the nine spaces in the matrix. Now is the time to have these discussions.

Some examples

The 1991 Chemical Bank/Manufacturers Hanover transaction is a classic case of an "in-market" efficiency deal that would sit squarely in the lower-left corner of figure 9-3a. Thus, it would also be represented, in figure 9-3b, in the area of predominantly cost synergies. At the opposite extreme, in the upper right, is an expeditionary deal like AOL's acquisition of Time Warner, which brought together the internet and traditional media—and would be expected to yield mainly revenue synergies, as indicated in figure 9-3b. Where a deal spans a variety of different spaces in the matrix, its Synergy Mix will be the weighted average of these underlying revenue and cost synergy combinations based on their individual proportions. The resulting point—all cost, all revenue, or some combination of benefits—is the appropriate %SynR/%SynC point consistent with the assets being combined, which will lie above or below the MTP Line shown earlier in figure 9-1. Investors will want to be able to plot the point an acquirer is suggesting.[19]

Viewing deals in terms of capabilities/market access "spaces" as being the same, better, and/or new has two main benefits: Deals can be broken down and valued by their individual components; and, perhaps more important, the plausibility of projected revenue and cost synergies can be evaluated based on an assessment of whether these spaces are likely to yield cost or revenue synergies. It forces management to address the following question: In the case of a proposed deal, what point above the MTP Line makes sense, given the nature of the individual pieces that comprise the overall transaction? And if management presents a combination of revenue and cost synergies that is clearly inconsistent with the spaces a given deal occupies on the matrix, that should send a warning signal. For example, if a deal plots largely in the top-right box of figure 9-3a and management is projecting significant cost savings, with no or poorly described revenue synergies, the deal should come under intense scrutiny.

Beyond the reasonableness of the Synergy Mix, figure 9-3a also allows us to gain some insight into the likelihood of achieving improved performance in various deals. The concentration of the components of the matrix that a deal spans in figure 9-3a essentially gives what can be viewed as the *center of gravity* of the deal. As noted earlier, projections of cost synergies are generally more reliable than projections of revenue synergies. And thus, for a given premium, deals with a center of gravity closer to the lower left are generally more likely to achieve projected synergies and are easier to justify a premium—that, at least, is likely to be the perspective of investors.

Such strategic analysis has major implications for a board assessing the value of a deal, for integration planning, and for guidance in writing a winning investor presentation. When a major transaction is announced, investors are trying to understand where the value is going to come from and whether the acquirer has a plan to achieve that value. Too often, deals are brought to market with one big synergy number, without a timetable, and with a statement that the deal will be accretive to earnings. The problem, however, is that investors can't understand or track one number. Going to market with just one number also suggests that the acquirer doesn't have a credible plan, which in turn gives investors more reason to sell shares than buy, particularly when a significant premium is being offered.

A Model of How to Do It

A good example of a transaction that gave investors trackable and defendable synergy forecasts, and thus signaled the acquirer truly had a plan, was PepsiCo's $13.4B all-stock acquisition of Quaker Oats announced in December 2000.[20] (We discussed PepsiCo's investor presentation for the deal in chapter 5.)

PepsiCo's management described in detail where it expected synergies, distinguishing highly probable gains from those it anticipated but did not include in the investor model. Recall that they identified a total of $230M of synergies, which they expressed in terms of the following contributions to operating profit: $45M from increased Tropicana revenues (same capability with better market access); $34M from Quaker snack revenues sold through the Frito-Lay system (same capability with better market access); $60M from procurement savings (same/same); $65M from cost savings derived from SG&A expenses, logistics, and hot fill manufacturing (same/same); and $26M saved by eliminating corporate redundancies (same/same).

Thus, the deal had a center of gravity relatively close to the core businesses (and the lower-left spaces of figure 9-3a), and it was clear what investors—and employees—could expect in the parts of the business from where synergies were to come. They could easily see how the deal would produce improvements in operating profit and more efficient use of capital that would more than justify the modest 22 percent acquisition premium.

The management team also articulated clearly how they planned to integrate Quaker Oats and several of its brands into PepsiCo and how capabilities from both companies would be leveraged to achieve additional growth. Moreover, Roger Enrico, PepsiCo's outgoing chairman, stressed that management used conservative estimates for cost savings and revenue synergies.

PepsiCo's announcement was received positively by investors. Its shares rose by over 6 percent (nearly $4B) in the days following the announcement and continued to outperform the shares of its industry peers throughout the decade after the transaction closed in August 2001.

Like PepsiCo, Nexstar Media's $6.4B (with assumed debt) all-cash acquisition of Tribune Media, at a 20 percent premium, offered a compelling investor presentation with trackable synergies of $20M in corporate overhead savings, $65M of expense reduction from stations, and $75M of revenue synergies from net retransmission revenue applying Nexstar rates to Tribune's subscriber counts—or $160M of synergies all realized in the first year after close. (We also addressed the Nexstar acquisition in chapter 5.) Nexstar CEO, Perry Sook, emphasized the company's disciplined management team with a strong track record of M&A integration and delivering synergies (at close Nexstar increased its synergy projection to $185M).

Placing these synergy projections into figure 9-3a shows that the deal had a center of gravity close to the bottom left with $85M (same/same) from efficiencies and $75M (same capability/better market access) from revenue. That yielded a Synergy Mix consistent with the assets coming together and investors could easily plot the point of revenue and cost synergies that was above the MTP Line for an 11 percent increase (nearly $400M) in Nexstar's shares at anouncement.[21]

And Some Contrast

A different picture is provided by AOL's acquisition of Time Warner announced in January 2000, and Hercules's acquisition of BetzDearborn announced in July 1998. The AOL/Time Warner deal involved a $51B premium (56%) and brought together radically different businesses, and yet the investor presentation projected $1B in cost synergies—without any guidance as to where those synergies would come from. That deal was what we would classify as an "expedition," and thus there was no plausible basis for projecting that level of cost synergies.

The Hercules/BetzDearborn all-cash transaction involved a whopping 95 percent premium (nearly $1B) and brought together businesses that appeared to have some overlap in paper process chemicals, where $100M of cost synergies was projected in the investor presentation. But a closer look shows that Hercules competed in functional paper chemicals that improved the properties of paper while BetzDearborn sold paper process chemicals that improved the performance of paper machinery. In addition, more than half of BetzDearborn's $1.3B of revenues came from a large water treatment business in which Hercules had no presence.

While both Hercules and BetzDearborn had significant channel overlap with paper customers, the deal would have mapped mainly into the expansion and expedition spaces on the right side of our matrix in figure 9-3a. Thus, according to the Synergy Mix diagram in figure 9-3b, we would have expected to see management projections mainly of revenue synergies from cross-selling initiatives but only a modest amount of cost reduction (e.g., corporate overhead).

Figure 9-4 illustrates the case for each of the four deals.[22] The lines on the graph represent the MTP Lines as noted for each deal, and the dots represent the corresponding combination of revenue and cost synergies that were presented in the

FIGURE 9-4

Announced %SynR / %SynC points relative to MTP Lines

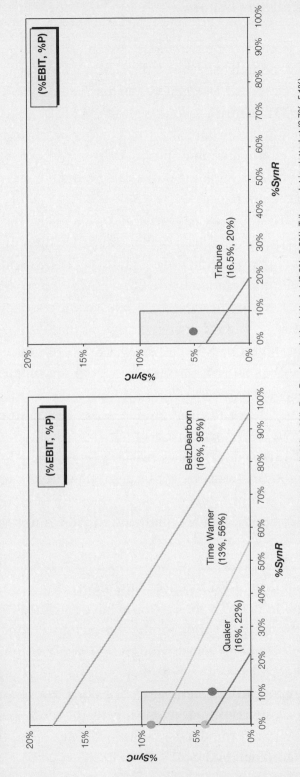

Note: Quaker dot is plotted at (10.0%, 3.6%); Time Warner dot is plotted at (3.7%, 5.1%); BetzDearborn dot is plotted at (0.0%, 4.2%); Tribune dot is plotted at (0.0%, 9.2%).

respective investor presentations.[23] While all four of those points fall within our hypothetical plausibility box from figure 9-2, only the proposed Synergy Mixes for the PepsiCo/Quaker and Nexstar/Tribune deals lie above the MTP Line. More important, the points for both PepsiCo/Quaker and Nexstar/Tribune indicate a combination of projected cost and revenue synergies that is consistent with the deal strategy and the assets that were brought together.

The $1B of pre-tax cost synergies announced for AOL/Time Warner put the deal well below the MTP Line in figure 9-4. Moreover, the resulting projected %SynC of roughly 5 percent is difficult to substantiate given the expeditionary nature of the deal (i.e., "new/new" in figure 9-3a). Not surprisingly, the initial market reaction to the announcement of the AOL/Time Warner deal was significantly negative—a 15 percent decline (or more than $30B)—and the synergies had been discounted to almost zero by the time the deal closed.[24]

Similarly, the $100M of pre-tax cost synergies projected for the Hercules/BetzDearborn deal put that transaction far below the MTP Line and without a sensible Synergy Mix. The announcement of the deal was met with a nearly 14 percent reduction (or $485M, almost half the premium) in the price of Hercules shares and the company's shares continued to fall from there.

Conclusion: The Duty of Care Imperative

Major acquisitions are only one of many governance issues on the plate of today's boards—but it is a big one. Directors now understand they will be held accountable by shareholders, especially for "bet the company" decisions. Poorly planned and executed acquisitions have almost certainly destroyed far more investor value than managerial acts of fraud. (See the sidebar, "Questions from the Board.")

Questions from the Board

We offer the following list of straightforward questions that any board can go through with its CEO on a proposed deal. If the CEO cannot answer these questions, then they are clearly not prepared to talk to investors—or the board.

- Is there evidence this deal emerged from a clear strategic process?

- How is the deal consistent with our long-term objectives for customers, markets, and products or technologies?

- What are the stand-alone expectations of the acquirer and target?

- Where will performance gains emerge as a result of the merger?

- Are the projected performance gains in line with the premium being paid?

- Which competitors are likely to be affected by the deal?

- How will those and other competitors likely respond?

- What are the milestones in a 12–18 month implementation plan?

- What additional investments (one-time costs) will be required to support the plan?

- Who are the key executives responsible for implementing the plan?

- Which pieces of either company are good candidates for sell-off or spin-off?

- Why is this deal better than alternative investments or other deals?

Although the methodology we've presented here is by no means a substitute for thorough due diligence of the deal thesis, a proper DCF analysis of a proposed deal value (see chapter 4 for our analysis of DCF valuations), and early PMI planning, it is a useful complement, and we hope it can be used to provide CEOs and boards with relatively simple but reliable guidance and the basis for active discussions with senior leadership. Where the results of our methods are at odds with the DCF analysis (or EVA assessment) and the logic of the inputs, then the *assumptions* of the DCF analysis should be investigated.

The key issue that boards must address is: *How will this deal affect our stock price and why?* The time to stress test the deal strategy, proposed benefits, valuation, integration preparation, and communications plans of the senior team is not after the deal is announced. Implementing our approach may seem challenging, but it translates to some minimum basic considerations for directors. Before approving a deal and recommending it to shareholders, directors should ensure that senior management offers a clear business case and has an operating model—and a plan—in place. And, knowing this, senior executives must be prepared to withstand such scrutiny.

CHAPTER 10

Conclusion

Getting M&A Right

Sometimes it seems like companies have a stricter approval policy for T&E expenses than they do for M&A. That's a bit of an exaggeration, but it is certainly true that most companies have capital allocation approval processes where even small investments may take months of review to get approved, while multibillion-dollar M&A deals get approved in a fraction of the time—without the same controls, processes, or discipline.

Over-eagerness to seize a target during a bidding process almost inevitably leads to a disappointing result. Wanting to get a deal done—where any deal could sound strategic, and there aren't other alternatives on the table—can lead to a willingness to race to the finish line. Due diligence glosses over problems and a valuation exists somewhere that justifies the price. It's the "Wow! Grab it! acquisition locomotive."

Predictably, Announcement Day leads to a decline in stock price when investors (including employees) realize that the numbers don't add up. The acquirer loses its focus after the celebration at announcement and can't effectively execute on pre-close planning, leading to scrambled post-close execution, demoralized employees, and disappointed customers and shareholders.

It may seem crazy, but this is the world of M&A—even though a bad deal can undo decades of smart management and growth. And all of this happens very publicly.

Initial investor reactions, positive or negative, are persistent and indicative of future returns. Investors do a pretty good job of assessing deals at announcement because that's their job. Returns on portfolios of positive reaction deals and negative reaction deals stay that way, respectively. And although some individual deals turn around, and while a positive start is no *guarantee* of future success, a negative start is very tough to reverse, with nearly two of three deals still negative a year later.

In fact, the most important practical finding from our research is the "persistence spread" of nearly 60 percentage points that separate the one-year returns on persistently positive deals—deals that have a positive market reaction and deliver—from the persistently negative ones that confirm investors' initial negative forecast. The huge benefit of starting in the right direction and delivering on that forecast should be an eye opener for any acquirer.

The problem with a bad acquisition is not just the initial market reaction and the persistence of that negative result. It's also the fact that you will drag your whole organization through the pain of the acquisition for years before a disappointing divestment—along with high exit costs to unwind the mistake. That's a tough way to learn.

We're not deal killers—quite the contrary. The promise of M&A is sustained profitable growth, an energized workforce, delighted customers, and superior shareholder returns. Trust us: If we didn't believe in the promise of M&A, we wouldn't have spent our time writing this book.

So if it's clear you should prefer a sustained positive reaction over a negative one, then the question is how to achieve it. We've argued that failures, on balance, are the result of a lack of preparation, methodology, and strategy. Most acquirers do deals only sporadically. As a consequence, they have no system in place to manage them. They lack both a strategic process that regularly refreshes their pipeline of the most important deals and a detailed integration approach for realizing projected value.

The solution we've proposed is that you become a prepared acquirer throughout the M&A cascade. Our approach applies regardless of your M&A experience and will help you achieve that initial and sustained positive reaction when you pay up front to play the acquisition game.

By working through our cascade, and becoming prepared, you greatly improve your chances of avoiding the common mistakes of the *synergy trap*—when acquirers mix up synergies that can only be achieved as a result of the deal with performance improvements already expected for the stand-alone companies. As we've seen, confusing synergies with that base case will haunt you and your employees through the entire process. Acquirers who don't fully understand the performance improvements they are paying for—the old and new—will get into trouble from the beginning. You must have the capabilities, resources, discipline, and a credible plan to deliver on those promises from Day 1 because that's when the cost-of-capital clock starts ticking on that luxurious new capital, whether or not you are prepared. Remember, an acquisition won't make you a stronger or more efficient competitor just because you say it is so, and synergies don't come for free.

It's only by understanding the whole of the process *before you even start listing targets* that you can truly be prepared. As should be clear from chapters 6–8, which focused on pre-close planning and post-close execution, you should know what you're getting into before greenlighting a deal as a path toward growth. The last thing you want to hear the day after Announcement Day is the all-too-common refrain, "I'm just coming to terms with how much work this is going to be."

Despite the enormous amount of work that's involved in becoming prepared, the good news is it's not a one-shot process— it's repeatable, so if you do it right, you can continue your M&A program. Once you've absorbed the new acquisition, you're not done. If you're executing on your overall growth thesis, then you'll already have on your watch list other important deals, with the right sets of assets, that should be part of your ongoing M&A program and fulfill the thesis.

Recap

We've laid out the book in a logical, coherent flow: from M&A strategy and the deal thesis through diligence, synergy imperatives driven by the DCF valuation, Announcement Day, pre-close planning, and post-close execution, and implications for boards. Each step is built on the lessons and decisions of the ones that came before.

In chapter 1, we named five fundamental premises of successful acquisitions. They're worth revisiting now that we've worked through the entire M&A cascade:

1. Successful acquisitions must both enable a company to beat competitors while rewarding investors.

2. Successful corporate growth processes must enable a company to find good opportunities and avoid bad ones *at the same time.*

3. Prepared acquirers (what we call "always on" companies) are not necessarily active acquirers. They can be patient because they know what they want and are prepared to act when a priority target becomes available.

4. A good post-merger integration (PMI) will not save a bad deal, but a bad PMI can ruin a good one (i.e., one that is strategically sound and realistically priced).

5. Investors are smart and vigilant. They can smell a poorly considered transaction right from announcement and they will track results.

The point is, successful M&A is challenging, but there are clear principles that will differentiate how successful acquirers think about M&A from the beginning. Now that we've worked through the cascade, the traps should be apparent and the lessons clear and actionable.

M&A strategy

The cascade exists in service of becoming prepared throughout. That begins with developing a proactive M&A strategy—the antithesis of being a reactor who leaps at deals that may appear superficially good without considering others and wastes a lot of time and money on diligence for deals they shouldn't have considered in the first place. Reactors have few priorities.

Prepared "always on" acquirers play to win instead of only playing not to lose.

They fully use their power of choice to bring strategic integrity to M&A by developing a thoughtful agenda for their capital. And they don't outsource their strategies to bankers. Prepared acquirers treat capital like it is luxurious—expensive to touch. They have developed a disciplined process allowing them to find good opportunities and avoid predictably poor or inferior ones. Most important, prepared acquirers have established priorities for their M&A program: They know what they want—and why—and how they will create value.

In short, they have determined what role M&A plays in their company's growth. They have a watch list of companies or divisions that they want to buy, and they know why each target is on the list. They also know what they *don't* want to buy and what kind of deals they seek to avoid. They have hypotheses about their competitors' strategies and, based on that, know what auctions they may need to enter for strategic reasons. Finally, they know the *next step* in their M&A growth plans, whether or not the current deal closes.

Armed with an identifiable M&A strategy, and a watch list of their most important targets, prepared acquirers enable themselves to accomplish the twin objective of successful corporate development: beating competitors and rewarding investors.

Becoming "always on" is learnable, but you must commit time and resources to the process. That includes performing an assessment of your organic growth versus investor expectations and the M&A activity of your competitors, aligning the top team on the strategic priorities and most important pathways for M&A, developing a master list of targets along priority pathways, and iteratively screening that list based on criteria that allow you to determine a watch list of the most attractive and plausible targets.

By following those steps, if you haven't done them before, you will have detailed profiles of the most important targets and documented your decisions throughout, especially for those deals that don't merit your attention. Along the way, you'll have identified the capability gaps for future growth and decided which pathways (businesses, products or services, end markets, etc.) are the most important for M&A—helping avoid the reality of the "pay me now or pay me later" problem where pathways get mixed up with more fine-grained screening criteria and questions later emerge on what the strategy was in the first place. You'll know what you want and how you'll create value and be able revisit and refresh decisions (just like your business strategies). And you'll be ready for due diligence.

Due diligence

Once you have developed an M&A strategy and are pursuing prioritized targets on your watch list, you must be prepared to test a target's potential against your investment thesis (the business case). You'll sometimes be wrong about the attractiveness of a target, and that's OK. After all, you're not looking to rush into deals. Each possible deal is an opportunity to learn and sharpen both your thesis and priorities for M&A. Some of our best advice has been to identify problems that led our clients to walk away.

Sellers will present you with pictures of their future revenues and margins—rosy ones, which is why robust diligence is necessary. The future is filled with uncertainty for both the stability of the target's current business and profitable revenue growth, and the potential of the combined entity. As a consequence, you must do diligence on both the target's current business and its future growth because you will pay not only for both but also the premium, which is based on a range of potential outcomes.

Additionally, you must earn a cost-of-capital return on all of that luxurious invested capital to satisfy investors. Remember, on Announcement Day investors will almost instinctually multiply the premium by the cost of capital to see if your synergy promises make sense.

As a consequence, take diligence seriously. A strategic due diligence process focuses on understanding a target's business, confirming how the candidate fits with your strategic objectives, discovering what cost and revenue synergies exist between the two entities and how they can be captured, and setting a purchase price. You are aiming to create a combined entity that better serves customers and produces results that beat the cost of capital on your investment.

In chapter 3, we focused on three kinds of due diligence that are at the core of a strategic process: financial, commercial, and operational. FDD goes beyond the mere baseline audited financials of the target to understand the normalized financial performance of the target's business—the baseline from which forecasts will be built. Acquirers need to have conviction about the accuracy of historical numbers and understand the business implications of those numbers.

CDD tests the growth thesis of the deal, encompassing the future revenue assumptions for recurring revenues, margins from pricing, stand-alone growth, and the benefits of the combination through a new go-to-market strategy. Primary research is the secret sauce for CDD because, as we say, all of the answers are in the market.

ODD tests the opportunity to capture cost synergies—and if they really are possible. That means assessing the current efficiency of a target's cost structure and its ongoing cost reduction initiatives, and building a bottom-up synergy model including one-time costs, timing of synergies, and interdependencies with the acquirer's operations that will either challenge or support the "magic 10 percent" offered by the target's bankers.

Diligence isn't intended to make you "comfortable"—the results will drive the inputs to your valuation and initial integration planning. At its heart, diligence is intended to reveal if *this* deal is the *right* deal. Diligence will allow you to get under the hood and identify market- and customer-related issues, as well as critical operational problems and opportunities. It is also—practically—intended to improve the sensibility of the offer price, identify operating model and integration priorities, increase confidence in your maximum bid, and minimize downside risk. If it makes you comfortable along the way, that's great.

How much do you need? No, really

Discounted cash flow (DCF) analysis is important, but it is extremely sensitive to the assumptions built into the analysis. As a consequence, it can lead to both inflated pricing of the target and the conclusion that the DCF analysis supports what you *have* to pay to do the deal rather than the maximum you *should* pay.

Evidence from our study suggests that the persistent negative group in our sample pays a higher premium than those with persistent positive results. The average premium paid by the persistent negative performers was 33.8 percent whereas the persistent positive performers paid an average premium of only 26.6 percent.

And the difference is even more pronounced in all-cash and all-stock deals. Proper valuation is essential because your model assumptions become your promises.

Instead of relying solely on DCF analysis, we introduced the well-accepted concept of economic value added (EVA) as a kind of sanity check of the DCF. The EVA approach will enable you to examine both the acquirer and target as stand-alone companies—their current operations value (COV) and future growth value (FGV)—to understand the performance trajectory already expected by investors.

The EVA approach will also allow you to understand what it means to pay the full market value of the target's shares plus an acquisition premium—a direct addition to FGV. The analysis also makes clear how the annual improvements you are promising (the synergies) translate into net operating profit after tax (NOPAT). All told, the results must show that you are properly using your capital—meaning that the promised synergies are sufficient to at least meet the cost-of-capital return on the premium. Understanding exactly what you're promising financially in the mechanics of the deal is an absolute must since your investors can, and will, do these calculations themselves—*in seconds*. This analysis will also feed the story you tell both the board when you seek its approval and the market on Announcement Day.

Dealing with the board

We put the board chapter at the end of the book, partly as an easy-to-find set of "tools for boards" but also as a summary of the kind of information you'll need to compile, analyze, and present during the process—information that is built into the M&A cascade. But of course, the board will need to approve the deal before you finalize and announce it. Both board approval and Announcement Day—and the materials that you prepare for them—are outcomes of the steps that came before: M&A

strategy formulation, landscape evaluation, target identification, and due diligence including synergies, valuation, and preliminary PMI plans.

The board should already be "read in" to your M&A strategy, so they should not be taken by surprise by the deals you
bring before them. On *this* particular deal, they're going to want
to know the answers to questions we laid out in chapter 9, questions the CEO and senior team must be prepared to answer. If
you cannot answer those questions well before the board meeting, you shouldn't be presenting the deal to the board—or to
investors.

The board should also use the tools in chapter 9 to dig into
the deal—not so much its bottom-up details but whether the deal
makes strategic and financial sense, and whether you have a sensible plan. Is this how the board thinks you should be spending
your capital relative to other possibilities?

Fundamentally, the board must know how much shareholder
value the deal will put at risk. They should be reassured about
the scope and feasibility of the plans for PMI. And the board
should also provide another sanity check on the deal as a whole,
using the Meet the Premium (MTP) Line and Plausibility Box,
reviewing whether the Synergy Mix of cost reductions and revenue increases that you are proposing is sensible given the assets
coming together, and assessing how investors will synthesize the
information they're presented.

Announcing the deal

The valuation process that was the detailed subject of chapter 4,
which also contributes to the board presentation, feeds right into
Announcement Day. That business plan is a story that you now
get to tell investors. Be ready.

In many ways, Announcement Day creates the atmosphere of
the deal: It's when you go public and address shareholders' ques-

tions, both the ones they ask and the ones they're only thinking about. Their questions are related to the ones the board asks, but investors are most especially interested in the deal logic and synergy targets, the plan to achieve them, and the premium paid. Employees and customers will have questions too. If you don't, or can't, address those fundamentals, you're in trouble. And the trouble will only compound.

Three questions take paramount importance when you're explaining a deal to investors and other stakeholders:

1. Is there a credible case with defendable and trackable synergy targets that can be accomplished by the acquirer, and monitored over time by investors?

2. Does the story help reduce uncertainty and give direction to the organization so employees can effectively deliver?

3. Does the presentation convincingly link PMI plans to the economics of the transaction?

Remember, if you *don't* answer them, investors will assume you *can't* answer them and that you don't have a plan—and they'll penalize you for it. At their heart, the three questions address one paramount issue that senior management and the board must be able to address: *How will this deal affect our stock price and why?*

Announcement Day is your first and best chance to get everyone on board—to explain the logic of the deal and how it benefits all parties—and signal you have a plan. Investor relations in M&A must contend with and help solve a classic asymmetric information problem: Management knows more about the transaction than investors, so investors can only go by what management tells them. Put another way, *you* know the deal thesis, *you* have evaluated the landscape, *you* have been through the logic of this deal repeatedly, *you* have written a board presentation, had seemingly endless discussions, done the math, prepared the premium—but no one on the receiving end of the investor presentation has.

All that means significant tactical preparation, including documenting the deal thesis and defining stakeholders to selecting communications channels and establishing the timing and presence of your leaders. Get started early and anticipate the critics.

All stakeholders will be paying attention—this is the zenith of attention the deal will get. Don't waste this pivotal moment. Use the attention carefully.

Pre-close planning

Announcement Day is not the finish line. It's the starting blocks. If you do garner an initial positive reaction—congratulations! Now the intense work begins: Pre-close planning and post-close execution are how you achieve and sustain value creation over the longer term.

Pre-close planning is rooted in the same story that started with the deal thesis and that flows into the board presentation and into Announcement Day. The topics involved in pre-close planning are themselves necessary to consider before going public with the deal. Knowing where synergies will come from and how, practically, they can be achieved should be central to the approval process for the deal, as is the new operating model—how the combined organization will run its businesses differently, and how it will generate value differently than either organization did before the merger. But the planning goes a huge step further toward the practical realization of all the things that will be necessary to integrate the workings of both companies to create the new organization—taking it from the theoretical to the practical.

That we spent two chapters on pre-close planning should tell you something about both the volume of work to do and its importance.

Because by its nature an acquisition is creating something new, few of the pre-close planning decisions are routine. From unveiling the details of a new operating model to determining how the go-forward leadership structure and roles should be created to meet deal objectives to planning for Day 1, acquirers will confront a range of issues from the large and operational, like implementing new enterprise management systems, to seemingly minor ones, like what happens to summer Friday schedules and the quality of the coffee.

Many of those non-routine decisions won't break the deal, but they all add up. Along with the big decisions, they'll need to be managed and tracked: Enter the Integration Management Office (IMO). The IMO requires influential leaders who understand the businesses. It drives the planning for the future-state operating model, prioritizes decisions, minimizes disruptions, and preserves momentum. It sets the meeting cadence for the entire process. The IMO follows up on the plans made before the deal was announced (that were developed during and after due diligence), and produces a finer-grained roadmap for success across the new organization for Day 1 and the end-state vision. It oversees the workstreams—where the real work gets done—and establishes the synergy targets for each, identifies critical interdependencies, and interfaces with the executive SteerCo on larger, more consequential decisions and approvals.

Under the IMO structure will be individual workstreams such as finance, IT, real estate, and marketing, each of which have their own leadership and charters of what they must accomplish as they build blueprints for their new functional organizations, or businesses, and how they will deliver or exceed their assigned synergy targets.

We spent an entire chapter on the major cross-functional workstreams that will involve regular coordination across the individual workstreams. Organization design works with the new enterprise operating model, the new L1 leadership, synergy targets, and the functional and business operating model choices as they design the structure and roles. Organization design will choose between two process options: 1) design roles and pick the people layer by layer; or 2) design the organization structure and roles all the way down to the ground and then pick the people.

Synergy planning—the heart of the economics of the deal logic—begins with the handoff from the deal team that did the commercial and operational due diligence and built the valuation model. Those projected synergies will be converted into actual bottom-up workplans for each workstream that has synergy targets. The synergy team works with FP&A from both companies to develop a combined functional or business baseline budget; the synergy plan is built on top of that baseline. Synergy plans evolve from initial ideas into prioritized initiatives and detailed project plans aiming to confront the dreaded leakage that can derail synergy programs.

Communication and employee experience works under the presumption that you have borrowed trust you haven't yet earned. The communications team will develop plans for all relevant stakeholders—employees, customers, vendors, unions, retirees and, of course, investors. Employee experience planning recognizes that you are not onboarding employees; they are not new recruits. The team aims to build employee confidence, establish early trust in leadership, reduce anxiety through targeted communications, and allow a mechanism for feedback so employees feel heard throughout their journey and ready for the forthcoming changes.

All of this leads to Day 1 readiness. Day 1 may seem like a daunting milestone and a never-ending list of decisions and activities. And while it is, it should be, operationally speaking, a quiet one. It is a laser-focused exercise separating absolute must-haves from nice-to-haves. Day 1 is a prioritization exercise and should be flawless because any major hiccups can spell serious consequences for morale and in kicking off the work of post-close execution.

Post-close execution

All of that pre-close planning pays off. It forms the foundation for a series of post-close transitions, when plans are put into effect.

Post-close, the IMO structure shrinks over time as workstreams graduate and the combined organization transitions to business as usual. Graduation signifies that workstreams no longer require active coordination by the IMO—and workstream leads don't have to go to any more IMO meetings. Workstreams must complete all their integration objectives and achieve their synergy targets, and interdependencies with others should be concluded such that nothing else relies on them.

The organization design team, which has been considering and planning how to combine the two workforces, moves to the talent selection and workforce transition phase. Once L2 or L3 leadership has been announced, talent selection will be based on applying agreed criteria for the new roles consistent with the chosen design option and not at odds with legal guidelines. The process must avoid "death by a thousand cuts." The team also develops leadership and employee transition plans that facilitate the knowledge transfer that must happen for the smooth operation of businesses as employees move into their new roles.

Synergy planning moves to synergy tracking and reporting. Synergy plans and results that are not managed and tracked aggressively will likely go off plan. The synergy team installs three major mechanisms: financial reporting that tracks benefits realized and their associated costs, milestone tracking for each initiative, and leading indicators that serve as a forward-looking health check that major initiatives are on track. The IMO and synergy team push an aggressive cadence for reporting results, and significant financial bonuses for achieving synergies can be a very valuable incentive.

The growth team(s) will focus on growth opportunities and designing the customer experience—achieving results that neither company could have achieved on its own. Revenue synergies present a special case of go-to-market strategy challenges and M&A can offer myriad opportunities for approaching customers and realizing new growth from cross-selling existing products, new valuable bundled offers, and new innovative products that will delight customers.

Finally, the employee experience team moves on to managing change and creating a new culture to guide all other activities. Executive teams are expected to quickly create inspiring points of view about the possibilities for the future that investors and customers find believable and demonstrate progress. They must simultaneously calm the workforce's anxieties and inspire employees as they move up their hierarchy of needs and see themselves and their futures with the new organization. These two goals require two carefully crafted—but different—messages. We said that "culture begins at announcement." Acquirers have to be careful because they, whether they realize it or not, send signals about the new culture—how work gets done around here—with their actions.

Post-close execution moves from the theoretical to empirical, from planning to doing. The merger is all about managing myriad decisions guided by all of the work that came before to fulfill the promise of the deal.

The Promise Fulfilled

In M&A, you are buying the future—recurring revenues, margins, and growth. It can be a monumental amount of work to do this right, but it's worth it. Acquisitions can create tremendous value, and value that persists.

There's something that we've heard too often when we're brought in to help with PMI or to analyze a deal gone wrong: "I raised this before we did the deal." That phrase represents the recrimination that comes from not having an effective process, or not listening to your executive team that is being signed up to lead and execute your vision.

With *The Synergy Solution* you'll have that process, which will raise and address issues, help you do the right deals, and bring your vision to reality. By working through the book, and taking the cascade seriously, you will be both informed and prepared— and able to fulfill the promise of M&A.

But getting M&A right is not just a project. It's a state change, a transformation that will affect how you approach acquisitions going forward, improving your chances of getting them right. M&A can and should produce enduring value—for the acquirer and its stakeholders, and also for the economy as a whole.

ACKNOWLEDGMENTS

Writing *The Synergy Solution* was in many ways a labor of love during our three-year journey. Contemplating the scope and essential topics for boards, executives, and managers; developing the content and examples; assessing the vast literature on M&A; and completing a major study all amounted to a grueling undertaking. *We didn't make the journey alone, however.* We benefited greatly from the depth of experience in the Deloitte M&A and Restructuring practice and several outside experts who willingly offered their time, wisdom, and, often, critiques of our many drafts.

We owe a huge debt of gratitude to our core team whose invaluable contributions made this a different book: Ami Rich, Anupam Shome, Ben Kotek, David Nathan, James Rabe, John Forster, Madhavi Rongali, Philip Garbarini, and Sauvik Kar.

But there are more—when we said we didn't make this journey alone, we were serious. The following professionals contributed their insights, perspectives, and leading practices, and we truly enjoyed working with them:

Alfredo Sakar
Amarjot Singh
Andrew Grimstone
Ayesha Rafique
Barb Renner
Bob Glass
Brian Kunisch
Brian Pinto
Brice Chasles
Bryan Barnes
Cesar Kastoun
Chris Gilbert
Chris Hutnick
Danielle Feinblum

Danny Tong
Dave McCarthy
David Hoffman
David Lashley
Deepak Subramanian
Derek Lai
Enrique Gutierrez
Eric Overbey
Franz Hinzen
Gary Levin
Gillian Crossan
Guillermo Olguin
Ian Lundahl
Ian Turner

Jared Bricklin
Jayant Katia
Jeff Kennedy
Jeffrey Canon
Jennifer Lee
Jiak See Ng
Joe Ucuzoglu
Joel Schlachtenhaufen
John Peirson
Jonathan Cutting
Joost Krikhaar
Jörg Niemeyer
Julia Rutherford
Karen Werger

Karsten Hollasch
Karthik Krishnamoorthy
Kazuhiro Fukushima
Kim Wagner
Lara Treiber
Lisa Iliff
Liz Fennessey
Mark Garay
Mark Jamrozinski
Martin Reilly
Matt McGrath
Mengyuan Hou
Michael Jeschke
Mohammad Obeidat

Monika Rolo
Orlando Taylor
Phil Colaço
Rachel McGee
Raghav Ranjan
Ram Sriram
Randall Hottle
Richard Bell
Richard Houston
Richard Paul
Ronaldo Xavier
Ryan Gordon
Saadat Khan
Samantha Parish

Sandeep Gill
Shashi Yadavalli
Simon Howard
Sridhar Kollipara
Stephanie Dolan
Stephen Dapic
Stephen O'Byrne
Steve Lipin
Steven Wolitzer
Sumit Sahni
Susan Goldsmith
Toby Myerson
Uday Bhansali
Vincent Batlle

Additionally, over the last 25 years we've been fortunate to work closely with many Deloitte leaders in the M&A and Restructuring practice who have collectively served on tens of thousands of deals and complex restructuring projects. These leaders include Adam Reilly, Andy Newsome, Andy Wilson, Anna Lea Doyle, Asish Ramchandran, Bhuvy Abrol, Chris Caruso, Dan Gruber, David Carney, Faisal Shaikh, Glen Witney, Iain Macmillan, Ian Thatcher, Jack Koenigsknecht, Jason Caulfield, Jay Langan, Jeff Bergner, John Powers, Larry Hitchcock, Mark Walsh, Mike Dziczkowski, Olivier May, Punit Renjen, Rob Arvai, Russell Thomson, Sandy Shirai, Susan Dettmar, Tanay Shah, Tom Maloney, Trevear Thomas and William Engelbrecht— our heartfelt thanks for their wisdom, encouragement, and sense of partnership.

We owe special thanks to our editor at Harvard Business Review Press, Kevin Evers, for thorough reviews and helpful suggestions; to our amazing production editor, Angela Piliouras, for tireless assistance; and to our exceptional executive assistants, Diane Kavanaugh and Kari Liljequist, and chief of staff, Sharon Piech, for their patience and flawless support.

Mark L. Sirower
Jeffery M. Weirens

Shareholder Returns from M&A

There have been hundreds of M&A studies published over the past 40 years. The articles published in volume 11 of the *Journal of Financial Economics* (1983) launched a flood of academic papers across many disciplines, resulting in now vast M&A literatures across finance, economics, management, accounting, and beyond. Academics have studied everything from shareholder performance for acquirers and targets to incentives and motivations of managers to the impact of acquisition experience and different accounting treatments.

Although studies of M&A performance tend to focus on acquirer shareholder returns around announcement (measured with different periods of days), some studies measure performance over longer periods of time. Moreover, the measurement of shareholder returns itself has varied from raw returns to market-adjusted returns, mean-adjusted returns, and the common cumulative abnormal returns (CARs) generated from so-called event studies. Scholars have also extensively studied before and after accounting-based returns such as return on assets (ROA) or return on equity (ROE).

It is also important to recognize that different studies examine different periods of time, which is natural because we have lived through several major M&A waves, and there are lots of choices on how many years to cover, which can generate varying results.

For our study, we set out to explore how acquirers' investors fared around deal announcement, which we measured as the 11-day return of five trading days before and after announcement, and how they fared over the course of one-year post announcement (including the announcement period). Both measures were adjusted by a peer index (i.e., industry adjusted) within the S&P 500, as classified by the Capital IQ platform. We used shareholder returns because companies are often judged by whether they are superior performers based on that measure. We report the mean industry-adjusted returns, often called relative total shareholder returns (RTSRs).

We drew from widely used databases and used straightforward measures that both characterize shareholder returns from M&A and are readily replicable. (Note that our overall announcement return to acquirers of –1.6% is close to Graffin, Haleblian, and Kiley's 2016 finding of –1.4% in a study that used CARs from 770 deals.)[1]

We decided to begin where Mark had left off in *The Synergy Trap* with deals announced from January 1, 1995, through December 31, 2018—a 24-year period. We assembled a preliminary sample of roughly 2,500 deals worth over $100M using Thompson ONE, where we applied the following criteria: Both companies had to be listed on a US stock exchange, the relative size of the seller to the buyer had to be at least 10% based on pre-deal equity market capitalization, and the buyer could not have completed another material deal in the year following, so that the one-year performance measurement period was not affected by other material deals.

These criteria yielded a sample of 1,267 deals representing $5.37 trillion of equity value and $1.13 trillion of premiums paid. Capital IQ was the source for buyer and seller share prices, market capitalizations, and shareholder and industry returns data (adjusted for stock splits and dividends). All data and results are reported at the mean (average value).[2]

Shareholder Returns to Acquirers: Overall Results

Adding combo deals (mix of cash and stock) to our overall findings table on shareholder returns to acquirers from chapter 1, we find a similar pattern as for all-cash ("cash") and all-stock ("stock") deals, as shown in table A-1.

Highlights

- For the 1,267 deals, industry-adjusted announcement returns are negative (–1.6% return) with 60% of deals met with a negative reaction (percent negative reaction (PNR) of 60%); 56% of deals have negative one-year returns (–2.1% return). Overall, nearly 40% of all deals are persistently negative while 23% of all deals are persistently positive.

- Cash deals significantly outperform stock and combo deals on announcement (+1.8% vs. –2.9% and –2.1%, respectively) and one-year returns (+3.8% vs. –5.7% and –1.9%, respectively). That outperformance for cash deals is also reflected by the cash PNR of only 43% versus 65% and 64% for stock and combo deals, respectively. That contrast is also shown by the percentage of persistently negative cash, stock, and combo deals (27%, 46%, and 39%, respectively) versus persistently positive deals (35%, 20%, and 19%, respectively).[3]

- Initially positive and initially negative portfolios remain significantly positive and negative over the course of one

TABLE A-1

Shareholder returns to acquirers

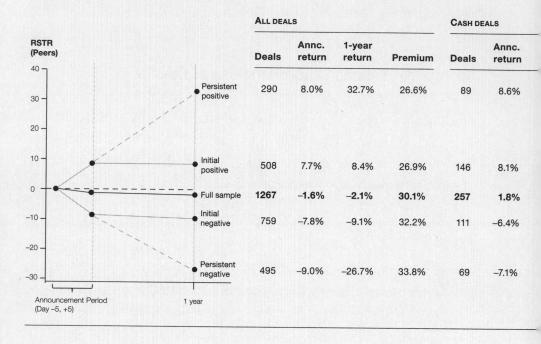

RSTR (Peers)	ALL DEALS				CASH DEALS	
	Deals	Annc. return	1-year return	Premium	Deals	Annc. return
Persistent positive	290	8.0%	32.7%	26.6%	89	8.6%
Initial positive	508	7.7%	8.4%	26.9%	146	8.1%
Full sample	1267	–1.6%	–2.1%	30.1%	257	1.8%
Initial negative	759	–7.8%	–9.1%	32.2%	111	–6.4%
Persistent negative	495	–9.0%	–26.7%	33.8%	69	–7.1%

Announcement Period (Day –5, +5)   1 year

year, respectively, for each deal type—*market reactions matter.* For example, overall, the initially positive portfolio with a +7.7% return maintains a strong positive one-year return of +8.4%, and the initially negative portfolio with a –7.8% return maintains a strong negative return of –9.1%.

- Negative reactions are more persistent than positive reactions, with 65.2% of initially negative deals remaining negative and 57.1% of initially positive deals remaining positive. Negative reaction stock deals are the most persistent with 71.1% remaining negative.[4]

- The persistence spread (the difference between the one-year returns on the persistently positive and persistently

1-year return	Premium	STOCK DEALS				COMBO DEALS			
		Deals	Annc. return	1-year return	Premium	Deals	Annc. return	1-year return	Premium
36.2%	27.6%	92	7.3%	31.1%	22.5%	109	8.0%	31.0%	29.3%
12.6%	28.6%	160	8.1%	7.2%	23.3%	202	7.2%	6.4%	28.4%
3.8%	31.1%	451	−2.9%	−5.7%	28.2%	559	−2.1%	−1.9%	31.1%
−7.8%	34.5%	291	−8.9%	−12.8%	30.9%	357	−7.4%	−6.5%	32.6%
−29.1%	36.6%	207	−9.9%	−27.4%	32.8%	219	−8.7%	−25.3%	33.7%

negative portfolios) is 59.4% overall, with cash deals having the largest persistence spread of 65.3%.

- Premiums paid get progressively higher as we move from the persistently positive through persistently negative portfolios. Overall, the premium paid for persistently negative deals is 27% higher (33.8% vs. 26.6%) than those paid for persistently positive deals. That contrast is even more pronounced for cash and stock deals, with 33% higher (36.6% vs. 27.6%) and 46% higher (32.8% vs. 22.5%) premiums paid, respectively, for the persistently negative versus persistently positive deal portfolios.[5]

Table A-2 offers some illuminating characteristics of the 1,267 deals, adding details behind the overall results.

TABLE A-2

Overview of the sample data

SAMPLE DETAILS OVERALL ($M)

	No. of deals	% deals	Annc. return	1-year return	PNR-% negative reaction	Persistence spread	Premium
All deals	1267	100%	−1.6%	−2.1%	60%	59.4%	30.1%
Cash	257	20%	1.8%	3.8%	43%	65.3%	31.1%
Stock	451	36%	−2.9%	−5.7%	65%	58.5%	28.2%
Combo	559	44%	−2.1%	−1.9%	64%	56.3%	31.1%

Highlights

- Overall, the average size of buyers is $9.3B and the average size of sellers is $3.3B.

- Cash buyers are smaller ($7.2B) than stock and combo buyers ($10.8B and $9B, respectively).

- Deal size (Day −5—five trading days before announcement—seller market cap plus the dollar premium) for cash buyers is much smaller ($2.3B) than the deal sizes for stock and combo deals ($5.3B and $4.3B, respectively).

- Premium paid is 30.1% or $902M overall. Dollar premiums paid for stock and combo deals are much higher than for cash deals because those deals are much larger as is their relative size.

- Relative size (seller to buyer market cap 5 days before announcement) is 46%. Cash deals have a much lower relative size (37%) than stock and combo deals (49% and 48%, respectively).

Buyer market cap D −5	Seller market cap D −5	Dollar premium	Deal size	Relative size	PP/ IP	PN/ IN	TSVA%
$9,289	$3,341	$902	$4,243	46%	57%	65%	1.45%
$7,220	$1,722	$549	$2,271	37%	61%	62%	3.73%
$10,806	$4,218	$1,041	$5,259	49%	58%	71%	0.07%
$9,017	$3,379	$952	$4,331	48%	54%	61%	2.05%

- Stock deals are the most persistent for initially negative reactions (Persistently Negative/Initially Negative or PN/IN of 71%) and cash deals are the most persistent for initially positive reactions (Persistently Positive/Initially Positive or PP/IP of 61%).

- Total shareholder value added percentage (TSVA%)—the sum of the dollar announcement returns to buyers and sellers as a percentage of their combined market caps—is positive (+1.45%), with cash deals having the highest TSVA% (+3.73%). *Mergers create value overall*; see the section on TSVA below.

Shareholder Returns to Acquirers over Time

Time period is an important consideration, so we divided the sample into three eight-year periods: 1995–2002, 2003–2010, and 2011–2018. Admittedly, these three periods are arbitrary, but each period contains a wave of M&A activity, and there is a fairly even distribution of deals across the three periods (410, 415, 445, respectively). Table A-3 shows the overall results for the 1,267 deals across the three periods.

TABLE A-3

Shareholder returns to acquirers across three periods

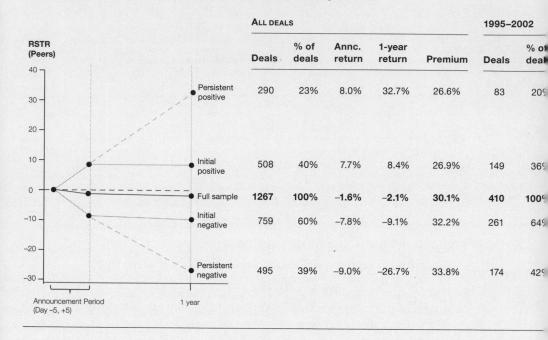

RSTR (Peers)		ALL DEALS					1995–2002	
		Deals	% of deals	Annc. return	1-year return	Premium	Deals	% of deal
Persistent positive		290	23%	8.0%	32.7%	26.6%	83	20%
Initial positive		508	40%	7.7%	8.4%	26.9%	149	36%
Full sample		1267	100%	–1.6%	–2.1%	30.1%	410	100%
Initial negative		759	60%	–7.8%	–9.1%	32.2%	261	64%
Persistent negative		495	39%	–9.0%	–26.7%	33.8%	174	42%

Announcement Period (Day –5, +5)   1 year

Highlights

- Announcement returns have improved over time (a trend consistent with the 2017 finding of Alexandridis, Antypas, and Travlos) from –3.7% in the first period to nearly zero in the third.[6] However, one-year returns, after a significant improvement from –3.3% to +1.3% in the first to second period, remain challenged in the third period with a –4.1% return.

- PNRs have improved across the three periods (64%, 60%, 56%, respectively).

- Initially positive and initially negative portfolios remain significantly positive and negative, respectively, as represented by their one-year returns across the three periods

Annc. return	1-year return	Premium	2003–2010					2011–2018				
			Deals	% of deals	Annc. return	1-year return	Premium	Deals	% of deals	Annc. return	1-year return	Premium
6.5%	40.7%	27.7%	101	24%	8.0%	31.5%	24.7%	106	24%	9.1%	27.5%	27.6%
7.2%	9.9%	29.6%	166	40%	7.5%	10.7%	23.5%	193	44%	8.4%	5.2%	27.6%
–3.7%	**–3.3%**	**35.5%**	**415**	**100%**	**–1.3%**	**1.3%**	**26.4%**	**442**	**100%**	**0.1%**	**–4.2%**	**28.4%**
–10.0%	–10.9%	38.9%	249	60%	–7.1%	–5.0%	28.4%	249	56%	–6.4%	–11.5%	29.1%
–11.5%	–28.2%	40.6%	153	37%	–7.8%	–25.4%	30.1%	168	38%	–7.4%	–26.3%	30.0%

(+9.9%, +10.7%, +5.2% vs. –10.9%, –5.0%, –11.5%, respectively)—*market reactions matter.*

- Persistence for initially positive deals across the three periods (56%, 61%, 55%, respectively) emphasizes the need for acquirers to effectively deliver and report results. Persistence for initially negative reactions, in contrast, remains compelling across the three periods (67%, 61%, 67%, respectively), further supporting the point that negative reactions are tough to turn around.

- The persistence spread has decreased from 68.9% in the first period to 56.9% in the second to 53.8% in the third period—there remains an enormous spread of returns between the persistently positive and persistently negative portfolios.

- The relationship of higher premiums paid as we move from persistently positive through persistently negative portfolios has maintained, although the differences in the extremes have narrowed and premiums overall have declined from their overall highs of 35.5% in the first period to 28.4% in the third period.

Table A-4 provides an overview of additional details of the sample of 1,267 deals across the three time periods.

Highlights

- Overall, the average size of buyers and deal size has declined from the first period, largely attributable to stock deals, which fell sharply from $15.3B and $7.6B in the first period to $4.3B and $2.6B in the third period, respectively. Also notable, in the other direction, the size of cash buyers and their deal size more than doubled from $4.1B and $1.3B in the second period to $10.7B and $2.9B in the third period, respectively.

- Cash deals have increased as a percentage of total deals from their low of only 10% during the 1990s merger boom to 26% and 25% in the second and third period, respectively.

- Announcement returns have improved for stock and combo deals, though still negative, from −4.9% and −3.6% in the first period to −0.7% and −0.9% in the third period, respectively. Announcement returns for cash deals have been positive across the three periods (+2.1%, +0.8%, +2.7%, respectively).

- One-year returns have varied by deal type, and by period, but are showing sharp declines in returns in the third period for all deal types, especially for stock and combo deals (–7.0% and –5.1%, respectively). That reflects our point in chapter 1 that we are not out of the woods on buyer performance; see also the overall year-by-year charts below.

- PNRs have increased for cash deals from 38% in the first period to 43% in the second and 45% in the third period but are still significantly lower than PNRs for stock and combo deals in each period. PNRs for stock deals are 68%, 62%, and 61% across the three periods, respectively, and for combo deals are 64%, 68%, and 60%.

- Premiums paid have declined overall from their high of 35.5% ($1.3B) in the first period to 28.4% ($748M) in the third, especially for stock and combo deals, which declined from their highs of 33.2% and 38.6% in the first period to 22.9% and 29.2% in the third period, respectively. Premiums paid for cash deals have approached their first period level of 35.7% in the third period at 33.3%—along with a higher PNR.

- Positive reaction cash deals were the most persistent (PP/IP of 75%) in the first period in contrast to negative reaction stock deals, which were strongly persistently negative (PN/IN of 74%) in the same period. Stock deals, after an improvement in the second period leading to their best one-year returns of +4.4% with an improved PP/IP (66%) and PN/IN (57%), dropped sharply to a –7.0% return in the third period and were again the most strongly persistently negative (PN/IN of 77%) and the weakest persistently positive (PP/IP of 53%) in the third period.

- The narrowing persistence spread of returns for persistently positive versus persistently negative deals occurred for cash, stock, and combo deals from 81.7%, 64.5%, and 68.5% in the first period to 63.8%, 44.1%, and 54.3% in

TABLE A-4

Overview of the sample data across three periods

SAMPLE DETAILS: 1995–2002 ($M)

	No. of deals	% deals	Annc. return	1-year return	PNR-% negative reaction	Persistence spread	Premium
All deals	410	100%	–3.7%	–3.3%	64%	68.9%	35.5%
Cash	39	10%	2.1%	15.6%	38%	81.7%	35.7%
Stock	212	52%	–4.9%	–10.2%	68%	64.5%	33.2%
Combo	159	39%	–3.6%	1.2%	64%	68.5%	38.6%

SAMPLE DETAILS: 2003–2010 ($M)

	No. of deals	% deals	Annc. return	1-year return	PNR-% negative reaction	Persistence spread	Premium
All deals	415	100%	–1.3%	1.3%	60%	56.9%	26.4%
Cash	106	26%	0.8%	2.6%	43%	59.6%	27.2%
Stock	109	26%	–1.5%	4.4%	62%	63.4%	24.8%
Combo	200	48%	–2.2%	–1.1%	68%	50.7%	26.9%

SAMPLE DETAILS: 2011–2018 ($M)

	No. of deals	% deals	Annc. Return	1-year return	PNR-% negative reaction	Persistence spread	Premium
All deals	442	100%	0.1%	–4.2%	56%	53.8%	28.4%
Cash	112	25%	2.7%	0.8%	45%	63.8%	33.3%
Stock	130	29%	–0.7%	–7.0%	61%	44.1%	22.9%
Combo	200	45%	–0.9%	–5.1%	60%	54.3%	29.2%

Buyer market cap D −5	Seller market cap D −5	Dollar premium	Deal size	Relative size	PP/ IP	PN/ IN	TSVA%
$12,156	$4,549	$1,327	$5,876	46%	56%	67%	−0.26%
$5,766	$2,366	$634	$3,000	48%	75%	53%	4.94%
$15,253	$5,962	$1,636	$7,598	46%	56%	74%	−1.47%
$9,594	$3,199	$1,086	$4,285	45%	47%	58%	1.59%

Buyer market cap D −5	Seller market cap D −5	Dollar premium	Deal size	Relative size	PP/ IP	PN/ IN	TSVA%
$8,096	$2,687	$646	$3,333	48%	61%	61%	1.41%
$4,129	$1,034	$290	$1,324	36%	58%	65%	3.85%
$9,880	$3,209	$646	$3,855	53%	66%	57%	1.21%
$9,226	$3,279	$835	$4,114	51%	60%	62%	1.00%

Buyer market cap D −5	Seller market cap D −5	Dollar premium	Deal size	Relative size	PP/ IP	PN/ IN	TSVA%
$7,750	$2,836	$748	$3,584	45%	55%	67%	4.00%
$10,651	$2,149	$764	$2,913	34%	58%	62%	3.41%
$4,329	$2,219	$402	$2,621	50%	53%	77%	6.33%
$8,349	$3,621	$963	$4,584	49%	54%	63%	3.53%

the third period, respectively—the persistence spreads remain enormous between the "good guys" and "bad guys" across the board.

- TSVA% overall has improved across the three periods to +4.0% overall in the third period, with the largest improvement coming in stock deals, from −1.47% in the first period (thanks largely to the very large loss on the AOL/Time Warner deal) to +6.33% in the third period—supporting the interpretation that mergers continue to create value overall and that has increased over time.

Year-by-Year Results for Selected Data

The results overall and across the three periods are informative but looking at some of the data year-by-year offers a more granular view of the variation over time, and offers some additional perspective. Even with year-by-year variations (as should be expected), our major findings are supported.

Figure A-1 indicates that announcement and one-year shareholder returns to acquirers, after an improvement, are both trending lower in the last four years of the study period.

Figure A-2 shows that PNRs and percentages of negative one-year shareholder returns to acquirers have increased significantly from 43.3% and 46.3% in 2014 to 64.6% and 76.9% in 2018, respectively—after some improvement following the 2008 downturn—a negative and disappointing trend.

The results in figure A-3 show that the announcement returns to acquirers on the initially positive and initially negative portfolios (the market reactions) have remained not only remarkably different, but also relatively stable and close to their overall means over time, respectively (+7.7% for the initially positive portfolio and −7.8% for the initially negative portfolio).

FIGURE A-1

Announcement and 1-year returns to acquirers

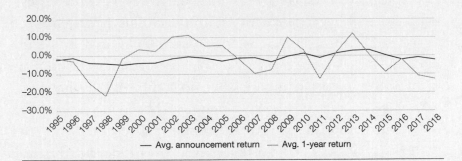

— Avg. announcement return   — Avg. 1-year return

FIGURE A-2

Percentage negative reaction and percentage negative 1-year returns to acquirers

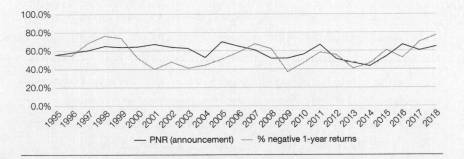

— PNR (announcement)   — % negative 1-year returns

FIGURE A-3

Announcement returns to acquirers on the initially positive and initially negative portfolios

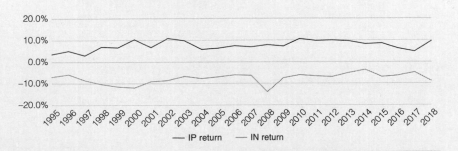

— IP return   — IN return

Although a positive investor reaction is no guarantee of sub-sequent returns, if positive news and results are not forthcoming, a negative reaction is very difficult to reverse. The rising persistence of negative reactions, and declining persistence of positive reactions, in the last two years (2017 and 2018) in figure A-4 is a partial explanation of the corresponding decline in overall one-year returns (shown in figure A-1). Combined with increasing PNRs (shown in figure A-2), the increasing PN/IN creates a sobering picture. It is important to note that even with the variations in persistence levels over time, for the initially positive and initially negative portfolios, that the shareholder returns on the respective market reaction portfolios remain indicative of the returns on those portfolios over the course of one year (largely due to the size of the returns on the persistent portfolios), as we reviewed in the previous sections.

Although the persistence spread—the difference between industry-adjusted one-year shareholder returns to acquirers on the persistently positive and persistently negative deal portfolios—has varied (with 1999 having a handful of very positive persistent deals), it's clear that enormous benefits accrue to being a persistently positive versus a persistently negative performer. Figure A-5 illustrates the persistence spread over time.

FIGURE A-4

Persistently positive/initially positive and persistently negative/initially negative deals (PP/IP and PN/IN)

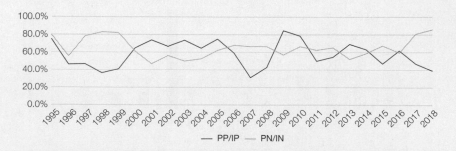

FIGURE A-5

The persistence spread

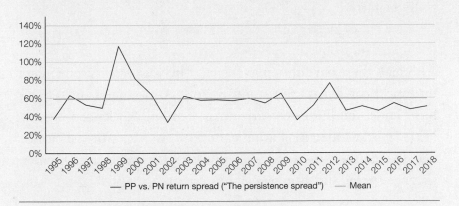

PP vs. PN return spread ("The persistence spread")   Mean

Distribution of returns

The view that initial market reactions are a forecast of the future and the effects of positive and negative persistence, and the persistence spread, are illustrated in figure A-6. These two charts illustrate how the announcement returns—investor reactions—appear to be a forecast of the future and that returns fan out over the course of a year as additional information is released and investors reconsider their initial forecast. Not surprisingly, 71% of the most negative one-year returns

FIGURE A-6

Distribution of announcement and 1-year returns to acquirers

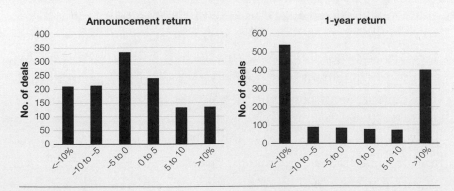

(those with returns lower than negative 10% in the one-year return chart, representing 42% of the total sample) were initially negative.

Although there is variation in the year-by-year results, our major findings hold across the study period: Announcement returns have improved but one-year returns remain challenged overall, initial market reactions are meaningful forecasts of the future, negative market reactions are very tough to reverse, and the persistence spread has been enormous over the years.

Total Shareholder Value Added

Often, when mergers are debated, the level of analysis of the discussion gets confused. There is a difference between whether M&A is good for buyers or for sellers and whether M&A creates value overall. In other words, mergers may not benefit buyers, on average, but the question is: Does adding the gains or losses to the buyer and gains to the seller result in a positive number at the aggregate level? The answer appears to be yes.

We calculated the TSVA as the sum of the 11-day peer-adjusted dollar return around deal announcement for all buyers and sellers. In effect, TSVA is the sum of the buyer and seller SVAs (their individual dollar announcement returns). We summarize the average dollar returns for the full sample, and by method of payment and portfolio type (initial reactions and subsequent persistence) for the 24-year period of our study in table A-5.

We then used our TSVA dollar values, for the full sample and by method of payment and portfolio type (which we reported in table A-5), and divided by two different denomina-

TABLE A-5

TSVA for deals by method of payment and portfolio type ($M)

Method of payment	Acquirer SVA	Target SVA	TSVA
All deals	−285.15	468.67	183.52
Cash	−55.03	388.14	333.11
Stock	−434.51	446.63	11.12
Combo	−270.44	524.28	253.83

Portfolio type	TSVA All Deals	Cash	Stock	Combo
Persistent positive	1005.33	669.88	1082.10	1214.44
Initial positive	995.49	671.06	1194.78	1072.14
Full sample	**183.52**	**333.11**	**11.12**	**253.83**
Initial negative	−359.94	−111.40	−639.69	−209.19
Persistent negative	−446.72	−35.60	−650.96	−383.20

tors for two perspectives: 1) TSVA divided by combined pre-deal market caps of the buyers and sellers for a percentage change in the total combined market cap, and 2) TSVA divided by pre-announcement seller market cap plus the premium paid (or total price paid) for a return on investment (ROI) measure. That yields a TSVA% based on total market capitalization change and a TSVA% as an ROI based on the total price paid for the target, respectively. The results using both measures are shown in table A-6.

We also calculated TSVA% on an equally weighted basis—that is, using the TSVA for each deal (the sum of the SVA of the buyer and the SVA of the seller) and dividing by the two denominators (for our two perspectives) for each deal separately, and then

TABLE A-6

TSVA% for deals from two perspectives by method of payment and portfolio type

Portfolio type	COMBINED PRE-DEAL MARKET CAPS				PRE-DEAL SELLER MARKET CAP PLUS PREMIUM			
	All deals	Cash	Stock	Combo	All deals	Cash	Stock	Combo
Persistent positive	9.42%	8.88%	8.79%	10.27%	26.23%	38.53%	20.39%	28.27%
Initial positive	9.11%	9.40%	8.28%	9.85%	25.10%	39.07%	20.45%	26.11%
Full sample	1.45%	3.73%	0.07%	2.05%	4.32%	14.66%	0.21%	5.86%
Initial negative	−2.61%	−0.98%	−4.17%	−1.58%	−8.13%	−3.71%	−12.95%	−4.69%
Persistent negative	−3.08%	−0.35%	−4.29%	−2.52%	−9.76%	−1.34%	−13.16%	−7.94%

TABLE A-7

Equally weighted TSVA% for deals from two perspectives by method of payment and portfolio type

Portfolio type	COMBINED PRE-DEAL MARKET CAPS				PRE-DEAL SELLER MARKET CAP PLUS PREMIUM			
	All deals	Cash	Stock	Combo	All deals	Cash	Stock	Combo
Persistent positive	11.26%	11.58%	9.97%	12.09%	38.33%	44.34%	32.33%	38.48%
Initial positive	10.98%	11.30%	10.49%	11.15%	36.90%	41.85%	33.83%	35.76%
Full sample	3.63%	6.95%	1.33%	3.96%	10.44%	23.77%	3.28%	10.08%
Initial negative	−1.29%	1.24%	−3.71%	−0.11%	−7.28%	−0.02%	−13.52%	−4.44%
Persistent negative	−2.21%	0.87%	−4.41%	−1.10%	−9.53%	−0.47%	−15.68%	−6.56%

taking an average for the full sample and by method of payment and portfolio type. We find a very similar pattern of results, as shown in table A-7.

The major takeaway from this TSVA section is that M&A overall, based on our announcement-return results, creates value in the aggregate, but the initially negative and persistently negative portfolios of deals do not.

M&M 1961 and the Origins of Economic Value Added

Virtually everyone in business is familiar with the famous equation 11, the discounted cash flow (DCF) approach to valuation, from Miller and Modigliani's (M&M) 1961 *Journal of Business* article, "Dividend Policy, Growth, and the Valuation of Shares." Equation 11 is as follows:

$$MV_0 = \sum_{t=0}^{\infty} \frac{X_t - I_t}{(1 + \rho)^{t+1}}$$

where MV_0 is the market value today, X_t is net operating profit after taxes (NOPAT) at the end of year t, I_t is new investment at the end of year t, $X_t - I_t$ are the free cash flows (FCFs) in year t, and ρ is the cost of capital. But M&M also described their so-called Investment Opportunities Approach (IOA), equation 12, which they proved was equivalent to DCF (equation 11). In fact, M&M thought the IOA was the more natural from the standpoint of an investor considering an acquisition because it offered a view of value based on whether the return on new investments would exceed their cost of capital.[1]

The IOA proposed that a firm's value can be broken into the value of its recurring business operations today and expectations of additional value that will be created from new investments in the future—that is, the known and expectational components of current market value. This approach is the foundation of what became known as the economic value added (EVA) concept, popularized by Bennett Stewart in the 1990s and refined and extended by Stephen O'Byrne.[2]

Serious finance practitioners will know the IOA equation, equation 12:

$$MV_0 = \frac{X_0}{\rho} + \sum_{t=0}^{\infty} \frac{I_t(\rho^*(t) - \rho)}{\rho(1 + \rho)^{t+1}}$$

where X_0 is the uniform perpetual "earnings" on the current asset base, I_t is the new investment at the end of year t, $\rho^*(t)$ is the constant rate of return on I_t in the year immediately following the investment, and ρ is the cost of capital. Equation 12 assumes that return on current investments is constant.

Equation 12 essentially separates current market value into two components: the value from maintaining current operations (the perpetuity value of the uniform perpetual stream of "earnings" on the current asset base) and the value of future growth *expected* from new investment, expressed as the capitalized present value of the constant annual spreads between the return on invested capital and the cost of capital for each new investment (in the year following the investment). Recasting what investors would be willing to pay for a company in this way allows us to thoughtfully consider how much better a company would be expected to perform, in terms of creating additional value, than it does today.

Maintaining current performance, the uniform perpetual stream of earnings will yield only a cost-of-capital return on the perpetuity value of that stream $(X_0/\rho \times \rho = X_0)$ each year but would not justify any additional value for an investor. Thus, the only way for a company to justify value above the value of current operations is to achieve performance *improvements* that exceed the cost of capital on new investments. This logic forms the underpinnings of the EVA approach.

From a strategy perspective, that would imply creating or exploiting advantages relative to competitors. That is the economic essence of a go-forward business plan, as M&M explained in 1961:

> Formula (12) has a number of revealing features and deserves to be more widely used in discussions of valuation. For one thing, it throws considerable light on the meaning of those much abused terms "growth" and "growth stocks." As can readily be seen from (12), a corporation does not become a "growth stock" with a high price-earnings ratio merely because its assets and earnings are growing over time. To enter the glamor category, it is also necessary that $\rho^*(t) > \rho$. For if $\rho^*(t) = \rho$, then however large the growth in assets may be, the second term in (12) will be zero and the firm's price-earnings ratios will not rise above a humdrum $1/\rho$. The essence of "growth," in short, is not expansion, but the existence of opportunities to invest significant quantities of funds at higher than "normal" rates of return.

Equation 12 offers several uniquely helpful qualities. First, it allows the perpetuity value of recurring "earnings" to be easily separated from growth value. Second, it allows value added from growth to be considered on a periodic basis by taking an explicit charge for any additions of capital in each year. Finally, and more fundamentally, it makes two things perfectly clear: 1) maintaining current performance only justifies a company's value equal to the present value of current operations (its perpetuity value), and 2) future investments must earn a return on investment greater than the capital charge for those investments to justify a market value greater than the present value of current operations.

Economic Value Added Model Development

In chapter 4, we defined current market value (MV_0) as beginning capital plus the present value of future EVAs. Many will recognize this as consistent with the popular MVA (market value added) concept where the MVA of a firm is its market value less invested capital. We have:

$$MV_0 = \text{Invested Capital} + \text{Present Value of Future EVAs}$$

We broke future EVAs into two parts: maintaining current EVA and achieving EVA improvements (ΔEVAs). We employed the following expression for current total market value based on beginning invested capital, capitalized current EVA, and the capitalized present value of expected EVA improvements:

$$MV_0 = Cap_0 + \frac{EVA_0}{c} + \frac{1+c}{c} \times \sum_{t=1}^{\infty} \frac{\Delta EVA_t}{(1+c)^t}$$

We referred to the sum of the first two terms as "current operations value" (COV) and the third term as "future growth value" (FGV). Investors expect a cost-of-capital return (c), the WACC, on both COV and FGV. Merely maintaining current EVA (EVA_0) will yield a cost-of-capital return on COV but no return at all on FGV. Thus, justifying FGV will require EVA improvements.

Although the EVA equation for market value is a straightforward adaptation of M&M's equation 12 (reviewed in appendix B), it is useful to develop the intuition of the EVA equation.[1] Let's say that a firm has EVA of EVA_0 today, which is expected to change by ΔEVA in the first period. What does that mean? It means that this period's ending EVA (i.e., next period's beginning EVA) is $EVA_1 = EVA_0 + \Delta EVA$.

If we assume constant FGV and define ΔEVA as an equal annual improvement and each change persists in perpetuity, EVA in each period should be higher by ΔEVA of the previous period. So,

$$EVA_1 = EVA_0 + \Delta EVA,$$
$$EVA_2 = EVA_1 + \Delta EVA = EVA_0 + 2 \times \Delta EVA,$$
$$EVA_3 = EVA_2 + \Delta EVA = EVA_0 + 3 \times \Delta EVA,$$
$$EVA_4 = EVA_3 + \Delta EVA = EVA_0 + 4 \times \Delta EVA, \text{ and so on.}$$

In EVA terms, the net present value (NPV) of a business is the present value of its per-period EVAs (the present value of future EVAs) because we take a capital charge for investments. Using that concept, we have:

$$NPV = EVA_1/(1+c) + EVA_2/(1+c)^2 + EVA_3/(1+c)^3$$
$$+ EVA_4/(1+c)^4 + \cdots$$

Expanding EVA_1, EVA_2, EVA_3, and so on gives us following:

$$NPV = (EVA_0 + \Delta EVA)/(1+c) + (EVA_0 + 2 \times \Delta EVA)/(1+c)^2$$
$$+ (EVA_0 + 3 \times \Delta EVA)/(1+c)^3 + (EVA_0 + 4 \times \Delta EVA)/(1+c)^4 + \cdots$$

We can separate all the EVA_0 terms from the ΔEVA terms and group the EVA_0 terms together. We do the same for the ΔEVA terms. This creates two series from the equation:

(1) $NPV = EVA_0/(1+c) + EVA_0/(1+c)^2 + EVA_0/(1+c)^3$
$\qquad + EVA_0/(1+c)^4 + \cdots$

$\qquad\qquad\qquad +$

(2) $\Delta EVA/(1+c) + 2\times\Delta EVA/(1+c)^2 + 3\times\Delta EVA/(1+c)^3$
$\qquad + 4\times\Delta EVA/(1+c)^4 + \cdots$

The first series represents the present value of a perpetuity of EVA_0 dollars starting its payoff at the end of the first period (where today is time zero). Thus, its value will converge to EVA_0/c, the present value of a level perpetuity. So, we now have:

$$NPV = EVA_0/c + \Delta EVA/(1+c) + 2\times\Delta EVA/(1+c)^2$$
$$+ 3\times\Delta EVA/(1+c)^3 + 4\times\Delta EVA/(1+c)^4 + \cdots$$

The second series involving ΔEVA is also quite intuitive once it is simplified and broken down into its components.

Let's rewrite the second series (the series of ΔEVA) in an intuitive way that helps us get a closed-form expression:

$$\Delta EVA/(1+c) + \Delta EVA/(1+c)^2 + \Delta EVA/(1+c)^3 + \Delta EVA/(1+c)^4 + \cdots +$$
$$\Delta EVA/(1+c)^2 + \Delta EVA/(1+c)^3 + \Delta EVA/(1+c)^4 + \cdots +$$
$$\Delta EVA/(1+c)^3 + \Delta EVA/(1+c)^4 + \cdots +$$
$$\Delta EVA/(1+c)^4 + \cdots$$

You will notice that this new rewritten series is identical to the previous ΔEVA series. However, it is easier to solve. Notice the first row of the above series: it represents the present value of a perpetuity of ΔEVA dollars starting its payoff at the end of the first period. Similarly, the second row represents a perpetuity of ΔEVA dollars starting its payoff at the end of the second period, and so on.

We already know the closed forms for these kinds of perpetuities. The present value of a $1 perpetuity starting its payoff at the end of the first period is $1/c. The present value of a $1 perpetuity starting at the end of the second period is $(\$1/c)/(1+c)$, which is exactly the same perpetuity value as the previous perpetuity but with an extra period of discounting to account for the one-period delay in beginning its payoff. Similarly, the present value of a $1 perpetuity starting at the end of the third period is $(\$1/c)/(1+c)^2$, and so on.

Substituting these values, we get a simplified second series:

$$\Delta EVA/c + \frac{\Delta EVA/c}{(1+c)} + \frac{\Delta EVA/c}{(1+c)^2} + \frac{\Delta EVA/c}{(1+c)^3} + \cdots$$

Now, we need one more step to get a simplified expression for this series. Since we've assumed that the ΔEVAs are equal annual improvements, then, excluding the first term, we see that the second term and onwards represents a perpetuity of ΔEVA perpetuities starting at the end of the second period. Thus, its present value will be $(\Delta EVA/c)/c$.

So, the total value of this series becomes:

$$\Delta EVA/c + \frac{\Delta EVA/c}{c} = \frac{\Delta EVA \times (1+c)}{c \times c}$$

We combine this expression for the second series (the ΔEVA series) with the expression for the first series (the EVA_0 series) to arrive at a simplified formula that describes the NPV of a business in terms of its current EVA and expected future annual EVA improvements.

$$NPV = \frac{EVA_0}{c} + \frac{\Delta EVA \times (1+c)}{c \times c}$$

or,

$$NPV = \frac{EVA_0}{c} + \frac{(1+c)}{c} \times \left(\frac{\Delta EVA}{c}\right)$$

Relaxing the assumption of constant FGV and allowing for different EVA changes in each year t yields the second and third components of our EVA equation for market value:

$$NPV = \frac{EVA_0}{c} + \frac{1+c}{c} \times \sum_{t=1}^{\infty} \frac{\Delta EVA_t}{(1+c)^t}$$

So, for example, if each ΔEVA_t is \$100 in perpetuity, and with constant FGV, then $\sum_{t=1}^{\infty} \frac{\Delta EVA_t}{(1+c)^t}$ would simply reduce to $\left(\frac{\Delta 100}{c} \right)$ or $\left(\frac{\Delta EVA}{c} \right)$.

Adding beginning invested capital (Cap_0) yields our EVA equation for MV_0—invested capital plus the present value of future EVAs (or NPV of investments):

$$MV_0 = Cap_0 + \frac{EVA_0}{c} + \frac{1+c}{c} \times \sum_{t=1}^{\infty} \frac{\Delta EVA_t}{(1+c)^t}$$

Now, let's review and solve for $\Delta EVAs$, or required EVA improvements, to justify a given FGV. A company's current market value can be expressed as the sum of its COV and FGV:

$$MV = COV + FGV$$

The first two terms in our general MV_0 formula above— beginning capital (Cap_0) and capitalized current EVA (EVA_0/c)— or invested capital plus the capitalized current EVA that a company is generating today, represent the COV:

$$COV = Cap_0 + \frac{EVA_0}{c}$$

The third term contains future required $\Delta EVAs$ and captures the FGV of the business (the capitalized present value of expected EVA improvements). Thus, assuming equal annual improvements in EVA and constant FGV:

$$FGV = \frac{\Delta EVA \times (1+c)}{c \times c} = \frac{(1+c)}{c} \times \left(\frac{\Delta EVA}{c} \right)$$

Solving for ΔEVA gives us:

$$\Delta EVA = \frac{c \times FGV}{\dfrac{(1 + c)}{c}}$$

This is the method for calculating required perpetual EVA improvements (uniform ΔEVAs), assuming constant FGV, which we introduced in chapter 4. Allowing for different ΔEVAs, for example the ramp up for synergy realization required to justify the FGV created by paying a premium, relaxes the assumption of constant FGV and yields our general expression (as we discussed above). In either case, these EVA changes (ΔEVAs) become additions to COV. Not achieving these required EVA improvements might drive investors to doubt projected future growth and lower the value of the company accordingly. Changes in market value in either direction reflect changes in investor expectations.

Relationship between ΔEVA and ΔNOPAT

We know that ΔEVA is the change in EVA from the prior year (or period), thus if EVA of the firm today is EVA_0 and EVA one year from now is EVA_1, then by definition:

$$\Delta EVA_1 = EVA_1 - EVA_0$$
$$= (NOPAT_1 - Cap_0 \times c) - (NOPAT_0 - Cap_{-1} \times c)$$

$NOPAT_0$ and $NOPAT_1$ are the NOPAT numbers for the prior year and year 1, respectively. Cap_{-1} and Cap_0 refer to the capital invested at the beginning of these periods, respectively. Rearranging terms give us the following expression for ΔEVA_1:

$$\Delta EVA_1 = (NOPAT_1 - NOPAT_0) - (Cap_0 \times c - Cap_{-1} \times c)$$
$$= \Delta NOPAT_1 - (Cap_0 - Cap_{-1}) \times c$$

$Cap_0 - Cap_{-1}$ is the net new capital (i.e., gross new investment less depreciation expense) invested in the business. We can represent it by ΔCap_0:

$$\Delta EVA_1 = \Delta NOPAT_1 - \Delta Cap_0 \times c$$

This is also an intuitive result. When there is no net new capital invested in the business ($\Delta Cap = 0$), ΔEVA will be equal to $\Delta NOPAT$ because EVA can only change when there is a change in NOPAT in this case. Our objective here is to put a spotlight on future NOPAT—the heart of operating results.

However, when there is net new investment, then ΔEVA is $\Delta NOPAT$ less the additional cost-of-capital charge on the net new investment made in the prior period. If a company raises new funds (e.g., through new equity or debt) or reinvests NOPAT cash flows as net new investments in the business, then it must create an additional cost-of-capital return on that new investment before it can add economic value.[2]

NOTES

Chapter 1

1. See, for example, Mark L. Sirower, "Bankruptcy as a Strategic Planning Tool," *Academy of Management Best Papers Proceedings* (1991): 46–50.

2. Philip L. Zweig, "The Case Against Mergers," *BusinessWeek*, October 29, 1995. The 65% figure comes from Mark L. Sirower, *The Synergy Trap: How Companies Lose the Acquisition Game* (New York: Free Press, 1997).

3. It is interesting to note that these issues have been known and recognized for decades. For example, a JPMorgan advertisement from the early 1990s titled, "What does finding the right price mean if it isn't the right thing to do," closed with the statement, "Turning your back on the difference between price and value is like turning your back on reality," suggesting that many CEOs might either be following bad advice or simply did not understand the promises they were making when they paid more than anyone else in the world was willing to pay for an already existing set of assets, people, and technologies.

4. This quote comes from Charles Shoemate, former CEO of Bestfoods.

5. David Henry, "Why Most Big Deals Don't Pay Off," *BusinessWeek*, October 13, 2002.

6. See, for example, Mark L. Sirower and Stephen F. O'Byrne, "The Measurement of Post-Acquisition Performance: Toward a Value-Based Benchmarking Methodology," *Journal of Applied Corporate Finance* 11, no. 2 (Summer 1998): 107–121; Jim Jeffries, "The Value of Speed in M&A Integration," *M&A Blog*, November 17, 2013, https://www.macouncil.org/blog/2013/11/17/value-speed -ma-integration; Decker Walker, Gerry Hansell, Jens Kengelbach, Prerak Bathia, and Niamh Dawson, "The Real Deal on M&A, Synergies, and Value," *BCG Perspectives*, November 16, 2016, https://www.bcg.com/publications/2016 /merger-acquisitions-corporate-finance-real-deal-m-a-synergies-value.

7. The returns are similar to the S&P 500 benchmark overall and all values are statistically significant at $p < 0.05$ or better.

8. Around announcement, peer-adjust acquirer returns ranged from −50% to 60%, and one-year returns ranged from −116% to 281%. See also Scott D. Graffin, Jerayr (John) Haleblian, and Jason T. Kiley, "Ready, AIM, Acquire: Impression Offsetting and Acquisitions," *Academy of Management Journal* 59, no. 1 (2016): 232–252. Using a sample of 770 deals over $100M in value from the period 1995–2009, these authors find announcement returns of −1.4% based on cumulative abnormal returns methodology, which is similar to our announcement return of −1.6%.

9. See, for example, Roger L. Martin, "M&A: The One Thing You Need to Get Right," *Harvard Business Review,* June 2016, 42–48, https://hbr.org /2016/06/ma-the-one-thing-you-need-to-get-right. Martin states, "But these are the exceptions that prove the rule confirmed by nearly all M&A studies: M&A is a mug's game, in which typically 70% to 90% of acquisitions are abysmal failures." See also Graham Kenny, "Don't Make This Common M&A Mistake," hbr.org, March 16, 2020, https://hbr.org/2020/03/dont-make-this -common-ma-mistake. Kenny begins with, "According to most studies, between 70 and 90 percent of acquisitions fail."

10. For data on the merger wave of the 1980s and 1990s, see Sirower, *The Synergy Trap,* chapter 7 and appendices.

11. Our results provide further support of Greg Jarrell's summary of the literature in "University of Rochester Roundtable on Corporate M&A and Shareholder Value," *Journal of Applied Corporate Finance* 17, no. 4 (Fall 2005): 64–84, where he states, "The evidence we have suggests that the initial market response is a fairly reliable predictor of how the deals are going to turn out" (p. 70).

12. To be clear, "closing" is the event when the transaction is complete and ownership transfer has occurred. The process of closing could be a day or occasionally multiple days on very large or complex deals. "Day 1" is the first date of combined operations, the day the transfer of ownership has taken effect, normally immediately following close. For public companies Day 1 is often denoted as the day the stock ticker goes into effect referring to the combined company, and the day when payroll responsibilities and supplier payable responsibility is assumed by the controlling entity. We will use "Day 1" and "close" interchangeably.

Chapter 2

1. Mark L. Mitchell and Kenneth Lehn, "Do Bad Bidders Become Good Targets?," *Journal of Political Economy* 98, no. 2 (1990): 372–398. See also Jeffrey W. Allen, Scott L. Lummer, John J. McConnell, and Debra K. Reed, "Can Takeover Losses Explain Spin-Off Gains?," *Journal of Financial and Quantitative Analysis* 30, no. 4 (1995): 465–485.

2. For the more complete story of Amazon, see Brad Stone, *The Everything Store: Jeff Bezos and the Age of Amazon* (New York: Little, Brown, 2013). Data source for deals: AlphaSense search engine, as of August 2020. See also Zoe Henry, "Amazon Has Acquired or Invested in More Companies Than You Think," *Inc.,* May 2017, https://www.inc.com/magazine/201705/zoe-henry /will-amazon-buy-you.html; "Infographic: Amazon's Biggest Acquisitions," *CBInsights,* June 19, 2019, https://www.cbinsights.com/research/amazon -biggest-acquisitions-infographic/.

3. Laura Stevens and Annie Gasparro, "Amazon to Buy Whole Foods for 13.7 Billion," *Wall Street Journal,* June 16, 2017, https://www.wsj.com/articles /amazon-to-buy-whole-foods-for-13-7-billion-1497618446; Amazon, "Amazon

.com Announces Minority Investment in Homegrocer.com," press release, May 18, 1999, https://press.aboutamazon.com/news-releases/news-release -details/amazoncom-announces-minority-investment-homegrocercom. The Piper Jaffray analyst comment appears in Robert D. Hof, "Jeff Bezos' Risky Bet," *Bloomberg Businessweek*, November 13, 2006.

4. On the Kindle figure, see Consumer Intelligence Research Partners, 2013, as cited in "Kindle Device Owners Spend 55% More Every Year with Amazon," https://www.geekwire.com/2013/kindle-owners-spend-55-amazon-study/.

5. Steven Levy summarized Amazon's acquisition of Evi in "Inside Amazon's Artificial Intelligence Flywheel," *Wired,* February 1, 2018, https://www .wired.com/story/amazon-artificial-intelligence-flywheel/.

6. Tara-Nicholle Nelson, "Obsess over Your Customers, Not Your Rivals," hbr.org, May 11, 2017, https://hbr.org/2017/05/obsess-over-your-customers-not -your-rivals.

Chapter 3

1. For example, the seller might have disposed of a business through a purported tax-free spin-off that wasn't executed properly, thus resulting in actual unpaid tax liabilities the buyer would be stepping into.

2. Subsequent adjustments might include such issues as allowance for doubtful accounts, obsolete inventory reserves, litigation, restructuring charges, severance, closing costs for facilities, or lease payments on closed stores.

3. In the past, if an acquirer discovered that one of the target's representations or warranties was false, they would go after the seller for the claimed damages, which may or may not be recoverable through an escrow account. Today, acquirers purchase insurance policies so they can put in an insurance claim. As part of the insurance underwriting process, the underwriters will want to read all the diligence reports and exclude facts that were identified in diligence.

4. This quote comes from Charles Shoemate, former CEO of Bestfoods.

5. Net Promoter Scores are a popular metric for assessing customer sentiment—a dimension of stickiness—of brands or particular products. Typically executed through an online survey, respondents are asked to score, "How likely are you to recommend Product X to a friend or colleague?" on a scale of 1–10 (10 being the highest), and the Net Promoter Score is the percentage of promoters less the percentage of detractors.

Chapter 4

1. This chapter has been adapted from Mark Sirower and Stephen O'Byrne, "The Measurement of Post-Acquisition Performance: Toward a Value-Based Benchmarking Methodology," *Journal of Applied Corporate Finance* 11, no. 2 (Summer 1998): 107–121.

2. Enterprise value is generally defined as market capitalization of the equity + net debt + preferred shares + minority interests.

3. *Smith* v. *Van Gorkom*, 488 A.2d 858 (Del. 1985). This was a landmark judgment against Van Gorkom and the directors of the Trans Union Corporation. In a meeting lasting only two hours, the directors approved a leveraged buyout offer presented as fair by Van Gorkom, owner of 75,000 shares of the company. The court found the directors grossly negligent because they did not make an *informed* decision. Specifically, the directors did not seek to inform themselves as to Van Gorkom's motives, they did not adequately inform themselves as to the intrinsic value of the company, and the decision was made in a two-hour meeting in the absence of an emergency situation. See M. R. Kaplan and J. R. Harrison, "Defusing the Director Liability Crisis: The Strategic Management of Legal Threats," *Organization Science* 4, no. 3 (1994): 412–432.

4. Warren Buffett in the *1981 Berkshire Hathaway Annual Report*.

5. On EVA, see G. Bennett Stewart, *The Quest for Value: A Guide for Senior Managers* (New York: HarperCollins, 1991); and S. David Young and Stephen F. O'Byrne, *EVA and Value-Based Management: A Practical Guide for Implementation* (New York: McGraw-Hill, 2000). For extensive discussion of EVA Math, see Stephen O'Byrne, "A Better Way to Measure Operating Performance (or Why EVA Math Really Matters)," *Journal of Applied Corporate Finance* 28, no. 3 (2016): 68–86.

6. Merton H. Miller and Franco Modigliani, "Dividend Policy, Growth, and the Valuation of Shares," *Journal of Business* 34, no. 4 (1961): 411–433.

7. See Stephen F. O'Byrne, "EVA and Market Value," *Journal of Applied Corporate Finance* 9, no. 1 (1996): 116–126.

8. In this example, we have held capital constant from the prior year. Where there is an increase in capital from the prior year, maintaining current EVA will require an increase in NOPAT to compensate for the additional capital charge and thus, maintaining current EVA (with the commensurate increase in NOPAT) will provide a cost-of-capital return on COV but no return on FGV. In our model, only maintaining current EVA implies that $\Delta EVA = 0$.

9. Using EVA math, $c \times FGV = \Delta EVA + \Delta EVA/c + \Delta FGV$; thus, with constant FGV yields:

$$c \times FGV = ((1 + c)/c) \times \Delta EVA, \text{ or } \Delta EVA = c \times FGV/((1 + c)/c).$$ (See appendix C for additional details.)

10. We use the weighted average WACC as a good approximation. There are more technical approaches where we would go through an exercise of unlevering the "betas" in the cost of equity of each company and then relevering to calculate a new beta, based on the new capital structure of the combined company, and arrive at the new WACC for the pro-forma merger. See Susan Chaplinsky, "Methods of Valuation for Mergers and Acquisition," Darden Graduate School of Business, University of Virginia, 2000 (Case: UVA-F-1274).

11. This is a simplified example where the WACCs of both companies are the same and beginning capital is unchanged from the prior year for both companies. And, in all tables, we refer to capitalized present value of expected

EVA improvements simply as "Capitalized PV of expected EVA improvements."

12. This method is discussed in Sirower and O'Byrne, "Measurement of Post-Acquisition Performance." Calculating new current EVA by taking a capital charge as if the combined acquirer and target had all the new capital on its balance sheet in the prior year—that is, including the market value of the target plus the premium along with the acquirer's prior year beginning capital—effectively creates a "pro-forma base year." That is, we create a level playing field for future EVA improvements such that the capital charge in future ΔEVAs is only impacted by the change in the acquirer's capital from the prior year and additional capital growth following the acquisition. Otherwise, the first year ΔEVA would have a huge negative impact because of the large capital increase from the deal. The name of the game is *improvements*.

13. New COV = Homeland COV + Affurr COV = 3,900 + 1,200 = 5,100; New FGV = Homeland FGV + Affurr FGV = 1,100 + 800 = 1,900.

14. To be precise, the value is actually 24.545, which we rounded down for simplicity so that 17.27 + 7.27 = 24.54.

15. Please note that we are using prior year beginning capital to calculate current EVA (NOPAT less the capital charge). So, for Future, current EVA is $(1,889.34 - (32,009.84 \times 0.08)) = -671.45$ and for Cabbāge, current EVA is $(3,151.33 - (29,888.60 \times 0.076)) = 879.80$. We round each calculation to two decimal places.

16. We used market values for the weighted average WACC. For the denominator we used $(40,924.41 + 45,799.24 + 10,000) = 96,723.65$, which is Future's total market value plus Cabbāge's total market value plus the premium. The numerator for Future at its 8% WACC is 40,924.41 (its market value), and the numerator for Cabbāge at its 7.6% WACC is 55,799.24 (its market value plus the premium).

17. For those of you who are following through in Excel, we have rounded to two decimal places after each step. In either case we arrive at the same answers except for "Expectations of ΔEVA driven up using our method" value, which would round to 57.41 instead of 57.42.

18. The sum of the independent COVs is not equal to the new COV from our method because the former is calculated on the target's prior beginning capital whereas the new COV effectively assumes the target, and ultimately the acquirer, had all the capital (market value and the premium) on its balance sheet in the prior year; the usefulness of creating this "pro-forma base year" is that the first year ΔEVA is only impacted by the change in the acquirer's prior year capital and changes in NOPAT. The new COV is also impacted by the new (weighted average) WACC, which can create slight differences in the pro-forma COV and resulting FGV.

19. This is a simplification to make the point and put the spotlight on NOPAT. Of course, if there are meaningful planned additional capital investments, then NOPAT would need to be higher to cover the capital charge on that new invested capital to achieve the required ΔEVAs.

20. $10B = ((1 + 7.77\%)/7.77\%) \times [\$194.25/(1 + 7.77\%) + \$293.08/(1 + 7.77\%)^2 + \$360.97/(1 + 7.77\%)^3]$

21. Another example to illustrate the point: If the new Future Industries realized 50% of required synergies in the second year and 50% in the third year, that would yield required EVA improvements of $419M and $451M, respectively, for a run rate of $870M of after-tax improvements after the third year onward—again not even close to announced $500M of pre-tax synergies.

22. In the case of all-stock and combo deals (a mix of cash and stock), the value to the seller can fluctuate pre-close based on the movements of the buyer's shares because the seller will be joint owners in the new enterprise (more on this in chapter 9). In any case, the movement in the buyer's shares is based largely on expectations of whether the buyer can realize the performance improvements embedded in the offer price and especially the premium.

Chapter 5

1. This chapter is adapted from Mark L. Sirower and Steve Lipin, "Investor Communications: New Rules for M&A Success," *Financial Executive* 19 (January–February 2003). For more on the board's evaluation of the deal, see chapter 9.

2. Acquirers must recognize that investor relations in M&A must contend with and help solve a classic asymmetric information problem: Management knows more about the transaction than investors, so investors can only go by what management *signals* to them through investor communications. Investors around the world will listen to management and then make the decision to hold their shares of the acquirer, buy, or sell. Target shareholders will want answers if the deal involves stock because their board has essentially recommended an investment decision that is presumably in the best interests of their shareholders.

3. The quotation comes from "University of Rochester Roundtable on Corporate M&A and Shareholder Value," *Journal of Applied Corporate Finance* 17, no. 4 (Fall 2005): 70. Recognizing this, some CEOs attempt to surround announcements with unrelated good news, and recent evidence suggests those CEOs engage in this strategy when they perceive a deal as riskier, and subsequently exercised more options than those who did not offer unrelated news. Findings suggest that CEOs who issue unrelated positive news exercise 6.7% more options in the next quarter than CEOs who did not, suggesting a lower level of confidence in the outcomes of those deals. Daniel L. Gamache, Gerry McNamara, Scott D. Graffin, Jason T. Kiley, Jerayr Haleblian, and Cynthia E. Devers, "Why CEOs Surround M&A Announcements with Unrelated Good News," hbr.org, August 30, 2019, https://hbr.org/2019/08/why-ceos-surround-ma-announcements-with-unrelated-good-news.

4. Not only will a negative market reaction jeopardize the success of the merger, but it can also distract managers and employees from ongoing business activities, threatening the growth value already built into the acquirer's share

price—potentially causing losses in the share price far beyond the amount of the premium.

5. On Conseco, see Leslie Eaton, "Conseco and Green Tree, an Improbable Merger," *New York Times*, April 8, 1998.

6. Information drawn from Nexstar Media Group acquisition of Tribune Media investor presentation and conference call, December 3, 2018. Subsequent calls at closing raised the projected synergy number to $185M.

7. For a review of our evidence on the disappointing returns to stock deals, see appendix A. Presumably, the board of the seller would also have done that before recommending their investors take the acquirer's stock, but that doesn't appear to be the case, on average. For additional details, see chapter 9.

8. Information drawn from Avis Budget Group acquisition of Zipcar investor presentation and conference call, January 2, 2013.

9. David Harding and Sam Rovit, "Building Deals on Bedrock," *Harvard Business Review*, September 2004, https://hbr.org/2004/09/building-deals-on -bedrock.

10. Information from PepsiCo press release at close on August 13, 2001, "PepsiCo Raises Estimate of Quaker Merger Synergies to $400 Million," and cited in *Chicago Tribune* story, "Quaker Savings, Sales Growth Expectations Double for PepsiCo," August 14, 2001.

Chapter 6

1. HSR filing goes to either DOJ or the Federal Trade Commission. All deals go through preliminary review, when regulating agencies make a determination of which agency does the investigation. As a consequence, the deal moves forward and can potentially close in less than 30 days. If the 30-day waiting period expires then the deal is deemed "approved without objection." Within 30 days the agency can come back and ask for a meeting or additional data to satisfy their concern. They may have an anti-trust concern, which will trigger additional investigation through a second request. There can be many requests, responding to which can take many pages and many months. The waiting period can expire, or an agency can provide explicit approval, or it can come back and challenge the deal, requiring some divestment, or a governance review, or an injunction that the acquirer will have to contest.

2. On the distinction between "close" and "Day 1," see chapter 1, note 12, above.

3. David Carney and Douglas Tuttle, "Seven Things Your Mother Never Told You about Leading as an Integration Manager," Deloitte M&A Institute white paper from the Deloitte publication, "Making the Deal Work," 2007.

Chapter 7

1. This section is drawn from Ami Louise Rich and Stephanie Dolan, "Please Excuse My Dear Aunt Sally: The Order of Operations for Organization

Design during an M&A Event," Deloitte M&A Institute working paper, July 2019, and from many helpful discussions.

2. The levels and reporting relations may appear different, depending on the size of the company, its divisions and constituent business units, and the CEO's preference.

3. Exiting leaders may still have a significant positive impact. Retaining them for a period of time may make employees feel more comfortable, confident, and valued. Acquirers can also draw on their knowledge of the business, and they can advocate for the exciting new chapter. But toxic people have to go. Very large organizations have employment contracts, so acquirers should be careful that they don't trigger change of control clauses sooner than desirable. Employees will also need to know the next layer of the organization that directly impacts them so they can discern the direction, broad policies, interaction models with customers those leaders will adopt. Absent that information there will be a power struggle between both organizations because people don't know who will win.

4. Option 1 yields precise costs layer by layer. Option 2 allows "napkin math" for approximate costs because names aren't yet in the boxes; it also gets us quicker to the fact that we may not hit our synergy targets.

5. For example, a $3M cost baseline would quickly reveal a $2M synergy target is not reasonable. Further, if legal has a baseline of $9M and a synergy target of $2M, the combined cost structure post synergy realization should be $7M. There are two ways to get there, either direct reduction from the baseline or reduction in the legal budget by the synergy target.

Chapter 8

1. On the difference between "close" and Day 1," see chapter 1, note 12, above.

2. See, for example, Val Srinivas and Richa Wadhwani, "Recognizing the Value of Bank Branches in a Digital World," *Deloitte Insights*, February 13, 2019, https://www2.deloitte.com/us/en/insights/industry/financial-services/bank-branch-transformation-digital-banking.html; Rob Morgan, "The Future of the Branch in a Digital World, *ABA Banking Journal,* June 15, 2020, https://bankingjournal.aba.com/2020/06/the-future-of-the-branch-in-a-digital-world/; and Kate Rooney, "Despite the Rise of Online Banks, Millennials Are Still Visiting Branches," *CNBC*, December 5, 2019, https://www.cnbc.com/2019/12/05/despite-the-rise-of-online-banks-millennials-still-go-to-branches.html.

3. Jay W. Lorsch and Emily McTague, "Culture Is Not the Culprit," *Harvard Business Review*, April 2016, https://hbr.org/2016/04/culture-is-not-the-culprit.

4. Todd D. Jick, "On the Recipients of Change," in *Organization Change: A Comprehensive Reader,* ed. W. Warner Burke, Dale G. Lake, and Jill Waymire Paine (San Francisco: Jossey-Bass, 2009), 404–417.

5. For additional background, see the M&A classics, David M. Schweiger, John M. Invancevich, and Frank R. Power, "Executive Actions for Managing

Human Resources before and after Acquisition," *Academy of Management Executive* 1, no. 2 (1987): 127–138; and Mitchell L. Marks and Philip H. Mirvis, "The Merger Syndrome," *Psychology Today*, October 1986, 35–42.

6. Joel Brockner, *The Process Matters: Engaging and Equipping People for Success* (Princeton, NJ: Princeton University Press, 2015).

7. For a review with implications for M&A, see Gary B. Gorton, Jill Grennan, and Alexander K. Zentefis, "Corporate Culture," National Bureau of Economic Research, working paper 29322 (October 2021).

8. Robert Iger, *The Ride of a Lifetime: Lessons Learned from 15 Years as CEO of the Walt Disney Company* (New York: Random House, 2019).

9. John Kotter, "Leading Change: Why Transformation Efforts Fail," *Harvard Business Review*, May–June 1995, https://hbr.org/1995/05/leading-change-why-transformation-efforts-fail-2.

10. Lorsch and McTague, "Culture Is Not the Culprit."

Chapter 9

1. The business judgment rule is primarily a tool of judicial review and only indirectly a standard of conduct. The rule applies if directors have met specific conditions. See, for example, Donald G. Kempf Jr., "'Can They Take My House?': Defending Directors and Officers," *Illinois Bar Journal* 81 (May 1993): 244–248.

2. Adapted from Alfred Rappaport and Mark L. Sirower, "Cash or Stock: The Trade-offs for Buyers and Sellers in Mergers and Acquisitions," *Harvard Business Review*, November–December 1999, https://hbr.org/1999/11/stock-or-cash-the-trade-offs-for-buyers-and-sellers-in-mergers-and-acquisitions.

3. The prevalence of cash, stock, or combinations of the two have shifted dramatically over the decades of merger waves. For example, 1980s were dominated by all-cash deals representing nearly 70% of all deals by the end of the decade. That trend dramatically shifted to the rise of all-stock deals in the 1990s, particularly for large deals. From our data of 1,267 deals we have the following percentage breakdown of cash, stock, or combination for each eight-year period, respectively. 1995–2002: 10%, 52%, 38%; 2003–2010: 26%, 26%, 48%; 2011–2019: 25%, 30%, 45% (please excuse the rounding).

4. See appendix A and, for example, Tim Loughran and Anand M. Vijh, "Do Long-Term Shareholders Benefit from Corporate Acquisitions?," *Journal of Finance* 52, no. 5 (December 1997): 1765–1790. See also Mark L. Sirower, *The Synergy Trap: How Companies Lose the Acquisition Game* (New York: Free Press, 1997); and Richard Tortoriello, Temi Oyeniyi, David Pope, Paul Fruin, and Ruben Falk, *Mergers & Acquisitions: The Good, the Bad, and the Ugly (and How to Tell Them Apart)*, S&P Global Market Intelligence, August 2016, https://www.spglobal.com/marketintelligence/en/documents/mergers-and-acquisitions-the-good-the-bad-and-the-ugly-august-2016.pdf.

5. A board that has determined to proceed with a share offer still has to decide how to structure it. That decision depends on an assessment of the risk

of a drop in the price of the acquiring company's shares between the announcement of the deal and its closing.

Research has shown that the market responds more favorably when acquirers demonstrate their confidence in the value of their own shares through their willingness to bear greater preclosing market risk. See, for example, Joel Houston and Michael Ryngaert, "Equity Issuance and Adverse Selection: A Direct Test Using Conditional Stock Offers," *Journal of Finance* 52, no. 1 (1997): 197–219.

A fixed-share offer is not a confident signal since the seller's compensation drops if the value of the acquirer's shares falls. Therefore, the fixed-share approach should be adopted only if the preclosing market risk is relatively low. But there are ways for an acquiring company to structure a fixed-share offer without sending signals to the market that its stock is overvalued. The acquirer, for example, can protect the seller against a fall in the acquirer's share price below a specified floor level by guaranteeing a minimum price. (Acquirers that offer such a "floor" typically also insist on a "ceiling" on the total value of shares distributed to sellers.)

An even more confident signal is given by a fixed-value offer in which sellers are assured of a stipulated market value while acquirers bear the entire cost of any decline in their share price before closing. If the market believes in the merits of the offer, then the acquirer's price may even rise, enabling it to issue fewer shares to the seller's stockholders. The acquirer's shareholders, in this event, would retain a greater proportion of the deal's NPV. As with fixed-share offers, floors and ceilings can be attached to fixed-value offers, in the form of the number of shares to be issued. See Rappaport and Sirower, "Cash or Stock"; and Carliss Y. Baldwin, "Evaluating M&A Deals: Floors, Caps, and Collars," Harvard Business School Background Note 209-138, March 2009.

6. Adapted from Mark L. Sirower and Richard Stark, "The PMI Board Pack: New Diligence in M&A," *Directors & Boards*, Summer 2001, 34–39.

7. On the re-emergence of hostile deals, see Kai Liekefett, "The Comeback of Hostile Takeovers," Harvard Law School Forum on Corporate Governance, November 8, 2020, https://corpgov.law.harvard.edu/2020/11/08/the-comeback -of-hostile-takeovers/.

8. Adapted from Mark L. Sirower and Sumit Sahni, "Avoiding the Synergy Trap: Practical Guidance on M&A Decisions for CEOs and Boards," *Journal of Applied Corporate Finance* 18, no. 3 (Summer 2006): 83–95. See also G. Bennett Stewart, *The Quest for Value: A Guide for Senior Managers* (New York: HarperCollins, 1991), chap. 2; and Eric Lindenberg and Michael P. Ross, "To Purchase or to Pool: Does it Matter," *Journal of Applied Corporate Finance* 12 (Summer 1999): 2–136.

9. We are not advocating an earnings accretion or multiples-based approach to valuing target companies. Rather, we use those perspectives by focusing on the target to highlight the relevant performance challenge regardless of whether a deal is accretive or dilutive to the short-term earnings of the acquirer.

10. A constant P/E implies the preservation of the base case expectations of the stand-alone business. Any downward change in the P/E of the acquirer at

announcement can be translated into an implied reduction in the target's P/E; it is an unfortunate reminder that synergies might be achieved but at the expense of the existing expectations of the forward plan. Alternatively, the drop could also be interpreted as an adjustment reflecting the expectations that synergies will not be awarded the growth value in the P/E of the target, or both.

11. This is a big assumption, but one that is made regularly by CEOs and security analysts. Applying the same P/E to synergies means that any accretion from synergies is capitalized in perpetuity along with any growth value component of the P/E. Awarding any synergies the full P/E multiple is potentially the largest factor in explaining why typical accretion analysis might not yield realistic valuations. For example, suppose the cost of capital (c) is 10% then the perpetuity value of current earnings without growth is 1/c or a multiple of 10. If the P/E is 20, then the additional multiple of 10 is the growth value based on expectations of future improvements. If the synergies have no growth value, applying the full P/E will lead to overvaluation of the target.

12. As in any simplifying finance model (including dividend growth models and the terminal value calculations used in DCFs), there are limitations at the extremes. The usefulness of the %*SynC* expression diminishes as the profit margin approaches extreme values. For example, as the profit margin approaches zero, %*SynC* tends to zero. This could lead to erroneous conclusions about the extent of profit improvements required to earn back the premium paid for a very low profitability target. Alternatively, as the profit margin approaches 50%, %*SynC* tends to 100%. This would suggest the elimination of all operating costs as a strategy to earn the acquisition premium.

13. Moving from concept to practice, if we were to use a "pure" earnings model then we would use the net income before tax margin in the numerator and denominator. But then we might base required synergies on an abnormally low pre-tax earnings number that includes extraordinary items and that would also yield an abnormally high P/E. On the other hand, modeling the equity market value on EBIT yields a lower effective P/E multiple and thus, a lower growth value assumption for synergies in the model. In practice, we generate MTP Lines for other pre-tax measures so we can discuss the different results and assumptions. For simplicity and practicality, here we use EBIT in both the numerator and denominator because it focuses on operations.

14. Over years of experience, we have found that the first estimate of cost reduction is from optimization of addressable overhead and SG&A costs, which are typically not more than one-third of the total cost base. A reduction of overhead costs by one-third is usually considered an upper bound, and the resulting third of a third gives us roughly 10% of the total cost base (what we called "the magic 10%" in chapter 3).

15. See Richard P. Rumelt, *Strategy, Structure, and Economic Performance* (Cambridge, MA: Harvard University Press, 1974); and Robert F. Bruner, *Applied Mergers and Acquisitions* (New York: Wiley, 2004).

16. Reviewed in Sirower, *The Synergy Trap*, chapters 5, 7, 8, and appendices A and B; and David J. Flanagan, "Announcements or Purely Related and Purely Unrelated Mergers and Shareholder Returns: Reconciling the Related-

ness Paradox," *Journal of Management* 22, no. 6 (1996): 823–835. See also Yasser Alhenawi and Martha L. Stilwell, "Toward a Complete Definition of Relatedness in Mergers and Acquisitions Transactions," *Review of Quantitative Finance and Accounting* 53 (2019): 351–396.

17. See, for instance, Chris Zook and James Allen, *Profit from the Core: Growth Strategy in an Era of Turbulence* (Boston: Harvard Business School Press, 2001) and their subsequent works.

18. Joseph L. Bower, "Not All M&A's Are Alike—And That Matters," *Harvard Business Review*, March 2001, https://hbr.org/2001/03/not-all-mas -are-alike-and-that-matters.

19. Charles Calomiris and Jason Karceski, "Is the Bank Merger Wave of 1990s Efficient? Lessons from 9 Case Studies," in *Mergers and Productivity*, ed. Steven N. Kaplan (Chicago: University of Chicago Press, 2000), 93–178. Banking analyst James Hanbury commented, "The reason to do the merger is to try to deal with the problems by developing a new income stream from savings, as you eliminate overlapping costs of two banks operating in the same marketplace." See Paul Deckelman, "Chemical Bank, Manufacturers Hanover Officially Merge," *UPI*, December 31, 1991, https://www.upi.com/Archives /1991/12/31/Chemical-Bank-Manufacturers-Hanover-officially-merge /3446694155600/.

20. Adapted from Mark L. Sirower and Steve Lipin, "Investor Communications: New Rules for M&A Success," *Financial Executive* 19 (January– February 2003): 26–30.

21. Although not discussed, the Avis Budget acquisition of Zipcar (described in chapter 5), which received a very positive market reaction even at 49% premium, is another good illustration. The combination of Zipcar assets with Avis Budget gave a center of gravity close to the bottom left in figure 9.3a. Zipcar offered expansion into adjacent markets but as CEO Ron Nelson stated during the investor call, "They share exactly the same core, allowing people to use the vehicles they don't own, when they want, where they want and how they want." Zipcar offered Avis Budget better market access and Avis offered Zipcar better capabilities and scale in fleet management (buying, financing, maintaining), optimization, and utilization. Across the three sources of value described in the investor presentation, roughly $30M was from cost reductions and $30M from revenue increases, yielding a (%*SynR*, %*SynC*) point of roughly (11%, 11%). Zipcar had a low EBIT margin (3.4%) largely because of the high costs of its fleet of cars. Its MTP Line intersects the %*SynC* axis at roughly 2% and at 49% on the %*SynR* axis, a line of much lower slope than our other examples. The point management proposed in their investor presentation lies well above the MTP line and just at the edge of our hypothetical Plausibility Box.

22. Data used in calculations is taken from last 10Ks available before the announcement deals—that is, 1997 for BetzDearbon, 1999 for Time Warner, 2000 for Quaker Oats, and 2018 for Tribune Media (the latter two deals were announced in December of their respective year). Revenue synergies projected for the PepsiCo/Quaker deal were calculated by grossing up the projected additions to operating profit from revenue synergies ($79M) by the 16% EBIT

margin of Quaker Oats. %*SynC* assumes an addressable cost base that includes COGS, SG&A, and D&A and these were the respective costs used to calculate the EBIT margin.

23. For BetzDearborn, %*SynC* of 9.2%; for Time Warner, %*SynC* of 4.2%; for Quaker Oats, a mix of %*SynC* of 3.6% and %*SynR* of 10.0%; for Tribune, a mix of %*SynC* of 5.1% and %*SynR* of 3.7%. Figures are calculated based on respective cost and revenue bases.

24. Mark L. Sirower, "When a Merger Becomes a Scandal," *Financial Times*, August 14, 2003.

Appendix A

1. Scott D. Graffin, Jerayr (John) Haleblian, and Jason T. Kiley, "Ready, AIM, Acquire: Impression Offsetting and Acquisitions," *Academy of Management Journal* 59, no. 1 (2016): 232–252.

2. All data and results significant at the $p < 0.05$ or better except for the overall one-year returns on combo deals ($p < 0.1$); and full sample 2003–2010 one-year returns, and full sample 2011–2018 announcement returns where we can't reject the null.

3. These findings reaffirm the widely reported underperformance of stock deals. See, for example, Nicolas G. Travlos, "Corporate Takeover Bids, Methods of Payment, and Bidding Firms' Stock Returns," *Journal of Finance* 42, no. 4 (September 1987): 943–963; and Tim Loughran and Anand M. Vijh, "Do Long-Term Shareholders Benefit from Corporate Acquisitions?," *Journal of Finance* 30, no. 5 (December 1997): 1765–1790.

4. Although much can happen to an acquirer over a two-year period of performance, it is interesting to note that for acquirers that had positive or negative one-year returns, regardless of the initial reaction, 72% and 82% were positive or negative for their two-year returns, respectively. Similarly, for persistently positive or persistently negative performers, 73% and 82% were persistent for their two-year returns, respectively.

5. Our findings of the absolute percentage point difference between the premiums paid for persistently negative and persistently positive portfolios are consistent with the findings of Sara B. Moeller, Frederik P. Schlingemann, and Rene M. Stulz, "Wealth Destruction on a Massive Scale? A Study of Acquiring-Firm Returns in the Recent Merger Wave," *Journal of Finance* 60, no. 2 (April 2005): 757–782. These authors find that the premium paid in large loss acquirers is 8% to 10% higher on average.

6. George Alexandridis, Nikolaos Antypas, and Nickolaos Travlos, "Value Creation from M&As: New Evidence," *Journal of Corporate Finance* 45 (2017): 632–650.

Appendix B

1. Merton H. Miller and Franco Modigliani, "Dividend Policy, Growth, and the Valuation of Shares," *Journal of Business* 34, no. 4 (1961): 411–433.

2. See G. Bennett Stewart, *The Quest for Value: A Guide for Senior Managers* (New York: HarperCollins, 1991); Stephen F. O'Byrne, "EVA and Market Value," *Journal of Applied Corporate Finance* 9, no. 1 (Spring 1996): 116–125 (where the author adapts M&M's equation 12 for the mechanics of EVA); Stephen F. O'Byrne, "A Better Way to Measure Operating Performance (or Why the EVA Math Really Matters)," *Journal of Applied Corporate Finance* 28, no. 3 (2016): 68–86; and S. David Young and Stephen F. O'Byrne, *EVA and Value-Based Management: A Practical Guide to Implementation* (New York: McGraw-Hill, 2000).

Appendix C

1. In their equation 12, M&M assume a uniform perpetual stream of earnings on the current asset base, what we call Cap_0. They presume, in effect, that prior year's NOPAT ($NOPAT_0$) will increase sufficiently to maintain what we call "current EVA" (EVA_0), which is based on prior year's NOPAT and the prior year's capital charge. Thus, maintaining current EVA in the EVA equation yields a cost-of-capital return on what we call COV, equivalent to a cost-of-capital return on the first term in M&M's equation 12. M&M's presumed "$NOPAT_1$" will equal $NOPAT_0$ when prior year's beginning capital is equal to Cap_0. Further, because we incorporate beginning capital, we can include a perpetual change in EVA (ΔEVA) beginning in the first year, where M&M assume the return on an investment and the capital charge are realized in the year immediately following the investment, so their assumption of constant return on the current asset base would yield $\Delta EVA_1 = 0$. Since the present value of a ΔEVA_1 perpetuity will be $\Delta EVA_1/c$ at time zero (today) and not $\Delta EVA_1/c(1+c)$, as might be incorrectly inferred from the second term in equation 12, we need to multiply the adapted second term by $(1+c)$ to account for that distinct possibility (a positive ΔEVA_1, for example, year 1 expected synergies) as represented in the third term of the EVA equation. To clarify, the first period change in the second term of equation 12 is the second period change in the EVA equation, and so on—but FGV, the third term of the EVA equation, and the second term in equation 12 are the same value. An important feature of the EVA equation is that it allows us to relax important assumptions in equation 12—that the return on the current asset base is constant, that new investments are required to create additional value, and that the returns on those investments are constant in perpetuity. Because ΔEVA is defined as $\Delta NOPAT$ minus the Δcapital charge, the EVA equation allows varying returns on the current asset base (such as synergies) and future investments (e.g., a cost transformation that yields higher NOPAT without necessarily increasing the capital base).

2. We owe special thanks to Anurag Srivastava, a former student of Mark's on the NYU Stern Executive MBA program, for his very helpful approach and comments on this alternative derivation of our EVA equation.

INDEX

Note: Figures are identified by *f* following the page number. Tables are identified by *t* following the page number. Endnote information is identified by *n* and note number following the page number.

ABOUT THE AUTHORS

MARK L. SIROWER is a US leader in Deloitte's M&A and Restructuring practice, which he joined in 2008 to launch the M&A Strategy practice. For more than 25 years, Mark has advised boards of directors and senior executive teams on hundreds of transactions, from strategy and diligence through post-merger integration. Previously, he built the Deals Strategy Group at PwC, and was global leader of the M&A practice at the Boston Consulting Group, where he developed innovative approaches to crafting M&A strategies, planning integrations, delivering synergies after the merger, and creating shareholder value.

Mark has taught M&A at the Wharton School and, for 30 years and counting, at the NYU Stern Executive MBA program as an adjunct professor. He is the author of the groundbreaking M&A bestseller *The Synergy Trap*, and his research and publications on M&A have been featured in *Harvard Business Review*, *BusinessWeek*, *Fortune*, *New York Times*, *Wall Street Journal*, *Economist*, *Financial Times*, *CFO*, and *Barron's*. He speaks worldwide on issues related to M&A.

Mark received his PhD from the Columbia University Graduate School of Business and MBA from the Kelly School of Business, Indiana University. He lives in Manhattan.

JEFFERY M. WEIRENS is the leader of Deloitte's global Financial Advisory business, which drives impact in defining moments for clients and society through mergers, acquisitions, divestitures, restructuring, and forensic services. He serves on Deloitte's Global Executive as well as the WorldImpact Steering Committee, setting Deloitte's strategy on critical topics including climate, diversity, equity, and inclusion.

For more than 30 years, Jeff has advised clients on several of the world's most iconic acquisitions and divestitures while growing and transforming Deloitte's Consulting and Advisory businesses. He has served in multiple leadership roles within Deloitte Consulting, including as a member of the Management Committee, as the US Leader of the Energy, Resources and Industrials Sector, and as the US and Global Leader of the M&A and Restructuring practice. He is a trusted adviser to senior client executive teams and boards of directors; has advised on hundreds of acquisitions, divestitures, and transformations; and is an expert on post-merger integration and divestitures.

Jeff has an MBA from the Johnson Graduate School of Management, Cornell University; a BSB from the Carlson School of Management, University of Minnesota; and is a Certified Public Accountant. He lives in North Oaks, MN.